Life-Span Developmental Psychology
Historical and Generational Effects

Life-Span
Developmental Psychology
Historical and Generational Effects

Edited by
KATHLEEN A. MCCLUSKEY
HAYNE W. REESE

Department of Psychology
West Virginia University
Morgantown, West Virginia

1984

ACADEMIC PRESS, INC.
(Harcourt Brace Jovanovich, Publishers)

Orlando San Diego New York London
Toronto Montreal Sydney Tokyo

155

L 722

COPYRIGHT © 1984, BY ACADEMIC PRESS, INC.
ALL RIGHTS RESERVED.
NO PART OF THIS PUBLICATION MAY BE REPRODUCED OR
TRANSMITTED IN ANY FORM OR BY ANY MEANS, ELECTRONIC
OR MECHANICAL, INCLUDING PHOTOCOPY, RECORDING, OR ANY
INFORMATION STORAGE AND RETRIEVAL SYSTEM, WITHOUT
PERMISSION IN WRITING FROM THE PUBLISHER.

ACADEMIC PRESS, INC.
Orlando, Florida 32887

United Kingdom Edition published by
ACADEMIC PRESS, INC. (LONDON) LTD.
24/28 Oval Road, London NW1 7DX

Library of Congress Cataloging in Publication Data

Main entry under title:

Life-span developmental psychology.

   (West Virginia University series on life-span develop-
mental psychology)
   Includes index.
   1. Developmental psychology--Methodology--Addresses,
essays, lectures. I. McCluskey, Kathleen A.
II. Reese, Hayne Waring, Date   . III. Series.
BF713.5.L527 1984   155   84-11061
ISBN 0-12-482420-X (alk. paper)

PRINTED IN THE UNITED STATES OF AMERICA

84 85 86 87   9 8 7 6 5 4 3 2 1

~~BRADFORD COLLEGE~~

MAR 1 0 1986
EBC   38.95
~~LIBRARY~~

OCLC 10777360

Contents

8. Hardship in Lives: Depression Influences from the 1930s to Old Age in Postwar America

GLEN H. ELDER, JR., JEFFREY K. LIKER, AND BERNARD J. JAWORSKI

9. Fatherhood: Historical and Contemporary Perspectives

ROSS D. PARKE AND BARBARA R. TINSLEY

10. Grandparenthood in Transition

NINA R. NAHEMOW

Contributors

Numbers in parentheses indicate the pages on which the authors' contributions begin.

AARON ANTONOVSKY (143), Department of the Sociology of Health, Center for Health Sciences, Ben-Gurion University of Negev, Beer-Sheva, Israel

NANCY DATAN (143), Human Development, University of Wisconsin-Green Bay, CHB ES-301, Green Bay, Wisconsin 54301-7001

LUTZ H. ECKENSBERGER (73), Universität des Saarlandes, Saarbrücken, Federal Republic of Germany

GLEN H. ELDER, JR.[1] (161), Departments of Human Development and Family Studies and Sociology, Cornell University, Ithaca, New York 14853

BERNARD J. JAWORSKI (161), Graduate School of Business, University of Pittsburgh, Pittsburgh, Pennsylvania 15261

ELISABETH KASPER (73), Universität des Saarlandes, Saarbrücken, Federal Republic of Germany

STEPHEN L. KLINEBERG (129), Department of Sociology, Rice University, Houston, Texas 77251

BERND KREWER (73), Universität des Saarlandes, Saarbrücken, Federal Republic of Germany

GISELA LABOUVIE-VIEF (109), Department of Psychology, Wayne State University, Detroit, Michigan 48202

JEFFREY K. LIKER (161), Department of Industrial and Operations Engineering, University of Michigan, Ann Arbor, Michigan 48109

BENJAMIN MAOZ (143), Center for Health Services, Department of Psychiatry, Ben Gurion University of Negev, Beer-Sheva, Israel

KATHLEEN A. McCLUSKEY (17), Department of Psychology, West Virginia University, Morgantown, West Virginia 26506-6040

JOHN A. MEACHAM (47), Department of Psychology, State University of New York at Buffalo, Buffalo, New York 14226

NINA R. NAHEMOW (249), Department of Sociology, Old Dominion University, Norfolk, Virginia 23508

---

[1]Present address: Carolina Population Center, University Square, Chapel Hill, North Carolina 27514.

ix

ROSS D. PARKE (203), Department of Psychology, University of Illinois, Champaign, Illinois 61820

HAYNE W. REESE (17), Department of Psychology, West Virginia University, Morgantown, West Virginia 26506-6040

K. WARNER SCHAIE (1), Individual and Family Studies, College of Human Development, The Pennsylvania State University, University Park, Pennsylvania 16802

BARBARA R. TINSLEY (203), Department of Psychology, University of Illinois, Champaign, Illinois 61820

Preface

The topic of the eighth West Virginia University life-span volume was chosen to complete our coverage of the three broad categories of influences on life-span development: normative age-graded influences were covered in the fourth life-span volume, published in 1975 (Datan & Ginsberg, 1975); nonnormative influences were covered in the seventh life-span volume, published in 1983 (Callahan & McCluskey, 1983); and history-graded influences are covered in the present volume. History-graded influences are by definition associated with definite time periods and affect significant portions of the population in similar ways, although the effects may differ for different age groups living at the time of such events. Examples of such events include economic depressions, wars, movements toward modernization, and changes in the demographic and occupational structure of a society. Much of the research relevant to this topic has been conducted within disciplines other than psychology—primarily within sociology. We have therefore departed from the tradition of previous volumes in the life-span series, in which most of the contributions were by psychologists, and have included herein contributions by sociologists as well as psychologists in about equal proportions.

History-graded influences reflect biological as well as environmental determinants of development. They are associated with historical time and therefore with changing contexts. They produce so-called cohort effects, which in turn often become functionally autonomous as cohort-graded influences. As Eckensberger, Krewer, and Kasper point out (Chapter 4 in this volume), the study of history- and cohort-graded influences demands explicit investigation of "the developing individual in a changing world," which has come to be the implicit motto of life-span developmental psychology and life-course sociology. Viewed in this way, history- and cohort-graded influences take on special significance in these disciplines, in that age-graded influences are by their nature resistant to historical change, and nonnormative influences are by definition related more to individual differences than to norms—whether they reflect age-graded stability or history-graded change. However, in spite of being fundamentally important for an understanding of life-span development, history- and cohort-graded influences are the least well-investigated category of influences. The chapters in this volume should facilitate expansion of relevant research by providing theoretical and methodological frameworks and by providing exciting examples of what can be learned.

REFERENCES

Callahan, E. J., & McCluskey, K. A. (Eds.). (1983). *Life-span developmental psychology: Nonnormative life events.* New York: Academic Press.
Datan, N., & Ginsberg, L. H. (Eds.). (1975). *Life-span developmental psychology: Normative life crises.* New York: Academic Press.
Eckensberger, L. H., Krewer, B., & Kasper, E. (1984). Simulation of cultural change by cross-cultural research: Some metamethodological considerations.

Acknowledgments

The success of the eighth West Virginia University Conference on Life-Span Developmental Psychology was facilitated by a large number of individuals. Stanley Wearden, Interim Dean of the College of Arts and Sciences, helped in providing university funds. Kennon A. Lattal, Acting Chairman of the Department of Psychology, was very generous with departmental resources and also helped to oversee the organization of the conference. Carrie Koeturius, in her role as director of the West Virginia University Conference Office, worked with us from the beginning to ensure the smooth operation of the entire conference. Dr. and Mrs. Franklin Parker deserve special recognition for their very charming and personal account of life events in the past three decades given in their keynote address. Thanks are in order for the graduate students in developmental psychology at West Virginia University who worked with the co-chair from the inception of this conference through the very end: Mary Kay August, Donna Barré, Linda Holt, Beverly Hummel, Jim Killarney, Nancy Meck, Dennis Papini, Gale Richardson, Rosellen Rosich, C. J. R. Simons, and Jeanne Thomas. Ann Davis provided many extra hours of secretarial work, for which we are grateful.

The contributors to this volume and the other participants who attended the conference deserve recognition for creating an invigorating intellectual climate that aided the creation of the essays published in this volume.

CHAPTER 1

Historical Time and Cohort Effects

K. WARNER SCHAIE

INTRODUCTION

Historical accounts of the life-span psychology movement are likely to point out that one of its major contributions may have been to shift the focus of concern from the search for purely developmental patterns of a normative nature to the context within which development occurs. This context, of course, not only refers to the characteristics of place and culture, but also includes as a major parameter the historical time during which development occurs. Concerns about the influence of historical period, however, have emerged largely from the study of adults. Children, as emergent organisms, might reasonably be assumed to possess some characteristics that are constant throughout history because those characteristics are involved in the establishment of behavioral competencies essential for survival. But few, if any, of these characteristics are important for development during much of adulthood, even though survival-relevant behaviors might again merit concern for the study of advanced old age. Therefore, I have in the past argued that scientific interest in age-related behavioral change recedes for those variables in which a behavioral asymptote is reached in young adulthood. Instead, close attention needs to be given to cohort and period effects (Schaie, 1973a, 1977).

In retrospect, it seems that much of the concern with methodologies designed to separate age, cohort, and period effects has stemmed from our preoccupation with the role of age as the independent variable of prime interest to developmentalists. Not unlike the early experimental psychologists who saw individual differences as a primary source of unwanted error variance, developmentalists have often treated historical time and genera-

LIFE-SPAN DEVELOPMENTAL PSYCHOLOGY
HISTORICAL AND GENERATIONAL EFFECTS

1

Copyright © 1984 by Academic Press, Inc.
All rights of reproduction in any form reserved.
ISBN 0-12-482420-X

tional effects as confounds to be controlled and explained away. Thus, it is not without a good deal of justification that Rosow (1978) could argue that the work on the sequential strategies (e.g., Baltes, 1968; Schaie, 1965) treated the effects other than age as nuisances and that any information developed on them was at best incidental.

Such a position, of course, has never been true for all developmentalists. Riegel, throughout the latter portion of his work, vehemently argued for a dialectic interplay of historical events with life-stage and cohort effects (1972, 1975, 1976). More recently, Sinott (1981) has considered implications of the theory of relativity for the study of development, which may provide considerable metatheoretical support for what we are about to consider. It should also be noted that several sociologists have addressed the interface of life stages and cohorts theoretically as well as substantively (e.g., Carlsson & Karlsson, 1970; Elder, 1974; Ryder, 1965). In my own work I have paid just as much attention to the estimation of period and cohort effects as to those of chronological age, perhaps at times even de-emphasizing the role of the age variable (e.g., Schaie, 1979, 1982b). But it remains quite true that not much has been done thus far to go beyond the description and identification of period and cohort effects, although attention has been called to the potential importance of these effects for fields as diverse as mental health, adult education, and the professional problems of engineers at midcareer (Schaie, 1978, 1981, 1982; Schaie & Willis, 1978).

The time has come then to remedy the lack of substantive attention given to the specific meaning of historical time and cohort. If this is to be done most constructively, it is not enough to appeal to sociologists and historians to provide definitions for what might be the most relevant societal changes and cohort boundaries for ordering developmental phenomena. It might be more constructive to begin by sketching out a framework that behavioral scientists can apply to the study of historical events that may be relevant to life-span development. To do this effectively, it may be necessary to broaden the concepts of cohort and period, to suggest methods for scaling the possible impact of historical events upon behavioral phenomena, and to suggest ways in which individual differences in position on space–time templates for diverse attributes might permit more creative uses of age as a dependent variable. In the course of this attempt, much of which is still highly speculative and provisional, it is possible that new insights may emerge on how the apparent stalemate in the estimation of age, cohort, and period effects could perhaps be finessed. But before we get too ambitious, let us begin far more humbly by recalling the kind of data that have persuaded at least some of us to leave the comforts of a static and ahistorical approach to the study of human development.

HISTORICAL TIME AND COHORT EFFECTS
IN PSYCHOLOGICAL DATA

Some concern had been expressed earlier regarding the impact of social change upon behavioral variables (e.g., Kuhlen, 1940), but fairly little formal attention had been given by developmental psychologists to the impact of generational or historical events. This lack of attention began to change when my concern with the discrepancies between cross-sectional and longitudinal findings on changes in adult intelligence led to the publication of my paper on the general developmental model (Schaie, 1965). What I had noted, essentially, was the fact that when I compared data from two cross-sectional samples drawn from the same parent population 7 years apart, the mean values on ability measures for the later sample exceeded those for the earlier sample with great regularity (Schaie & Strother, 1968). In addition, the overall mean for subjects at all ages also differed positively over time.

The implication of these findings suggested that there could either be the phenomenon of a unique period effect active across all cohorts studied, or that there was a long-term trend involving successively higher performance asymptotes in young adulthood (Schaie, 1983). It soon became obvious that to resolve these two alternatives it would be necessary to conduct an additional data collection, to permit construction of what we now call a longitudinal sequence (Schaie & Baltes, 1975). That is, data were needed that allow comparison of two or more cohorts followed over the same age range, a procedure that requires a minimum of three measurement points. This is what we did, and we were then persuaded that we were not faced with a period trend unique to the original time span, but that we were actually faced with substantial cohort differences (Schaie & Labouvie-Vief, 1974).

It will not surprise anyone that at the time of that study we lacked reasonable hypotheses with respect to the substantive meaning of either period or cohort effects (Schaie & Labouvie-Vief, 1974). The time period studied was an artifact of the timing of research funding; the cohort boundaries (and consequently the age ranges) were arbitrarily fixed to be equivalent to that time period. Because our initial interest was indeed the control of confounds for the age variable, this approach made sense. It simplified numerical analyses and permitted comparison of the magnitudes of variance components. In fact, this approach (perhaps inordinately directed toward attaining methodological sophistication) also gave rise to a number of methodological controversies (see Adam, 1978; Botwinick & Arenberg, 1976; Schaie & Hertzog, 1982), which may turn out to be of little substantive interest. For example, comparison of age and cohort effects, using equal chronological time units, may be appropriate only if it is possible to show that there are phenomena that can actually be scaled in comparable units, underlying the index variables of age and time.

In the life of adults, 7 years may actually not be an unreasonable age interval to detect behavioral change. The convention of using 5- or 10-year intervals relates to our use of the decimal system rather than to any psychologically meaningful dimension. It seems equally appropriate to segment the full age range over which adults can be found in reasonable frequency into 10 segments of 7 years each, 6 of which occur during the normal work life, and 4 after the typical retirement age. The reader who finds the latter justification somewhat strained might agree that cohort intervals selected to conform to age intervals for reasons of computational convenience have even less credibility! Nevertheless, the issue of meaningful cohort and/or period boundaries might still be neglected except that our data forcefully call attention to the absurdity of our present classification schemes.

This point is illustrated by Figure 1, which presents data on the variable of spatial orientation from the Primary Abilities Test for a data set in which all 162 participants were examined three times over 7-year intervals. The abscissa indicates their age at testing and the ordinate gives the mean performance in T-score points ($\bar{x} = 50$, $SD = 10$, based on a large sample at the first test occasion). The figure shows seven cohorts followed over a 14-year period, the youngest from mean age 25 to mean age 39 years, the oldest from mean age 67 to mean age 81 years. What becomes apparent immediately is that this figure does not portray seven *real* cohorts at all. Instead, considering the gaps between the arbitrary cohort boundaries, there appear to be three distinct cohort groupings. The three oldest cohorts seem quite distinct in level and slope from the next two, and those again are clearly

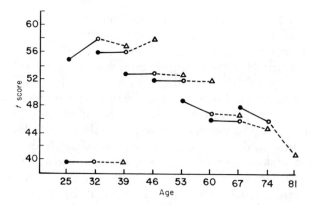

Figure 1. Longitudinal age gradients for spatial orientation measured in 1956 (darkened circles), 1963 (open circles), and 1970 (open triangles).

distinct from the youngest two. In this data set then, it appears empirically that there are three real cohorts. Given the constraints of our data set, the more appropriate time boundaries for the real cohorts ought to be 21 years for the oldest and 14 years for each of the youngest, empirically determined sets.

The gaps between these three sets seem curiously close in temporal contiguity to World Wars I and II. That is, the oldest group was educated prior to World War I, the second between the wars, and the youngest group during and after World War II. Calling attention ot such gross historical concomitants, however, is the rankest ad hoc approach to the interpretation of cohort effects. In the remainder of this chapter, consideration is given to some of the issues that must be addressed before historical time and cohort effects can seriously be related to human development.

The Concepts of Cohort and Period Revisited

Before we begin our attempt to delineate how behavioral scientists might go about measuring historical events, it might be prudent to give some attention to the manner in which the concepts have been defined, the meanings of which are clarified here. Most recently I have defined *cohort* as "the total population of individuals entering the specified environment at the same point in time," and *period* (time of measurement) as "the point in time at which the response of interest is actually recorded" (Schaie & Hertzog, 1982, p. 92). Footnoted to that paper is the suggestion that the point of common entry for a cohort need not necessarily be birth, and reference is made to relevant discussions in the sociological literature (Rosow, 1978). It now seems timely to begin to broaden the concepts of both cohort and period in a more explicit and formal manner. Such broadening may be useful in helping us reach a more genuine understanding of these concepts as they impact developmental phenomena. (For alternate but related conceptualizations of these issues, see Nesselroade, 1983; Nydegger, 1981; or Sorokin & Merton, 1937).

Cohort as a Selection Variable

Developmental psychologists have thus far utilized the cohort concept primarily as a mode of organizing individuals by birth year, but there are

TABLE 1

Alternative Cohort Definers: Some Examples

Age-graded	History-graded
Biological:	Initial staff of new college or corporation
Menarche	"Class" entering ranks of unemployed
Menopause	Class of technical or proprietary school
Birth of first child	Conscripts called up in a general mobilization
Becoming a grandparent	Nonnormative
Death	Divorce
Societal:	Infectious disease
Entry into school system	Accidental onset of disabling condition
Voluntary enlistment in armed forces	Membership in social group
First marriage	Purchase of home in new neighborhood
Retirement	

many other ways in which individuals can enter a common environment under study (see Table 1). Selection into such common environments may occur as the result of quite different influences. Baltes, Cornelius, and Nesselroade (1979) have classified such influences into three basic types: age-graded, history-graded, and nonnormative. The effects of the first of these influences will result in samples of subjects that are almost (but not entirely) as homogeneous by age as would be true for samples selected by birth year alone. Examples of age-graded cohort definers, other than the year of birth (in declining order of correlation with age) are entry into the public school system, menarche, menopause, enlistment in the volunteer armed forces, first marriage, birth of first child, becoming a grandparent, retirement, and death. Note that these cohort definers include both biologically and societally programmed events. They do have in common the attribute of being essentially normative in nature, and those among them that refer to societal norms are still largely constrained by relevant biological characteristics ordered by age.

There are other possible cohort definers that may be quite random with respect to age, at least over the broad range of middle adulthood. These include cohorts formed by influences that may be more or less history-graded in nature. For example, cohorts may be defined by events such as the staffing of a new corporation or college, the conscripts called up in a general mobilization, the cohort of persons entering the ranks of the unemployed during a depression and during periods of rapid technological change, the members of a given class of technical and proprietary schools.

Finally there are cohorts formed by the common experience of certain nonnormative events. This may sound paradoxical, but the fact remains that for members of a common species it is simply unlikely that there be a large variety of totally unique experiences of developmental consequence. Nonnormative events, therefore, are those favorable events that are not required for the adequate development of all (or even most) individuals and those unfavorable events that may impact some persons' development but may be avoidable for many. Again, temporally close experience of such nonnormative events may be influential in the formation of cohort groupings. Examples of such cohort definers (which typically are uncorrelated or only moderately correlated with age) include divorce, experience of an infectious disease, onset of a disabling condition by disease or accident, membership in a particular social group, purchase of residence in a particular neighborhood, and so on.

Some of these examples lend themselves to equal interval cohort boundaries, but others definitely do not. Moreover, it is important to note before leaving this topic that only the biologically determined age-graded influences permit assignment of all individuals to cohorts defined by a given influence. In all other instances cohort assignment is possible only for subtypes of the population displaying a particular biological, demographic, or behavioral attribute. This restriction might persuade some investigators to be rather cautious in trying out the proposed broadening of the cohort concept or to restrict broadening to universally assignable attributes. It should be stressed, however, that assignment to cohorts defined by influences holding only for limited subpopulations may actually yield more powerful predictions in individual cases than is possible from knowledge of universally defined characteristics.

Periods as Definers of Discrete Events

Thus far we have argued that there are many biological and societal influences that characterize entry into a common environment and that might consequently be suitable as selection variables for the definition of cohort groupings. Some of these influences might substitute meaningfully for year of birth, but would still be largely age-graded. Others, however, would largely be uncoupled from chronological age, albeit they might only be applicable to selected subpopulations. By analogy, we must now examine to what extent the concept of period is linked to particular calendar dates.

The objective of this exercise is to see whether the status of period can be converted from that of an index variable to that of an explanatory concept. What is of interest then is not the particular calendar date, but rather the historical event or events for which that date is the temporal indicator. It follows that just as organizational principles were needed to characterize alternate conceptions for cohorts, classes of influences are now wanted that would mark a given period. Here we immediately discover a most important conceptual distinction between period and cohort effects. Cohort effects may be history-graded, and many are, but cohorts can be defined by influences that may be quite ahistorical. By contrast, period effects are history-graded by definition! The Baltes *et al.* (1979) models then will not help in the reformulation of the period concept.

A beginning can be made by noting the range of impact of history-graded events. Some have universal impact, such as major wars or the introduction of major technological changes that achieve virtually immediate and universal acceptance. Others are of a far more parochial nature. They may affect certain localities, but not others, or even in a single region may only impact specific subsets of the general population. Of immediate concern is the recognition that all such events, whether general or specific, may impact different regions or even different individuals at different points in time. What we need then is some approach that will permit us to designate a calendar data at which a particular historical event, perceived to be a potential developmental influence, has had the opportunity to reach a specified proportion of our target population. Alternatively we may argue that for the most intensive study of individual development it may be necessary to assign to each individual a series of period indexes, one for each developmentally influential event under study, designating when such influence could have impacted our target person. Note immediately that a corollary of such an index of the initial impact on the target person would be a similar index reflecting the calendar date on which the impact ended!

Before consideration can be given to how the new definition of period designators is to be operationalized, attention must be given to the question of how a behavioral scientist would recognize historical events that are useful for this purpose. It is unlikely that we are really interested in political history as such; it is of no interest in this context who the president was, who fought, lost, or won what war. Instead, the kind of history to be considered is the chronicling of societal changes in technology, customs, and cultural stereotypes that might constrain behavior. A brief perusal of modern American history, conducted in preparation for writing this chapter, consequently eschewed the more formal treatments concerned with changes in our political fabric. What was of greatest interest were the far more journalistic accounts of the period that covered the life times of the people who have participated in my behavioral studies. These accounts not only conveyed the dramatic changes that have characterized the life of these individuals, but also helped to identify the calendar points at which particular events began to make broad impact (e.g., Allen, 1952).

Because most of my living research subjects were born no earlier than the turn of the century, I began by studying the immediate period preceding the First World War. For the behavioral scientist, a useful volume covering this period is provided by Lord (1960). Lord is most instructive in pointing to the vast differences in manner of living and in customs facing our older adult subjects in their youth from those experienced by our current cohort. For example, in the year 1900, radio was nonexistent, telephones were viewed as business tools, and the major means of personal transportation were horses and buggies for short distances and trains for long distances. Similar writings by Allen (1931, 1940) cover the decades of the boom following World War I and the Great Depression; and a useful account of the period immediately following the Second World War is provided by Goldman (1956).

What becomes clear then is that effective use of a broadened period concept requires (1) the identification of historical events that have developmental impact over the period in which subjects under study were alive, and (2) the scaling of temporal position of greatest impact of such events, perhaps as watershed dates.

How Do We Measure Historical Time?

It is now necessary to proceed from generalizations about the new directions that should be taken to specific prescriptions as to how the measurement of historical time can be operationalized. To begin with, a taxonomy of development-relevant events needs to be created by careful analysis of modern history texts, perhaps similar in scope to the approach taken by Allport and Odbert (1936) in their pioneering analyses of dictionaries, which they examined for the purpose of creating an exhaustive taxonomy of trait names. Professional judges can next be employed to classify the events as relevant to specific behavioral domains. Ratings of similarity may then serve to cluster events and to reduce to more manageable proportions the large number of events that could be studied.

Once events have been clustered along specified dimensions and a workable number of discrete events have been selected to mark each dimension, it is then necessary to do some further library research that will help obtain anchor points that can be used in assigning meaning to period analysis. The calendar dates need to be identified that bound those events that have been determined to be of most salient concern to developmentalists. For a number of temporally indexable social changes, it may be possible to note their date of first impact as well as the date when the change had become universally accepted (within the limits of the target population under study). Perhaps it would be prudent to define somewhat more conser-

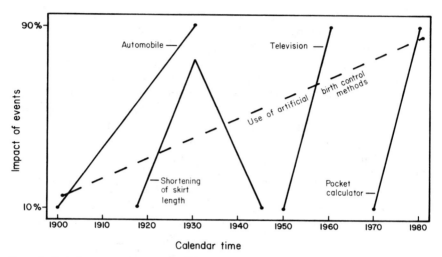

Figure 2. Period as event time, measured when 10–90% of the population adopted the change event.

vative boundaries, such as the year when 10% of the population had adopted a technological innovation (say the automobile, the telephone, or television) or accepted a changed custom or attitude (say minidresses, integration of schools, jogging) and the year when 90% of the population fully participated in the change event. For recursive phenomena by analogy, keeping in mind that event time is not necessarily unidirectional, an event would be deemed to have ceased when fewer than 10% of the target population remained impacted. Some examples of events showing various patterns of impact are depicted in Figure 2.

Another problem that requires solution is the manner in which relative impact values will be assigned to events that occur over the same or overlapping temporal periods. If data were available providing information on the individual timing (experience) of the historical events contiguous with behavioral measurements, it might then be feasible to determine the importance of the events by appropriate regression analyses. Lacking such data, it may not be unreasonable to rely once again upon expert scaling to obtain the needed parameters. Once this is done, calendar time can then be rescaled in terms of historical event impact density. Given a schema of multidimensional event classification, it might then be possible to develop a series of distinct time frames. For example, there might be one event-density based calendar for technological change, another for health-relevant interventions, a third for sexual mores, a fourth for information acquisition, and yet another for events enhancing self-awareness.

The broadened concept of period as a set of events marking historical

TABLE 2

Characteristics of Events Marking Historical Time

Type of event
  Technological
  Attitudinal
  Personal habits
  Knowledge diffusing
Impact of event
  Initial occurrence (impact on 10% of target population)
  Universal recognition (impact on 90% of target population)
  Dissipation (impact on less than 10% of target population)
Direction of the impact
  Linear
  Recursive
Event density
  Population effects
  Individual effects
Perception of event
  Objectively defined by professional judges
  Subjectively perceived by individual

time requires attention to a number of different characteristics that have not hitherto been given a great deal of attention. These characteristics have been summarized in Table 2.

Scaling, or rather rescaling, historical time would permit the assignment of psychological (or as some would term it, existential) rather than physical meaning to the construct of calendar time. Some might argue that moving away from the prevailing enslavement to the calendar (a purely physical time dimension) might bridge the gap between the hard-nosed experimental and the more humanistic approaches to life-span development (e.g., Schaie, 1973b; Sparks, 1973). This position does not specifically advocate a purely subjective calendar, although applying similar approaches to scaling the life history of a single individual would yield that result. What is advocated, however, is that historical time ought to be defined in terms of *event density*. That is, periods of time that are filled with behavior-relevant events ought to count more than those that are relatively event-free. If such an approach can be implemented, it seems likely that the new time units ought to correspond much more closely with those changes over age and time that are of interest to developmentalists. Moreover, reconceptualization of *period* as *event time* results in an important fringe benefit. As discussed next, it permits a new approach to resolving some of the methodological dilemmas that have plagued developmental researchers in recent years.

IMPLICATIONS FOR THE ESTIMATION OF AGE, COHORT, AND PERIOD EFFECTS

Broadening the concepts of cohort and period effects illuminate an important difference between them that may be fundamental to understanding them. This difference refers to the fact that *cohort* as a selection variable clearly must be and can only be an individual difference characteristic. One cannot belong to two cohort levels on the same selection variable, albeit under our broadened definition, one can simultaneously be a member of two or more cohort classifications. Period effects, by contrast, must be intraindividual change variables, whether calendar or event time, whether short or long; one cannot have the experience of an event commencing and terminating simultaneously. Although events are temporally bounded, it is nevertheless possible for two individuals to experience the same events on a different time scale or to experience different events at the same point in time. That is why I introduced the concept of event time.

The distinction just made sheds further light on the relation between cross-sectional and longitudinal data because chronological age has the status of an interindividual difference variable in the former, but of an intraindividual change variable for the latter. What is held in common by the two age indicators, therefore, must be other than cohort membership (now defined as a multiple selection variable) or experience of historical events (now considered as event time). What meaning does that leave for the concept of age? Most likely, it may be prudent to return to a fairly limited maturational view. Pure age effects, freed from cohort and period confounds, should reflect aggraded phenomena that are biological or ethological in nature because all other variance would be accounted for by group membership and experience of history-graded events. I am thus quite unabashedly returning to a position I took some time ago when I suggested that sequential methods might offer some contributions to the analysis of nature–nurture issues (Schaie, 1975).

Having allowed for cohort groupings, in which membership is not necessarily a function of chronological age, and having defined period effects as event time (which is no longer synonymous with calendar time), it now follows that the indeterminacies suggested by the general developmental model (Schaie, 1965) may no longer be inevitable. At least for extensive life stages, it is now possible to imagine research designs that permit specification of distinct age, period, and cohort dimensions. More often than not, these dimensions will fail to be orthogonal to each other, but it is possible to envision many circumstances (such as some of the examples given in this chapter for both cohort and event-time definers) in which, correlations will be quite low.

It would be beyond the scope of this chapter to indicate specific implications of these matters for technical aspects of sequential analysis. However, it appears to me that the earlier analysis of variance approaches (Schaie, 1977) will remain useful particularly in those instances in which cohort groupings are defined in such ways that the natural cohort boundaries are discrete or nonlinear in nature. Alternate approaches such as those suggested by Mason, Mason, Winsborough, and Poole (1973) and by Horn and McArdle (1980) would be preferred when all three dimensions are defined as continous variables, or when multiple definers of cohort and period are used.

In all of these instances it would seem to be most sensible to enter chronological age as the last variable because it alone retains the status of a pure index variable, unless it can be operationalized by physiological or other directly measurable age-related parameters. This leads to a cautious final comment that perhaps the time has indeed come to give more serious attention to Wohlwill's (1973) suggestion that chronological age might best be used as a dependent variable. That is the only approach that will ever provide the knowledge as to how chronological age manages to serve as a convenient index of the actual factors influencing human development!

SUMMARY AND CONCLUSIONS

Developmental psychologists and other developmental scientists, in recent years, have been spending a good deal of effort developing methodologies for a more valid description of developmental phenomena occurring over time. In that process they have recognized that chronological age as such has little explanatory power and is a rather empty indicator of the phenomena of interest. In the course of dealing with this problem the dimensions of cohort and historical period (time of measurement) were discovered, but were viewed at first primarily as unwanted confounds for the understanding of age changes. It was soon recognized, however, that rather than being merely inconvenient, these concepts may also be of great intrinsic interest to developmentalists.

In spite of the preoccupation with methods for separating cohort and period from chronological age, there have been few attempts to assign specific meaning to these concepts. In this chapter it is argued that before meaning can be assigned to the concept of cohort, it is necessary to broaden our view of how cohorts are selected; some organizing principles have been suggested for this purpose. Likewise, it is found to be desirable to transform the concept of period into one of event time. Once this is done, it then becomes possible and necessary to suggest an approach to the scaling of historical time to permit derivation of units of analysis useful for behavioral work. Finally, it is suggested that some of the methodological problems of age, time, and cohort estimation might be finessed by the redefinition of cohort and period, as their dependency upon chronological age can at least in some instances be partially broken by the new definitions.

REFERENCES

Adam, J. (1978). Sequential strategies and the separation of age, cohort, and time-of-measurement contributions to developmental data. *Psychological Bulletin, 85,* 1309–1316.

Allen, F. L. (1931). *Only yesterday: An informal history of the nineteen-twenties.* New York: Harper.

Allen, F. L. (1940). *Since yesterday: The nineteen-thirties in America.* New York: Harper.

Allen, F. L. (1952). *The big change: America transforms itself 1900–1950.* New York: Harper.

Allport, G. W., & Odbert, H. S. (1936). Traitnames: A psycholexical study. *Psychological Monographs., 47* (Whole No. 211).

Baltes, P. B. (1968). Longitudinal and cross-sectional sequences in the study of age and generation effects. *Human Development, 11,* 145–171.

Baltes, P. B., Cornelius, S. W., & Nesselroade, J. R. (1979). Cohort effects in developmental psychology. In J. R. Nesselroade & P. B. Baltes (Eds.), *Longitudinal research in the study of behavior and development.* New York: Academic Press.

Botwinick, J., & Arenberg, D. (1976). Disparate time-spans in sequential studies of aging. *Experimental aging research, 2,* 55–66.

Carlsson, C., & Karlsson, K. (1970). Age, cohorts and the generation of generations. *American Sociological Review, 35,* 710–718.

Elder, G. (1974). *Children of the great depression.* Chicago: University of Chicago Press.

Goldman, E. F. (1956). *The crucial decade: America, 1945–1955.* New York: Knopf.

Horn, J. L., & McArdle, J. J. (1980). Perspectives on mathematical/statistical model building (MASMOB) in research on aging. In L. F. Poon (Ed.), *Aging in the 1980s.* Washington: American Psychological Association.

Kuhlen, R. G. (1940). Social changes: A neglected factor in psychological studies of the life span. *School and Society, 52,* 14–16.

Lord, W. (1960). *The good years: From 1900 to the first World War.* New York: Harper.

Mason, K. O., Mason, W. M., Winsborough, H. H., & Poole, W. K. (1973). Some methodological problems in cohort analyses of archival data. *American Sociological Review, 38,* 242–258.

Nesselroade, J. R. (1983). *Temporal selection and factor invariance in the study of development and change.* In P. B. Baltes & O. G. Brim, Jr. (Eds.), *Life-span development and behavior* (Vol 5). New York: Academic Press.

Nydegger, C. N. (1981). On being caught up in time. *Human Development, 24,* 1–12.

Riegel, K. F. (1972). Time and change in the development of the individual and society. In H. W. Reese (Ed.), *Advances in child development and behavior,* (Vol 7). New York: Academic Press.

Riegel, K. F. (1975). Adult life crises: Towards a dialectic theory of development. In N. Datan & L. Ginsberg (Eds.), *Life-span developmental psychology: Normative life crises.* New York: Academic Press.

Riegel, K. F. (1976). *Psychology of development and history.* New York: Plenum.

Rosow, I. (1978). What is a cohort and why. *Human Development, 21,* 65–75.

Ryder, N. (1965). The cohort as a concept in the study of social change. *American Sociological Review, 30,* 843–861.

Schaie, K. W. (1965). A general model for the study of developmental problems. *Psychological Bulletin, 64,* 91–107.

Schaie, K. W. (1973a). Methodological problems in descriptive developmental research on adulthood and aging. In J. R. Nesselroade & H. W. Reese (Eds.), *Life-span developmental psychology: Methodological issues.* New York: Academic Press.

Schaie, K. W. (1973b). Reflections on papers by Looft, Peterson and Sparks: Intervention towards an ageless society? *Gerontologist, 13,* 31–35.

Schaie, K. W. (1975). Research strategy in developmental human behavior genetics. In K. W. Schaie, E. V. Anderson, G. E. McClearn, & J. Money (Eds.), *Developmental human behavior genetics.* Lexington, MA: Heath.

Schaie, K. W. (1977). Quasi-experimental designs in the psychology of aging. In J. E. Birren & K. W. Schaie (Eds.), *Handbook of the psychology of aging.* New York: Van Nostrand Reinhold.

Schaie, K. W. (1978). Impact of aging on the individual: Cognitive, intellectual and performance factors. In M. Hamburger & J. Arleo (Eds.), *The engineer at mid-career: Discrimination or utilization.* New York: Institute of Electrical and Electronic Engineers.

Schaie, K. W. (1979). The Primary Mental Abilities in adulthood: An exploration in the development of psychometric intelligence. In P. B. Baltes & O. G. Brim, Jr. (Eds.), *Life-span development and behavior* (Vol. 2). New York: Academic Press.

Schaie, K. W. (1981). Psychological changes from midlife to early old age: Implications for the maintenance of mental health. *American Journal of Orthopsychiatry, 51,* 199–219.

Schaie, K. W. (1982). *New directions for an applied developmental psychology of adulthood.* Invited lecture presented at the Annual Meeting of the Eastern Psychological Association, Baltimore.

Schaie, K. W. (1983). The Seattle Longitudinal Study: A twenty-one year exploration of psychometric intelligence in adulthood. In K. W. Schaie (Ed.), *Longitudinal studies of adult psychological development.* New York: Guilford Press.

Schaie, K. W., & Baltes, P. B. (1975). On sequential strategies in developmental research: Description or explanation? *Human Development, 18,* 384–390.

Schaie, K. W., & Hertzog, C. (1982). Longitudinal methods. In B. B. Wolman (Ed.), *Handbook of developmental psychology.* Englewood Cliffs, NJ: Prentice-Hall.

Schaie, K. W., & Labouvie-Vief, G. (1974). Generational versus ontogenetic components of change in adult cognitive behavior: A fourteen-year cross-sequential study. *Developmental Psychology, 10,* 303–320.

Schaie, K. W., & Strother, C. R. (1968). The effect of time and cohort behavior. *Multivariate Behavioral Research, 3,* 259–293.

Schaie, K. W., & Willis, S. L. (1978). Life-span development: Implications for education. *Review of Research in Education, 6,* 120–156.

Sinott, J. D. (1981). The theory of relativity: A metatheory for development? *Human Development, 24,* 93–311.

Sorokin, P. A., & Merton, R. K. (1937). Social time: A methodological and functional analysis. *American Journal of Sociology, 42,* 615–629.

Sparks, P. M. (1973). Behavioral versus experential aging: Implications for intervention. *Gerontologist, 13,* 15–18.

Wohlwill, J. F. (1973). *The study of behavioral development.* New York: Academic Press.

CHAPTER 2

Dimensions of Historical Constancy and Change

Hayne W. Reese
Kathleen A. McCluskey

Introduction

The purpose of this chapter is to survey the aims, methods, and problems of research on historical constancy and change and to emphasize the usefulness of dissecting the relevant independent and dependent variables into specific dimensions. Concern with historical constancy and change has been more prominent in sociology and history than in developmental psychology, although this concern has been fairly prominent in the psychology of adulthood and aging. One of our goals in this chapter is to increase this concern among developmental psychologists, and therefore we use herein the technical jargon of developmental psychology rather than that of sociology or of history.

Historical change refers to discontinuities across time or cohorts. It may be evolutionary or revolutionary; that is, it may be a gradual, cumulative effect of a series of historical events, or it may result from a relatively sudden and distinct historical event. *Historical constancy* is the absence of change despite the intuition that evolution should have occurred or that dramatic events which occurred should have produced revolutionary change. The focus of the research in this area has been on historical change, although the frequency of encountering historical constancy has often been noted.

Consider an analogy. The development of an ecosystem is subject to two kinds of disturbance: endogenous and exogenous. *Endogenous disturbances* are part of the normal course of development; *exogenous distur-*

Life-Span Developmental Psychology
Historical and Generational Effects

17

Copyright © 1984 by Academic Press, Inc.
All rights of reproduction in any form reserved.
ISBN 0-12-482420-X

bances are extrasystemic in origin and they deflect, at least for a time, the normal course of development. For example, in a terrestrial ecosystem such as a forest, the fall of a large, old tree is an endogenous disturbance, and severe winds and fires are exogenous disturbances (Bormann & Likens, 1979). The steady state of the system, or progress toward the steady state, is disturbed only locally by endogenous disturbances, but is disrupted by exogenous disturbances. Even in the latter cases, the usual finding has been that the normal course is eventually recovered in terrestrial ecosystems.

Historical events that affect human development are like exogenous disturbances. They deflect the life courses of individuals in the affected cohort; and they may deflect the cross-generational life course (history) of a larger social unit, such as a family, population, or even species. By analogy to the effects of exogenous disturbances in terrestrial ecosystems, however, the effects of such events should be transient in the cross-generational life or history of the larger unit if not in the life of the individual.

The historical events that are studied in research on human development are *historical* either in the sense of separating distinct stages of individual development in individual time or in the sense of separating distinct cohorts in historical time. The difference is between *idiographic* and *nomothetic events,* in Allport's (1961) senses of these terms, or in other words between events whose effects are unique to an individual and events whose effects are pervasive across many individuals. In both cases, the events are usually multidimensional. The "dimensions" of events are their "structural characteristics" (Danish, Smyer, & Nowak, 1980, p. 342), "properties" (Brim & Ryff, 1980, p. 371), or "attributes" (Hultsch & Plemons, 1979, pp. 20–21).

DIMENSIONS OF LIFE EVENTS

Baltes and his colleagues identified three categories of life events: non-normative, normative age-graded, and normative history-graded (Baltes, 1979; Baltes, Cornelius, & Nesselroade, 1978; Baltes & Nesselroade, 1979; Baltes, Reese, & Lipsitt, 1980; Baltes & Willis, 1979). The first two categories were covered respectively, in the 1974 and in the 1980 West Virginia University Conference on Life-Span Developmental Psychology (proceedings published in Datan & Ginsberg, 1975; Callahan & McCluskey, 1983), and the third was covered in the 1982 conference (proceedings contained in the present volume). Precise definition of the categories is unnecessary because they are not technical terms—they are "chapter heading" words. Nevertheless, they need at least rough definition if they are to have even this rough utility.

The Normative–Nonnormative Distinction

The normative–nonnormative distinction is somewhat ambiguous because in its strict sense *normative* refers to ideal standards, or "customs and jural rules" (Leach, 1968, p. 340), and in its loose sense it refers to norms, that is, average actual occurrences. In the strict sense, an event is normative if its occurrence is considered to be desirable, whether or not the event actually occurs and whether or not the occurrence would actually be welcomed. In this sense, *normative* refers to the life-event dimension of *desirability* defined as the perceived evaluation of an event by society at large or by whatever the relevant reference group is (Reese & Smyer, 1983, p. 6). In the loose sense referring to norms, *normative* refers to the life-event dimension of *prevalence*, defined as the number of individuals who experience a given event, relative to the number of individuals in the population (Reese & Smyer, 1983, p. 7).

The following examples given by Leach (1968) illustrate the difference between normative and normal on the desirability and prevalence dimensions. According to the normative standard of the Kurds, a man should marry his father's brother's daughter (his patrilateral parallel cousin— Schusky, 1972, pp. 20, 67); and according to the normative standard of the Trobriand Islanders, a man should marry his father's sister's daughter (his patrilateral cross cousin). Surveys done in 1951 showed that 45% of all Kurdish marriages conformed to the Kurdish ideal, but among the Trobriand Islanders, only one conforming marriage was found in several hundred marriages. For both groups, marrying the specified first cousin was high in desirability, but it was high in prevalence among the Kurds and very low in prevalence among the Trobriand Islanders.

Age Grading

Age grading is also called age relatedness, temporal predictability, and timing. It is measured by the strength of the correlation between age and the occurrence of an event (Reese & Smyer, 1983, p. 6). For example, being the victim of a crime seems to be low in age grading; its occurrence at any specified age is low in predictability. In contrast, entering school and entering the work force are high in age grading, the first more so than the second because the first if dictated by legislation and the second is dictated in part by custom.

The timing of age-graded events is expected to be relatively stable over historical time; and when their timing changes, causes of the change are sought. Put another way, age-graded events are not expected to exhibit *cohort specificity*. Cohort specificity is the extent to which the effect of an

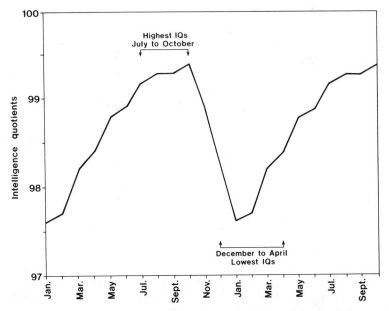

Figure 1. Average IQ in cohorts defined by month of birth, disregarding year of birth. (Adapted from Shuttleworth, 1949, Figure 275. Copyright 1949 by the Society for Research in Child Development. Adapted by permission.)

event is limited to one cohort (Reese & Smyer, 1983, p. 7). A *cohort* is a group of individuals who have a designated characteristic in common. In developmental psychology the defining characteristic is usually either the year of birth or a range of years of birth. Figure 1 illustrates an event that is age-graded and not cohort-specific. The "event" in this example is whatever causes the relation between month of birth and later IQ; the relation is presumably the same for all birth cohorts defined by year of birth, and therefore the "event" is presumably the same for all birth cohorts.

History Grading

History grading means that the events are associated with distinct periods of historical time. History-graded events are not age-graded, because although they may affect only one age group, their timing depends on history rather than age. History-graded events are always cohort-specific, even if only in the sense of a cohort consisting of everyone alive at the time of their occurrence; they are unique, one-shot events that affect *this* cohort, perhaps differently for individuals from different birth cohorts within the overall cohort. In any case, the events themselves are not expected to recur in the lives of later cohorts, and therefore they can affect these later cohorts only through cultural mediation. For example, Franklin Delano Roosevelt's four elections to the presidency led to the Twenty-Second Amendment in 1951, limiting presidents to two elected terms in office. This constitutional amendment is the cultural mediator of one effect of Roosevelt's presidency on subsequent cohorts.

Other Dimensions

So far, we have suggested that life events can be evaluated on the dimensions of desirability, prevalence, age grading, and cohort specificity. These four dimensions are not exhaustive; the effects of life events depend on a number of other dimensions, including duration, spacing, and sequence (Elder & Rockwell, 1979; for discussion of these and other dimensions, see Reese & Smyer, 1983). If an effect is produced, the stressfulness of the life event—or perhaps one should say the stressfulness of the effect—depends on the nature of the change and the personal context in which it occurs. The personal context includes the "life history of experience, expectations, and adaptive skills that one brings to the change . . . [and] the temporal context of the change—its position within the life course and relation to other events" (Elder & Rockwell, 1979, p. 15).

Other important dimensions—identified in disaster research—include the intensity, novelty, and unpredictability of the event (Logue, Hansen, & Struening, 1979), and its scope of impact (size of area and population affected) and speed of onset (Gleser, Green, & Winget, 1981). The cause of the event can also be important: According to Gleser *et al.,* "Disasters that are man-made are likely to result in a widespread feeling of having been betrayed by those who were trusted" (1981, p. 149).

Reese and Smyer (1983) surveyed the life-events literature and identified some 35 different dimensions. However, the 4 dimensions defined previously are an important subset, and they can be used to illustrate the dissection of life events into their constituent dimensions. We emphasize history-graded examples, to fit the theme of this volume.

Examples

As Reese and Smyer (1983) noted, being in the first class of women admitted to Yale University and being in the Black Death plague in fourteenth-century Europe and Asia are both history-graded events. They differ in desirability, obviously, but we would like to emphasize that desirability is culturally relative and therefore also historically relative. Kvale (1977) has pointed out that evaluation of past events is always done in the present and therefore the meanings of past events are determined by the present context. The Black Death was undesirable when it occurred, but to the extent that its consequences were eventually beneficial, its occurrence came to be desirable. Unfortunate for its victims, certainly, but fortunate in some ways for later cohorts. Its consequences may have included the emergence of "a new economy, that of mercantilist capitalism; a new political framework, mainly that of a centralized despotism or oligarchy, usually embodied in a national state; and a new ideological form, that derived from mechanistic physics" (Mumford, 1961, p. 345). These developments may now seem to have been undesirable, but consideration of what they replaced and what they in turn led to gives them a measure of desirability. Incidentally, if in fact the fourteenth-century Black Death had a causal role in these developments, they were long-range "sleeper effects" (e.g., Seitz, 1981), in that their emergence occurred between the fifteenth and eighteenth centuries.

The prevalence of being in the first class of women admitted to Yale University—in 1892 for doctoral students (Kelley, 1974, p. 283) and in 1969 for undergraduates (Lever & Schwartz, 1971, p. 30)—was extremely low in the population at large. In contrast, the prevalence of being in the Black Death plague was extremely high, in that even the survivors were affected in profound ways. The prevalence of dying in the Black Death was fairly high; for example, in Britain about one-third of the population died.

Both events were low in age grading and high in cohort specificity. The first undergraduate class of women admitted to Yale University consisted for the most part of women from the same late-adolescent birth cohort, and the population that experienced the Black Death plague consisted of a cohort defined by a range of birth years that was extremely wide relative to the average life span but not wide in the span of historical time. That is, the Black Death cohort consisted of everyone who was alive at any time during the plague years (1348–1350).

More narrowly defined Black Death cohorts can also be identified. Table 1 shows that the prevalence of mortality varied with age. This variation seems better identified as variation in cohort specificity than as age grading because age grading should imply that events are relatively stable over time. The prevalence of mortality also varied with other demographic characteristics that can be used to define cohorts: The mortality rate was much lower among the rich and powerful than among the rest of the population. For example, the mortality rate was 18% among English bishops and 40% among the clergy as a whole (Ziegler, 1969, p. 200).

A less dire example is illustrated in Figure 2, which shows a cohort change in the publishing output of psychologists. As shown in the figure, the

TABLE 1

Mortality in Britain in the Black Death[a]

Age	Number exposed to plague	Number who died	Mortality rate (%)
1–10	16	2	12
11–20	43	8	19
21–30	114	22	19
31–40	139	43	31
41–50	96	25	26
51–60	56	22	39
>60	41	16	39

[a]Based on "inquisitions post-mortem" (i.e., official inquiries regarding inheritance of property) conducted during the Black Death (1348–1350). Adapted from Russell (1948, Table 9.13, p. 216).

cohort of psychologists who obtained the PhD in 1963–1964 had a higher maximum level of output and maintained this level longer than the 1969–1970 cohort (Porter, Chubin, Rossini, Boeckmann, & Connolly, 1982). According to Porter *et al.*, the decline in output "is more a function of fewer people actively continuing to pursue research than of the same number of researchers producing less" (p. 479). In the face of increased pressures to publish, this finding suggests "a troubling erosion of commitment to research" (p. 480). The cause of this erosion is not apparent, especially because the fall off in the 1963–1964 cohort occurred 9–10 years after the PhD was obtained, and in the 1969–1970 cohort it occurred only 3–4 years after the PhD was obtained. The earlier cohort continued publishing beyond the time when tenure would ordinarily be obtained, but the later cohort slowed down the rate of publishing before that time. Incidentally, the later cohort may have had no more trouble obtaining tenure than the earlier cohort. According to a study by Lewis (1980), tenure was "perhaps not significantly" more difficult to obtain in the late 1970s than in the late 1960s (p. 381).

These examples show that cohorts can be defined on important bases other than age. As noted, a cohort is a group of individuals who have a designated characteristic in common, and the defining characteristic (in developmental psychology) is often age. However, characteristics that span age periods can define interesting cohorts.

We turn now to a more fully explicated example illustrating several additional dimensions of life events and illustrating dimensions of the effects of life events. The example also illustrates another event-related definition

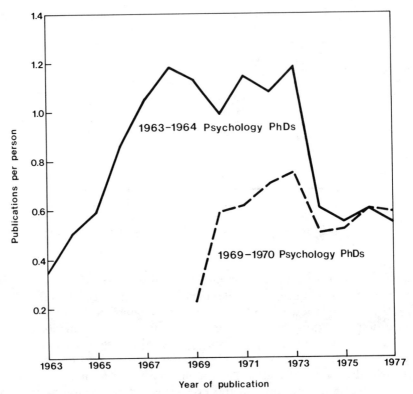

Figure 2. Mean number of publications per person in two cohorts of psychologists (PhD obtained in 1963–1964 or in 1969–1970). (Adapted from Porter, Chubin, Rossini, Boeckmann, & Connolly, 1982, Figure 2, p. 480. Copyright 1982 by Sigma Xi, The Scientific Research Society. Adapted by permission.)

of cohorts. We describe the example first and then the dimensions it illustrates.

THE NEW MADRID EARTHQUAKE

Summary of the Event

A prolonged earthquake occurred in the United States between December 16, 1811, and March 15, 1812. During that 91-day period (1812 was a leap year), 1874 tremors were counted, and "the area within which tremors could be felt without the aid of instruments approached one million square miles" (Penick, 1981, p. 6). The epicenter was near New Madrid,

Missouri, on the Mississippi River; but the prolonged tremors affected equilibrium in many individuals as far away as Richmond, Virginia; Savannah, Georgia; and Baltimore, Maryland. Nearer the epicenter (apparently), "a profile could be constructed of general and widespread physical symptoms resulting from the constant buffeting. These included giddiness, nausea, vomiting, debility, trembling knees, and pains in the knees and legs" (Penick, 1981, p. 107). Evidently, however, these physiological effects disappeared as the earthquake subsided and eventually came to an end.

Relatively short-lived psychological effects were also produced. For instance, in the multistate area in which the shocks were strong, membership in the largest religious sect, the Methodist Church, increased by 50% (from 30,741 in 1811 to 45,983 in 1812), while in the rest of the nation it increased by less than 1%. Penick (1981) commented:

> There was a relative decline in the next couple of years before the steady upward climb resumed, indicating a degree of backsliding as the unregenerate realized the world's end was not forthcoming. "Earth-quake Christian" was a phrase embittered preachers reserved for those whose devotions were more enthusiastic during the course of the shocks than before and after. (p. 118)

(Lachman and Bonk reported a similar phenomenon in Hawaii: "One unusually interesting class of 'security seeking' behavior emerges consistently during Hawaiian [volcanic] eruptions: rituals and offerings are made to the Hawaiian Volcano Goddess, Pele" [1960, p. 1095].)

In New Madrid County itself, the tremors continued for many years, and the residents gradually became inured to them (Penick, 1981, p. 48). The following anecdote illustrates what must have been relatively long-lasting physiological and psychological adjustment to the tremors, or "shakes" as they were called in the region:

> Several ladies and gentlemen, passengers on board a steam boat ascending the Mississippi in 1820, went on shore near New Madrid. In one of the houses, which they entered, they found a small collection of books. As they were amusing themselves with the examination of these, they felt the whole house so violently shaken, that they were scarce able to stand upon their feet. Some consternation was, of course, felt, and much terror expressed. "Don't be alarmed," said the lady of the house, "it is nothing but an earthquake." (James, 1966/1823, pp. 325–326)

Dimensions of the New Madrid Earthquake

The New Madrid earthquake produced some effects that were only temporary disturbances in affected individuals' life courses, and other effects that were perhaps more profound and certainly more long-lasting. In other words, it produced some transient time-of-measurement effects and some more lasting cohort effects, as the two types of effects are conventionally labeled (e.g., Baltes, Reese, & Nesselroade, 1977; Schaie, 1965). Actually, the New Madrid earthquake was part of a widespread upheaval. For example, on March 26, 1812, a week or so after the end of the generalized New Madrid earthquake, "the Venezuelan cities of Caracas and La Guaira were thrown down" with a loss of 20,000 lives (Penick, 1981, p. 46). Property damage and loss of lives were relatively light in the New Madrid region, and the differences on these two dimensions can be presumed to have produced differences in severity and persistence of the impact.

Table 2 shows our a priori assessment of the New Madrid earthquake and its effects, using 8 of some 35 dimensions that possibly could be used (Reese & Smyer, 1983). The *desirability* of the event was of course low and the *prevalence* was high. The event was related to historical time rather than individual time, and therefore *age grading* was low and *cohort specificity* was high, at least if cohort is given the broad meaning implied by the designation "New Madrid earthquake cohort." Cohort specificity was low with respect to birth cohorts. The *duration* of the event was long and its *impact* or severity was high, although surely not as high as that of the related earthquake in Venezuela. The *domains* affected included physiologi-

TABLE 2

An A Priori Dimensionalization of the New Madrid Earthquake

Dimension	Definition	Dimensional value
Desirability	Perceived social evaluation of event as good versus bad	Bad
Prevalence	Relative number of individuals experiencing the event	High
Age grading	Age relatedness	Low
Cohort specificity	Extent to which effect depends on person's cohort	Nonspecific for age cohorts; specific for "New Madrid earthquake" cohort
Duration	Amount of time for event to transpire	Long
Impact	Amount of change or stress induced; severity	High (?)
Domain	Type of functioning affected	Physiological, psychological, social
Stability of change	Degree to which change persists	Variable

cal processes such as equilibrium and psychological processes such as emotional reactions. Social processes were probably affected, in that residents who moved away were not fully replaced by new settlers and a sparsely settled area became more sparsely settled. The *stability* of the changes was variable: Some changes seem to have been transient time-of-measurement effects, abating and then disappearing as the shakes abated and disappeared. Other effects seem to have been longer-lasting, including the suppression of physiological and emotional responsiveness to the continued shakes in New Madrid County.

We deliberately chose this relatively uncomplicated example to make our point emphatic: Neither historical events nor their effects can be understood unless their multidimensional nature is recognized and, most importantly, unless the actual dimensions of the events and their effects are identified and evaluated. In some cases, relevant data sets may be comprehensive enough and sample sizes large enough to permit statistical identification and evaluation of the dimensions. In many cases—perhaps most cases, such as the examples given in this chapter—the identification and evaluation of the dimensions is speculative. However, the speculation should be theory-guided, for reasons that are discussed in the next section, in connection with the methods that are used for the study of historical change.

METHODS OF STUDY

Historiography

THE NATURE OF EXPLANATION

According to one philosophy of history, historians show not what caused an event but what made it possible—the causes cited are necessary but not necessarily sufficient. As Gardiner (1968) noted, this is a weak form of the covering law conception of historiography. In the *covering law* conception of explanation the occurrence of an individual event is explained by reference to antecedent conditions and to a "covering law," that is, a general law that relates such antecedents to outcomes (e.g., Hempel, 1967, pp. 80–81).

The covering law type of explanation can be either deductive or probabilistic (Hempel, 1967). In deductive explanation, the general covering laws (plus statements of antecedent conditions) serve as premises from which a given event is deduced as a conclusion through syllogistic reasoning. The truth criterion is verification of the conclusion. In probabilistic explanation, the event is shown to be expected or expectable with more or less high probability, given the relevant covering laws and the occurrence of certain antecedents. The truth criterion is verification of the expectation. Hempel and Oppenheim (1953/1948) gave the following example:

> In Northern France, there exist a large variety of words synonymous with the English "bee," whereas in Southern France, essentially only one such word is in existence. For this discrepancy, the explanation has been suggested that in the Latin epoch, the South of France used the word "apicula," and North the word "apis." The latter, because of a process of phonologic decay in Northern France, became the monosyllabic word "é"; and monosyllables tend to be eliminated, especially if they contain few consonantic elements, for they are apt to give rise to misunderstandings. Thus, to avoid confusion, other words were selected. But "apicula," which was reduced to "abelho," remained clear enough and was retained, and finally it even entered into the standard language, in the form "abbeille." While the explanation here described is incomplete . . . it clearly exhibits reference to specific antecedent conditions as well as to general laws. (pp. 325–326)

An alternative philosophy of history, according to Gardiner (1968), is the "theory of continuous series": "The historian traces, step by step, the relations between earlier and later phases of historical change, thereby building up an intelligible narrative whose various components can be seen to stand in 'intrinsic' or 'natural' connections with one another" (Gardiner, 1968, p. 432).

The continuous series type of explanation is the "pattern" type (Kaplan, 1964, p. 332) or "explanation by reasons" (Hempel, 1967, p. 87). In this type of explanation, an event is explained by arguing that it fits into a known pattern. The argument refers to relationships that have been discovered or invented. The truth criterion is not predictive but developmental—the ability to fill in and extend the pattern indefinitely and to fit the pattern into a larger whole (Kaplan, 1964, p. 335). In other words, the truth criterion refers to the plausibility of the postulated pattern or network of events.

According to Hempel, all scientific explanation is either deductive or probabilistic, and therefore requires covering laws. Even explanation by reasons, including teleological explanation, implies a general law about "the way the agent will behave under various circumstances" (Hempel, 1967, p. 88)—not only is the behavior necessary for the achievement of some end, but this agent is the type who will generally perform the required action. Therefore, the continuous series type of explanation actually fits the covering law conception, although the continuous series type is not necessarily "narrowly mechanistic" because explanations of this type "reach far beyond causal and mechanical explanation" (Hempel, 1967, p. 88).

Positivist philosophers of science have distinguished among three types of covering laws: process, developmental, and historical. (1) A *process* law—or "Newtonian lawfulness" (Bergmann, 1957, p. 89)—permits prediction of the state of a system at any moment, given assessment of the state of the system at any other moment. (2) A *developmental* law is "a crude sketch or anticipation of a process law" (Bergmann, 1957, p. 118). It states that if a system has Character B at a certain time, then under normal conditions it had Character A at an earlier time and will have Character C at a later time. Examples are the egg–caterpillar–cocoon–butterfly sequence, the sitting–crawling–standing–walking–running sequence, and the sequences of stages in Freud's and Piaget's theories (Spiker, 1966). (3) A *historical* law is a law in which the future state of a system is related to the present state *and* an earlier state (Bergmann, 1957, p. 126). That is, the future state is predictable only from knowledge of the past as well as knowledge of the present. If the past leaves a trace of some kind and the trace can be assessed in the present, then the law is developmental rather than historical because knowledge of the trace is present knowledge and knowledge of the history of the trace is not needed.

A fourth type of law is the *cross-sectional* or *syndromatic* type. Such laws refer to time-independent relations among variables. Some cross-sectional laws are deducible from process laws; others are not. For example, laws of the form "Whoever has personality trait A also has personality trait B" make no explicit reference to time, but would be deducible from the process laws of personality development if these laws were known (Bergmann, 1957, p. 118). Similarly, the law of the lever and Ohm's law make no reference to time, but they are *equilibrium* laws, which are deducible from process laws (Bergmann, 1957, p. 102). In contrast, the laws of interrelationship among the three angles of a triangle, for example, are not deducible from process laws. The nondeducible cross-sectional laws do not refer to antecedent–consequent relationships, but are nevertheless accepted as fully adequate explanations in empiricist sciences. They "are in no way logically subordinate to process laws. Rather, they represent a second, logically coordinate kind of lawfulness" (Bergmann, 1957, p. 118). However, the nondeducible cross-sectional laws are by their very nature not laws of *change;* interpreted within Aristotle's system they would be identified as laws of material or formal causality. That is, the nondeducible cross-sectional laws are synchronic, and the only diachronic laws in empiricist sciences are process, developmental, and historical laws, which therefore are the only kinds of laws that can serve as covering laws in explanations of change.

METHODS IN HISTORY

The sources used by developmental psychologists to document the occurrences and effects of historical events are not sources in the sense used by historians. According to Winks (1969), "By a 'source' the historian means material that is contemporary to the events being examined" (p. xx). However, the source used by a developmental psychologist is likely to be the historian's interpretation of such sources. In fact, the developmental psychologist's sources are sometimes one further step removed from the historian's sources, in that the developmentalist sometimes cites for documentation a fellow developmentalist's interpretation of the historian's interpretation. In Winks's (1969) view:

> The historian needs to assess evidence against a reasonably well-informed background. Is one writing of the Pullman Strike of 1894? One must, obviously, know quite a bit about general labor conditions, about business management, about employment opportunities and the nature of the economy, about Chicago and its environs, and about the railroad industry. But since many of the strikers were Welshmen, one needs also to know something of contrasting work conditions in that part of Wales from which the workmen came. Since the strike was compounded by inept police and militia work, one needs to know about the nature of such work in Illinois and, comparatively, elsewhere. One needs to investigate the judicial system, the rôle of President Grover Cleveland, the powers open to Governor John P. Altgeld, the ideas of Eugene V. Debs, and the effects of the Chicago World's Fair, which brought hundreds of drifters into the metropolitan area to contribute to the violence associated with the strike. Since the strike disrupted mail service throughout the nation, forcing letters north onto Canadian tracks, one needs to investigate at least briefly the Canadian rail network, the relationship with railwaymen elsewhere, and the applicability of the secondary boycott. One needs to know much of the general climate of opinion at the time to assess the meaning of the strike. One needs to look at company, city, union, judicial, militia, post-office, Presidential, legal, and gubernatorial records; at the private papers of Cleveland, Altgeld, Pullman, Debs; at the papers of the judges, magistrates, and strikers, if they can be found and, when found, if one can gain access to them. Much that one learns on such journeys will never appear in the final book, but every nuance, every sentence, will be better informed, closer to the truth, more protected against one's own biases (which can never be totally blocked out, and no responsible historian claims that they can be), than if such journeys were not taken at all. (pp. xvii–xix)

Winks (1969) also noted that American historians "tend to begin with the questions they wish to entertain first (Did failed farmers truly move West to begin life anew in the eighteen-forties? Did immigrants reinforce older patterns of life or create new ones?), confident that the data can be found. European historians, on the other hand, are likely to begin with the available source materials first, and then look to see what legitimate questions they might ask of these sources" (p. xxi). (The reason for the difference is a difference in the extensiveness of collections of historical source materials.)

Developmental Psychology

The methods used in history are either to start with the questions and find the answers or to start with the answers and find the questions. In developmental psychology—and other sciences such as epidemiology and sociology—the analogous methods are to start with an event and find its effects or to start with effects and find the determining events. The two methods have been labeled in various ways. For example, in epidemiology they have been called the "prospective" (p. 226) and "retrospective" (p. 194) methods (Lilienfeld & Lilienfeld, 1980). However, these terms can be confusing because *retrospective* has been used in psychology and sociology to refer to any method in which data about an event are derived from retrospective reports. An example is the Logue *et al.* (1979) study. The starting point of the study was a given event (the Wyoming Valley flood of 1972) and therefore the research was "prospective" in the epidemiological sense; but the data were collected 5 years after the event and therefore the study was "retrospective," as Logue *et al.* said (p. 496), in the other sense. To avoid confusion, we use herein the labels *anterograde* and *retrograde*. In the anterograde method, the question is about the effects of a given event; in the retrograde method the question is about the causes of a given effect. The given event or given effect could be in the present or in the past, or even in the future.

The Anterograde Method

Using the anterograde method, ideally, the investigator selects an event before it occurs and measures relevant variables before and after the event occurs. The relevant variables should include not only ones that are expected to change but also ones that should be unaffected, to provide the fullest evidence on the construct validity of the event. The event has construct validity if the variables that should be affected by its occurrence change in the expected way and if the variables that should be unaffected do not change.

The anterograde method has been used to study the effects of events that are planned to occur at times announced in advance, such as a factory closing (Cobb & Kasl, 1977) and an implementation of a law requiring that young children in automobiles be secured by safety devices (Cohen, Papini, Rodeheaver, & Thomas, 1982). More often, however, the method is modified so that the study begins after the occurrence of the event and the postevent measures are compared with whatever preevent measures are available. An example is the Berkeley study of the effects of the Great Depression. In some studies, the nature of the variables is such that preevent measures can be inferred or can be estimated after the event from retrospective reports that can be assumed to be accurate. An example is a study by Lachman, Tatsuoka, and Bonk (1961) of human behavior during a tsunami that hit Hawaii in 1960. The study was anterograde in that it dealt with the effects of a given event, but the measures were obtained after the event by interviewing a sample from the affected cohort. (We are deliberately using the phrase *affected cohort* instead of the more frequently used term *victims*. Our phrase is appropriate regardless of the intensity of the event that defines the cohort; *victims* is appropriate only if the intensity is extreme.) The retrospective reports obtained by Lachman *et al.* can be assumed to have been accurate because the interviews were conducted during a 7-day period soon after the event occurred—many of those interviewed were at a Red Cross disaster shelter.

If the delay between the occurrence of the event of interest and the beginning of the study of its effects is long, retrospective data are likely to be suspect. In these cases, the preevent measures of interest must often be inferred from limited preevent data. The design is then the usual ex post facto or "after-the-fact" design (Farrant, 1977, p. 359). We give several examples later.

A major problem in anterograde research is to assess possible *sleeper effects* (also called *delayed* and *lagged effects*). The precise meaning of *sleeper effect* has been debated (Clarke & Clarke, 1981, 1982; Seitz, 1981), but the debate seems unlikely to be fruitful unless the phrase is mistakenly interpreted to refer to causes (as, for example, when Clarke and Clarke [1981, p. 351] referred to it as "the concept proposed by Kagan and Moss to *account* for possible discontinuities in the personality domain" [emphasis added]). It is a descriptive concept and unless the description is made explicit, it is as empty as the phrase "significant difference" when the direction of the difference is not specified. Clarke and Clarke (1982) expressed doubt that a treatment can have long-range effects without having had earlier ones. Logically—except in the logic of radical pragmatism—Clarke and Clarke must be correct; but the point that should be made is not that the treatment effects are delayed, contrary to Seitz's (1981) position, but that the treatment effects are not detected until after a delay. Seitz asserted that "the essential feature of a delayed treatment effect [her suggested term for "sleeper effect"] is that differently treated groups do not differ at the end of a treatment but differ significantly at a later time on measures presumed to be assessing the same theoretical construct" (p. 365). That is, the label sleeper effect is used to refer to cases in which a treatment has no detected immediate effect on the variable of interest but has a detected delayed effect on this variable. Such cases evidently exist, but labeling them sleeper effects does not further the understanding of their causes.

THE RETROGRADE METHOD

Using the retrograde method, the investigator begins with an effect—the occurrence of change in some variable—and tries by retrospective, historical analysis to identify the event or events that caused it. Ideally, several variables will have been assessed concurrently with the variable that exhibited the change of interest, and the concurrent variables will have included ones exhibiting no change or different kinds of change. Given this ideal form, the method yields the fullest evidence on the construct validity of the event, by showing that the pattern of changes and nonchanges in the concurrently observed variables is expectable from the hypothesized causal event and is not expectable from other possible causal events.

A study by Super (1982a, 1982b) is a striking example of the retrograde method. He analyzed the contents of 499 articles published in *Child Development* between 1930 and 1979; and by statistical methods (multidimensional scaling and cluster analysis), he found that 1960 was "an apparent watershed for disciplinary concerns, and hence methodology, topic, and professional style as well" (1982a, p. 10). He suggested that "the dramatic changes around 1960 can probably be related to the post-Sputnik concern, at the national level, with our scientific development and hence our children's cognitive development [etc.]" (p. 11). Thus, Super identified several changes that occurred, determined the time at which the changes tended to occur, and indicated some of the events that occurred around this time and could plausibly have caused the identified changes.

A problem that is frequently encountered in retrograde research is that the historical records are incomplete, missing part or all of the information required to test the hypothesis. The retrograde study begins with an effect observed in a sample of individuals who are then hypothesized to have experienced some specified event that could have caused the observed effect. The problem is that the test of the hypothesis is often weak because of the lack of evidence that the individuals actually experienced or were affected by the hypothesized causal event.

Another frequent problem is the absence of some or all of the concurrent measures on other variables required for the best test of the hypothesis. For example, a decline in young children's imaginative play might be hypothesized to have resulted from the large increase in the popularity of video computer games. If so, then one might expect an increase in eye–hand coordination and perhaps, because many of the games have an element of violence, an increase in aggressiveness. Concurrent data on eye–hand coordination and aggressiveness might well be missing.

EXAMPLES

We turn now to a survey of actual studies that illustrate the problems encountered in using the anterograde and retrograde methods.

Anterograde Research

SELECTION OF THE INITIAL EVENT

The anterograde method begins with identification of a salient event and continues with measurement of changes that may have been caused by this event. The basis for the identification of a salient event varies. For example, one of the specializations in sociology deals with the effects of disasters. According to White and Haas (1975), the psychological effects of disasters on their victims were believed to be minimal until the 1970s, when research on floods and other disasters revealed long-lasting and significant psychological effects. Logue, Hansen, and Struening (1981) reported a five-year follow-up study of the effects of the June 1972 Wilkes Barre flood. They concluded that "stress arising from the flood experience is significantly associated with both mental and physical health problems measured 5 years after the flood" (p. 76). Gleser *et al.* (1981) found prolonged psychological effects of the Buffalo Creek flood; but Kilijanek and Drabek (1979) found no significant long-term (3-year) psychological effects of a tornado that struck Topeka, Kansas, in 1966, even though it was "the most destructive tornado in U.S. history up to that point in time" (p. 555).

Cohen and Poulshock (1977) concluded that within 100 days following the 1972 flood in Wilkes Barre, the community steady state was being restored and that the new steady state was "fully in place by the end of the first year following the disaster" (p. 266). Bolin's (1982) 18-month follow-up of the effects of tornadoes in Wichita Falls and Vernon, Texas, yielded consistent conclusions. Bolin noted that persisting effects are more likely to be detected in smaller social units, such as the family, than in larger social units, such as census tracts and communities, and that recovery is likely to be slower in the smaller units because the "impact ratio" (ratio of losses to available resources—p. 295) is greater for smaller units. (We cite these studies to illustrate selection of an event as the starting point for anterograde research, not to suggest any conclusions about the effects of disasters.)

An example of anterograde research starting with selection of a benign event is the Ball and Bogatz (1972) study of the effects of viewing *Sesame Street*. Ball and Bogatz selected this particular event because they were commissioned by the Children's Television Workshop to conduct an evaluation study of the program. The Children's Television Workshop was interested in this evaluation because of their involvement in the development of the program. As another example, Luria (1976) chose to study the effects of modernization—collectivization, education, and socialization—in Uzbekistan and Kirghizia in order to provide evidence relevant to Vygotsky's theory of the relationship between cognitive development and cultural development.

Problems of Interpretation

Regardless of the reasons for targeting a specific event, the methods employed tend to be similar. Variables are selected for assessment on the basis of hypothesized effects of the event. For example, the selection of most of the dependent variables in the Ball and Bogatz study (1972) was based on the purposes for which *Sesame Street* was designed. The majority of these variables were measures of symbolic representation and cognitive processes, which were the kinds of processes that *Sesame Street* was designed to influence. The study revealed significant impacts on a number of cognitive measures for preschool children who viewed *Sesame Street* regularly. Furthermore, as viewing increased, the cognitive superiority of the viewers over the nonviewers increased. Ball and Bogatz concluded that the viewing of *Sesame Street* was the causal event.

On the basis of the Ball and Bogatz report, Reese (1974) hypothesized that viewing *Sesame Street* would result in a cohort change in the effect of prompting preschool children to use a particular mnemonic operation, "elaboration." *Sesame Street* began national broadcasting on November 10, 1969 (Palmer, 1969), and Reese (1974) had conducted verbal learning research around that time, with about half the children tested in the summer of 1969 before the national broadcasting began, and with about half of the children tested afterwards, in the summer of 1970. As shown in Table 3, before *Sesame Street* began national broadcasting, younger children did not benefit from prompting but older children did; and after national broadcasting started, younger children were as good as older children in the

TABLE 3

Percentage Correct Responses
in the Reese (1974) Study[a]

Time	Age group[b]	No prompt	Prompt	p
Before	Younger	17.5	10.0	n.s.[c]
	Older	33.8	66.7	.01
After	Younger	36.7	70.0	.01
	Older	77.5	87.5	n.s.

[a]Adapted from Reese (1974, Table 1, p. 1177).
[b]Younger: 27–46 months old; older: 48–75 months old.
[c]n.s. = nonsignificant.

pre-*Sesame Street* cohort and older post-*Sesame Street* children did not need prompting. In other words, this research from an experimental child psychology laboratory seemed to confirm the conclusion of Ball and Bogatz's (1972) field research that viewing *Sesame Street* accelerated certain aspects of cognitive development.

Unlike Ball and Bogatz (1972), Reese (1974) had no direct evidence that his post-*Sesame Street* subjects actually watched *Sesame Street*. Furthermore, Reese later (1976) reported anecdotal evidence that was inconsistent with the conclusion that viewing *Sesame Street* was the cause of the cohort change he had observed:

> [Reese] discussed this study with several colleagues at a meeting in Ann Arbor in August, 1973, and two of them suggested similar cohort changes occurring at other times: J. P. Bronckart suggested that a cohort change was being reflected in Genevan research, which was revealing earlier transitions between Piagetian stages than had originally been observed; and L. Wilder suggested that an earlier instance of cohort change may be reflected in the failures of American investigators to replicate Luria's "squeeze, don't squeeze" research showing mediational deficiencies in young children. (p. 205)

Apparently, cognitive acceleration had begun in Geneva and the United States before the advent of *Sesame Street,* and therefore the cohort effect observed by Reese may have been the continuation of an evolutionary trend rather than a revolutionary effect of viewing *Sesame Street*.

These examples illustrate the main problem of the anterograde method—the difficulty of disentangling the postulated causal event from extraneous variables that occurred at the same time, or that occurred earlier and had sleeper effects, or that occurred later and produced an effect more rapidly. These associated variables could have been the cause of the change or could have been contributing conditions. In the Ball and Bogatz study (1972), for example, the changes reported could have arisen because the viewers of *Sesame Street* were watching proportionately less commercial television and their cognitive skills were less deadened than in children who continued to watch commercial television. Alternatively, perhaps the parents were the ones who were affected directly by *Sesame Street* and began interacting with their children in such a way as to encourage their cognitive growth. The change could also have been caused in a number of other ways.

Another example of this problem can be seen in Luria's (1976) study suggesting a cohort change from concrete to abstract thinking in Uzbeks and Kirghiz. Luria found that traditional peasant groups exhibited concrete thinking and that collective farm groups exhibited abstract thinking. The collective farm groups experienced collective living, education, division of labor, and so on, and they were apparently self-selected in moving to the collective farms. Any of these variables, or any combination, could have been the cause of the change in mode of thinking.

The anterograde method is therefore effective for determining possible effects of an event, but it is not completely sufficient for making such a determination because of the difficulty of separating cumulative, interactive, sleeper, and other associated effects.

Retrograde Research

Unfortunately, the retrograde method has equally difficult problems. Before illustrating the problems, we illustrate successful use of the method, using two examples from epidemiology.

EPIDEMIOLOGICAL EXAMPLES

The advent of modern medical procedures to treat infants born prematurely yielded an increase in the population of infants who suffered from impaired vision and blindness (Annis, 1978). For a number of years these visual defects were thought to be sequelae of premature delivery (Fraser & Friedman, 1968). Not until 1953 were the causes of this increase in blindness traced to the medical treatment used to keep premature infants alive. Because the major cause of death in premature infants is respiratory failure, oxygen was used generously in incubators to aid respiration and to prevent oxygen deprivation that could lead to brain damage or death. Nothing was known about the effects of oxygen on the developing retinal system. A common notion was that if a little bit of oxygen was good, more would be even better. Unfortunately, more was worse. The high concentrations of oxygen used caused a deterioration of the developing retina—a condition known as retrolental fibroplasia.

A second example of identifying the cause of change after discovery of the occurrence of change is the thalidomide disaster in 1960–1961 in Europe. In West Germany, 15 cases of phocomelia (the congenital absence of limbs) were reported in 1949–1959. In 1960, several hundred cases appeared, and in 1961 10 times more affected infants were born than in 1960. Epidemiologists began a concerted search for the cause of this change and eventually traced the cause to the use of a nonbarbiturate tranquilizer that was particularly effective in alleviating the symptoms of morning sickness. When ingested by the mother at any time between the twenty-seventh and fortieth days of pregnancy, phocomelia occurred. Although the identification of the causal variable was relatively rapid, 10,000 affected infants were born in West Germany, Great Britain, and Scandinavia during an 18-month period (Annis, 1978),

TABLE 4

Average Difference between Urban and Rural
Children in Height and Weight[a]

	Urban minus rural	
Time of measurement	Height (cm)	Weight (kg)
1870–1915	−1.2	−.6
1950–1959	1.6	.9
1960–1969	2.5	1.1
1970–1979	3.6	1.5

[a]Data reported by Meredith (1982). Means for
1870–1915 are unweighted means from six studies.

PROBLEMS OF INTERPRETATION

In these epidemiological examples, determination of the cause of the
change was relatively straightforward because of the direct influence of a
single cause on a specific effect. In developmental research, however, this
luxury is seldom encountered because of the multidimensionality of both
causes and effects.

Possibly because of these problems, developmental psychologists who
investigate cohort change tend not to speculate extensively on the causes of
historical change, but rather tend merely to describe the change. An example of this kind of retrograde approach is the extensive work by Meredith
(1982) on worldwide patterns of physical growth. Table 4 shows cohort
differences in human body size. The values in the table are differences
between means for urban and rural children, collapsed across age (7–17
years), gender, race, and so forth. The data are from a worldwide survey of
studies conducted at the times of measurement indicated in the table. As the
table shows, in 1870–1915 rural children were taller and heavier than
urban children, but by the 1950s the differences had reversed, and the
reversed differences steadily increased in magnitude in the 1960s and 1970s.
(The differences for the 1970s in British units were 1.4 inches and 3.3
pounds.) Meredith did not speculate about possible causes of the cohort
differences; and although he listed possible sources of the urban–rural differences, he noted that particulars for specific habitats are scarce in the
literature, and he did not speculate about which possible sources are probable causes.

A more common application of the retrograde method is in psychometric developmental research. Changes in psychometric measurements
over time and for specific cohorts are reported, and possible causal histor-

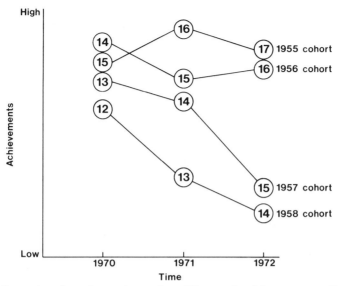

Figure 3. Separation of age changes from cohort differences in adolescent personality as measured by achievement. Ages are given in the circles. Connected circles show longitudinal data; vertical comparisons are cross-sectional. (Redrawn from Nesselroade & Baltes, 1974, Figure 9, p. 37. Copyright 1974 by the Society for Research in Child Development. Redrawn by permission.)

ical events may be suggested speculatively. An example is Nesselroade and Baltes's (1974) developmental study of intelligence and personality in Appalachian adolescents. Figure 3 shows a typical result obtained in this study. The cohorts born in 1955 and 1956 were similar to each other and showed little if any longitudinal change. The 1957 and 1958 cohorts were fairly similar to each other but markedly different from the 1955 and 1956 cohorts, showing either a marked decrease with increasing age or an increasingly interfering time-of-measurement effect. As in many applications of the retrograde method, Nesselroade and Baltes devoted little space—three-quarters of a page in 71 pages of text—to speculation about possible causes.

We suspect that one of the primary reasons developmental psychologists tend not to speculate about causes is the difficulty of making a compelling case when the retrograde method is used. Use of the method reveals change but may or may not indicate causes of the change. One difficulty that is frequently encountered is lack of the historical data needed to build a compelling case about causes. As Meredith (1982) pointed out:

> The existing reports of somatic research on urban and rural children and youths afford a paucity of information regarding regional differences in dietary content,

hygenic practice, disease treatment, environmental pollution, and gene pool heredity. Such particulars for specific habitats are needed to advance beyond general perspectives. (p. 133)

Meredith then cited 13 specific areas in which accurate, detailed information would be necessary for accurate identification of the variables that
caused the changes in human growth he had documented. Meredith's list
also illustrates a second problem with the retrograde method: the multidimensionality of the causal variables. Pinpointing a single causal variable
that would explain Meredith's data would be difficult if not impossible. As
Schaie and Labouvie-Vief (1974) pointed out, environmental causes interact
not only with one another but also with biological variables, which are also
difficult to identify.

The same problems with the identification of causes of change are
present in the Nesselroade and Baltes (1974) study. They briefly speculated
that the Vietnam War and increasing youth activism may have been the
cause of the cohort and time-of-measurement effects they found with Appalachian adolescents. Some of the dimensions of the change they suggested
are "a tendency to occupy themselves with ethical, moral and political
issues rather than with an orientation toward cognitive achievement" and
"a gradual decline in respect and confidence for public and educational
leadership" (p. 59). A problem with this speculation is that no data are
available to document that their specific sample was affected by the Vietnam War at all, much less affected in the specified way.

For the cohorts described by Nesselroade and Baltes (1974), the war
may have been viewed as a means of attaining status. One of the common
life courses of rural Appalachian males is to finish secondary schooling and
then to enlist in the military. A common phenomenon, referred to by a
physician at the 1980 Life-Span Developmental Psychology Conference as
the Pickup Truck Syndrome, is to find males enlisting in the military at an
early age, returning with their combat pay and savings in pocket, and buy-
ing the fanciest truck they can afford. Their worldly experience and more
importantly their ownership of the pickup truck make them highly desirable
to the young female population and heroes to the younger males. These
cohorts may have viewed the war as an ideal opportunity for an increase in
status and, in fact, probably saw many instances of it in their towns. The
war, then, may not have caused disillusionment with authority and concern
with moral and ethical problems but rather may have been an opportunity
to enhance social status. As this case illustrates, speculation about probable
causes without corroborating evidence is unlikely to be fruitful, unless it
leads to theory-guided empirical questions.

A final problem with the retrograde method is that the cause of any given change may not have been any one event; rather, the change may have been a dialectical leap. In other words, the change may have been the product of evolution rather than revolution. In dialectical terminology, the change may reflect the principle of the transformation of quantitative change into qualitative change. For example (B. Z. Hummel, personal communication, 1982), the passage of the disabled persons act (the Rehabilitation Act of 1973) in 1972 may have been caused in part by a marked increase that had occurred in the population of disabled adults and children. This increase occurred gradually over several decades and included victims of retrolental fibroplasia from the 1940s and early 1950s; disabled veterans from World War II, the Korean War, and the war in Vietnam; and the 20,000 multiple-handicapped persons born during the rubella epidemic of 1963–1965. No single disabling event was causal in this example, but rather the cause was the gradual increase in numbers until a critical mass was reached and the quantitative change led to a qualitative change—the change in legislation.

But as with the other examples of the identification of causal variables, this example is also open to alternative explanation. Perhaps the increasing number of disabled persons was not the cause of the disabled persons act; perhaps it was caused by other events occurring concurrently in the United States at that time. This was the period in U.S. history when the rights of a number of minority groups were being acknowledged, and legislation was being passed to insure the rights of these previously underrepresented groups. The disabled persons act may have reflected this movement independently of the increasing number of disabled persons in the two decades prior to the legislative change.

CONCLUSIONS

The methods used to investigate historical events and subsequent change are problematic when applied to life-span developmental psychology. The study of change in the individual or across cohorts is central to the goals of developmental psychology and is relatively easily accomplished in laboratory studies in which independent variables can be scrupulously controlled and selected dependent variables can be carefully measured. Unfortunately, this a priori systematic investigation of cause and effect is virtually impossible for exploration of historical change. Seldom do investigators have sufficient advance notice of an event to permit adequate planning of research and collecting of relevant preevent measures needed for the anterograde method. Also, the occurrence of the event itself may, in fact, change the conceptual framework that guided the selection of the original variables: The event itself may alter the nature of the questions asked. Even in cases where planned pre- and postevent measures are obtained, problems of interpretation can still plague the investigators. It may be difficult, if not impossible, to determine the specific dimensions of the event that caused specific change. Also, delayed effects of the event may never be adequately assessed or fully understood.

The reconstruction used in the retrograde analysis of an historical event postulated to be the cause of some measured change is even more problematic. The change analyzed for a given cohort is often one that was uncovered serendipitously in the course of other research. The investigators who wish to pursue such a finding are faced with the arduous task of determining the cause or causes of the change. This postdiction is necessarily theory-guided to permit conceptually valid inquiries into the past. Unguided attempts at reconstruction are likely to result in spurious or meaningless findings. Ideally, investigators employing the retrograde approach would apply a modified version of the anterograde method to validate their findings. If event x is postulated to have caused effect y, the investigators—working within the theoretical framework used to establish x—should select other variables (z) that should also have been influenced by x. Working forward from event x to measure corresponding changes in z would provide construct validity for conclusions concerning the causation of y. However, the major difficulty of the retrograde method also arises in this combined approach—the unavailability of relevant, usable documentation.

Although difficulties are inherent in these approaches to the investigation of historical change, no alternatives exist and therefore if developmental psychologists are to study historical change they must use one or both of these approaches. Historical change is an important aspect of psychological development (Baltes *et al.*, 1980); but one of the major gaps in the understanding of human development is about the impact of historical events on the life course. The current cohort of life-span psychologists seems to be in a unique historical position to undertake investigations to fill in this gap, because changes are occurring at a rapid rate in U.S. society and in other cultures (Bell & Hertz, 1976). Therefore, the investigation of historical change should not continue to be primarily the domain of nonpsychological sciences such as anthropology, history, and sociology. Life-span psychologists can and should increase their efforts in this domain.

REFERENCES

Allport, G. W. (1961). *Pattern and growth in personality*. New York: Holt.
Annis, L. F. (1978). *The child before birth*. Ithaca, NY: Cornell University Press.

Ball, S., & Bogatz, G. A. (1972). Summative research of *Sesame Street:* Implications for the study of preschool children. In A. D. Pick (Ed.), *Minnesota symposia on child psychology* (Vol. 6). Minneapolis: University of Minnesota Press.

Baltes, P. B. (1979). Life-span developmental psychology: Some converging observations on history and theory. In P. B. Baltes & O. G. Brim, Jr. (Eds.), *Life-span development and behavior* (Vol. 2). New York: Academic Press.

Baltes, P. B., Cornelius, S. W., & Nesselroade, J. R. (1978). Cohort effects in behavioral development: Theoretical and methodological perspectives. In W. A. Collins (Ed.), *Minnesota symposia on child psychology* (Vol. 11). Hillsdale, NJ: Erlbaum.

Baltes, P. B., & Nesselroade, J. R. (1979). History and rationale of longitudinal research. In J. R. Nesselroade & P. B. Baltes (Eds.), *Longitudinal research in the study of behavior and development.* New York: Academic Press.

Baltes, P. B., Reese, H. W., & Lipsitt. L. P. (1980). Life-span developmental psychology. *Annual Review of Psychology, 31,* 65–110.

Baltes, P. B., Reese, H. W., & Nesselroade, J. R. (1977). *Life-span developmental psychology: Introduction to research methods.* Monterey, CA: Brooks/Cole.

Baltes, P. B., & Willis, S. L. (1979). The critical importance of appropriate methodology in the study of aging: The sample case of psychometric intelligence. In F. Hoffmeister & C. Müller (Eds.), *Brain functions in old age.* Heidelberg: Springer.

Bell, R. Q., & Hertz, T. W. (1976). Toward more comparability and generalizability of developmental research. *Child Development, 47,* 6–13.

Bergmann, G. (1957). *Philosophy of science.* Madison: University of Wisconsin Press.

Bolin, R. (1982). *Long term family recovery from disaster* (Final report). Family Research Project, Grant No. PFR-802031, National Science Foundation.

Bormann, F. H., & Likens, G. E. (1979). Catastrophic disturbance and steady state in northern hardwood forests. *American Scientist, 67,* 660–669.

Brim, O. G., Jr., & Ryff, C. D. (1980). On the properties of life events. In P. B. Baltes & O. G. Brim, Jr. (Eds.), *Life-span development and behavior* (Vol. 3). New York: Academic Press.

Callahan, E. J., & McCluskey, K. A. (Eds.). (1983). *Life-span developmental psychology: Non-normative life events.* New York: Academic Press.

Clarke, A. D. B., & Clarke, A. M. (1981). "Sleeper effects" in development: Fact or artifact. *Developmental Review, 1,* 344–360.

Clarke, A. M., & Clarke, A. D. B. (1982). Intervention and sleeper effects: A reply to Victoria Seitz. *Development Review, 2,* 76–86.

Cobb, S., & Kasl, S. V. (1977). *Termination: The consequences of job loss.* National Institute for Occupational Safety and Health, Washington, DC: Government Printing Office.

Cohen, E. S., & Poulshock, S. W. (1977). Societal responses to mass dislocation of the elderly: Implications for Area Agencies on Aging. *Gerontologist, 17,* 262–268.

Cohen, S. H., Papini, D., Rodeheaver, D., & Thomas, J. (1982, August). The measurement and assessment of a child passenger restraint law: Observations on its implementation and effectiveness. In S. B. Fawcett (Chair), Interstate research collaboration: The case of child passenger safety legislation. Symposium presented at the meeting of the American Psychological Association, Washington, DC.

Danish, S. J., Smyer, M. A., & Nowak, C. A. (1980). Developmental intervention: Enhancing life-event processes. In P. B. Baltes & O. G. Brim, Jr. (Eds.), *Life-span development and behavior* (Vol. 3). New York: Academic Press.

Datan, N., & Ginsberg, L. H. (Eds.). (1975). *Life-span developmental psychology: Normative life crises.* New York: Academic Press.

Elder, G. H., Jr., & Rockwell, R. C. (1979). The life-course and human development: An ecological perspective. *International Journal of Behavioral Development, 2,* 1–21.

Farrant, R. H. (1977). Can after-the-fact designs test functional hypotheses, and are they needed in psychology? *Canadian Psychological Review, 18,* 359–364.

Fraser, G. R., & Friedman, A. I. (1968). *The causes of blindness in childhood: A study of 776 children with severe visual handicaps*. Baltimore: The Johns Hopkins Press.

Gardiner, P. (1968). The philosophy of history. In D. L. Sills (Ed.), *International encyclopedia of the social sciences* (Vol. 6). New York: Macmillan.

Gleser, G. C., Green, B. L., & Winget, C. (1981). *Prolonged psychosocial effects of disaster: A study of Buffalo Creek*. New York: Academic Press.

Hempel, C. G. (1967). Scientific explanation. In S. Morgenbesser (Ed.), *Philosophy of science today*. New York: Basic Books.

Hempel, C. G., & Oppenheim, P. (1953). The logic of explanation. In H. Feigl & M. Brodbeck (Eds.), *Readings in the philosophy of science*. New York: Appleton-Century-Crofts. (Reprinted from *Philosophy of Science*, 1948, *15*.)

Hultsch, D. F., & Plemons, J. K. (1979). Life events and life-span development. In P. B. Baltes & O. G. Brim, Jr. (Eds.), *Life-span development and behavior* (Vol. 2). New York: Academic Press.

James, E. (1823). *Account of an expedition from Pittsburg to the Rocky Mountains, performed in the years 1819 and '20*. Vol. 2. Philadelphia: Carey & Lea. (Reprinted Ann Arbor, MI: University Microfilms, 1966.)

Kaplan, A. (1964). *The conduct of inquiry*. San Francisco: Chandler.

Kelley, B. M. (1974). *Yale: A history*. New Haven: Yale University Press.

Kilijanek, T. S., & Drabek, T. E. (1979). Assessing long-term impacts of a natural disaster: A focus on the elderly. *Gerontologist*, *19*, 555–566.

Kvale, S. (1977). Dialectics and research on remembering. In N. Datan & H. W. Reese (Eds.), *Life-span developmental psychology: Dialectical perspectives on experimental research*. New York: Academic Press.

Lachman, R., & Bonk, W. J. (1960). Behavior and beliefs during the recent volcanic eruption at Kapoho, Hawaii. *Science*, *131*, 1095–1096.

Lachman, R., Tatsuoka, M., & Bonk, W. J. (1961). Human behavior during the tsunami of May 1960. *Science*, *133*, 1405–1409.

Leach, E. R. (1968). The comparative method in anthropology. In D. L. Sills (Ed.), *International encyclopedia of the social sciences* (Vol. 1). New York: Macmillan.

Lever, J., & Schwartz, P. (1971). *Women at Yale*. Indianapolis: Bobbs-Merrill.

Lewis, L. S. (1980). Getting tenure: Change and continuity. *Academe* (Bulletin of the AAUP [American Association of University Professors]), *66*, 373–381.

Lilienfeld, A. M., & Lilienfeld, D. E. (1980). *Foundations of epidemiology* (2nd ed.). New York: Oxford University Press.

Logue, J. N., Hansen, H., & Struening, E. (1979). Emotional and physical distress following Hurricane Agnes in Wyoming Valley of Pennsylvania. *Public Health Reports*, *94*, 495–502.

Logue, J. N., Hansen, H., & Struening, E. (1981). Some indications of the long-term health effects of a natural disaster. *Public Health Reports*, *96*, 67–79.

Luria, A. R. (1976). *Cognitive development: Its cultural and social foundations* (M. Lopez-Morillas & L. Solotaroff [Trans.], M. Cole [Ed.]). Cambridge, MA: Harvard University Press.

Meredith, H. V. (1982). Research between 1950 and 1980 on urban-rural differences in body size and growth rate of children and youths. In H. W. Reese (Ed.), *Advances in child development and behavior* (Vol. 17). New York: Academic Press.

Mumford, L. (1961). *The city in history: Its origins, its transformations, and its prospects*. New York: Harcourt.

Nesselroade, J. R., & Baltes, P. B. (1974). Adolescent personality development and historical change: 1970–1972. *Monographs of the Society for Research in Child Development*, *39*(1, Serial No. 154).

Palmer, E. L. (1969). Can television really teach? *American Education, 5* (August–September), 2–6.

Penick, J. L., Jr. (1981). *The New Madrid earthquakes* (rev. ed.). Columbia: University of Missouri Press.

Porter, A. L., Chubin, D. E., Rossini, F. A., Boeckmann, M. E., & Connolly, T. (1982). The role of the dissertation in scientific careers. *American Scientist, 70* (September–October), 475–481.

Reese, H. W. (1974). Cohort, age, and imagery in children's paired-associate learning. *Child Development, 45,* 1176–1178.

Reese, H. W. (1976). The development of memory: Life-span perspectives. In P. B. Baltes (Chair), Symposium on implications of life-span developmental psychology for child development. In H. W. Reese (Ed.), *Advances in child development and behavior* (Vol. 11). New York: Academic Press.

Reese, H. W., & Smyer, M. (1983). The dimensionalization of life events. In E. C. Callahan & K. A. McCluskey (Eds.), *Life-span developmental psychology: Nonnormative life events.* New York: Academic Press.

Russell, J. C. (1948). *British medieval population.* Albuquerque: University of New Mexico Press.

Schaie, K. W. (1965). A general model for the study of developmental problems. *Psychological Bulletin, 64,* 92–107.

Schaie, K. W., & Labouvie-Vief, G. (1974). Generational versus ontogenetic components of change in adult cognitive behavior: A fourteen-year cross-sequential study. *Developmental Psychology, 10,* 305–320.

Schusky, E. L. (1972). *Manual for kinship analysis* (2nd ed.). New York: Holt.

Seitz, V. (1981). Intervention and sleeper effects: A reply to Clarke and Clarke. *Developmental Review, 1,* 361–373.

Shuttleworth, F. K. (1949). The adolescent period: A graphic atlas. *Monographs of the Society for Research in Child Development, 14*(1, Serial No. 49).

Spiker, C. C. (1966). The concept of development: Relevant and irrelevant issues. In H. W. Stevenson (Ed.), *Concept of development. Monographs of the Society for Research in Child Development, 31*(5, Serial No. 107).

Super, C. M. (1982a, Spring). Secular trends in *Child Development* and the institutionalization of professional disciplines. *Newsletter, Society for Research in Child Development,* pp. 10–11.

Super, C. M. (1982b). Secular trends in *Child Development* and the institutionalization of professional disciplines. Judge Baker Guidance Center and Harvard University. Unpublished manuscript.

White, G. F., & Haas, J. E. (1975). *Assessment of research on natural hazards.* Cambridge, MA: MIT Press.

Winks, R. W. (1969). Introduction. In R. W. Winks (Ed.), *The historian as detective: Essays on evidence.* New York: Harper & Row.

Ziegler, P. (1969). *The black death.* New York: Day.

CHAPTER 3

The Individual as Consumer
and Producer
of Historical Change

John A. Meacham

Introduction

One can sense, within the discipline of psychology, a movement away from static conceptions of the individual toward a broadening understanding (1) that individuals change over their life spans; (2) that individuals develop not in isolation but within a social context; and (3) that this social context itself changes over the course of history. The purpose of the present chapter is to reflect upon the implications of this movement for the discipline of life-span developmental psychology, calling attention to some conceptual and methodological issues that arise when one inquires into the relationships between history-graded events and normative age-graded (ontogenetic) events (Baltes, Reese, & Lipsitt, 1980). Historical events include, for example, economic depression and affluence, war and peace, and changes in the demographic, political, and economic structure of society.

The plan for this chapter is to outline the processes or relationships from which sociohistorical and individual changes are derived, including changes both for the individual who is the subject of study in our discipline and for the observer—that is, for the researcher and for the discipline itself. Certain similarities between issues that arise in the study of history and issues that arise in the study of stages of cognition in adult development and aging (Labouvie-Vief, 1982; Meacham, 1983; Perry, 1970) and in the study of autobiographical remembering (Meacham, 1977b) are noted. These topics, because they are already familiar to many life-span researchers, may

Copyright © 1984 by Academic Press, Inc.
All rights of reproduction in any form reserved.
ISBN 0-12-482420-X

serve as a bridge to what will be said regarding the study of history. The chapter concludes with the argument that we need not, after all, be too much concerned with historical events in the past, for the aim of our discipline is to better understand not the past but the present.

A Framework for Discussion

Looking to the Future

Despite the common association of history with the past, our problem is not merely to understand the impact of past historical events upon the life-span development of individuals. Such a formulation of the problem is too restrictive, both in its unidirectional causality and in its emphasis on the past to the neglect of the present and future. The general problem is to understand, in their extension throughout the past, present, and future, the processes or relationships from which sequences of sociohistorical and individual life-course changes are derived.

Asimov's (1951, 1952, 1953) *Foundation* trilogy (winner of a special Hugo Award as Best All-Time Series in science fiction) provides a point of departure for exploration of this general problem. The setting for Asimov's novel is 50,000 years from now, 12,000 years after the millions of worlds in the galaxy have been united into a single empire. The events of the novel begin with Dr. Seldon, a psychohistorian[1] whose understanding of the processes of historical change was such that he could predict, with the aid of a pocket calculator and known probabilities of assassination, revolution, recurrence of periods of economic depression, and so forth, the fall of the empire, to be followed by a period of barbarism lasting 30,000 years, before a new empire would arise. However, Dr. Seldon was also able to predict that if the mass of historical events could be deflected just a little by the establishment of a foundation to preserve scientific knowledge, then the period of barbarism could be reduced to a mere 1000 years. (One must read Asimov's trilogy to learn whether Dr. Seldon's predictions were confirmed and whether his plan for the foundation was successful, especially after the arrival of a mutant human with extraordinary psychosocial powers and after the increased interactions with a hidden second foundation.)

Likely, more than a few developmentalists would regard Dr. Seldon's achievement as the end point toward which our present-day efforts to understand sociohistorical and individual changes are directed. Thus it is rea-

---

[1]Prisco (1982) maintained that Asimov invented the term psychohistory.

sonable to ask, what general understanding would it have been necessary for Dr. Seldon to have had in order to extrapolate from past events and predict, with a certain probability of being correct, the impact of present actions upon the future course of history? Asimov provides a clue in the third volume of the trilogy, in which two psychohistorians of the second foundation discuss an equation known as a Rigellian integral (Asimov, 1953, p. 89). Although the spelling has changed slightly over the course of 50,000 years, it seems that these two psychohistorians were discussing the ideas of Klaus Riegel, as presented at previous West Virginia Life-Span Developmental Psychology Conferences (Riegel, 1975, 1977). Thus what follows in this chapter will also be based to some extent on Riegel's prior work. (Is there an historical connection between the titles of Asimov's trilogy and Riegel's last book, *Foundations of Dialectical Psychology?* The similarity, I believe, is merely a coincidence.)

Riegel (1975; 1976a, pp. 376–382; 1979) suggested that historical and individual changes, described in terms of sequences of events along various arbitrary progressions labeled as psychological, sociohistorical, and so forth, could best be understood by examining the processes or relationships from which the progressions are derived. These relationships have the character of communication, dialogue, or conversation, in which each statement may be considered as a synthesis of a speaker's prior statement with the other speaker's antithetical response. Each speaker is both a *consumer* of the past statements of the conversation and a *producer* of statements that will be integrated within the future course of the conversation. The meaning of one speaker's sequence of statements is not intrinsic but is derived from the conversation within which the statements of the two speakers are related. Particular statements are not causal; rather, it is the relationships between statements that are primary and causal (Riegel & Meacham, 1978, pp. 31–34). This consideration of the relations from which historical and individual changes are derived is extended, in the present chapter, to the situation of two individuals, one observed and the other the observer.

A System of Relationships

In order to make his predictions, Dr. Seldon would have had to work with a system of relationships like that presented in Figure 1. The four event-sequences represent the life course of two individuals: an observer such as Dr. Seldon (B), including events pertaining to his family and career, as well as his shifting philosophical perspectives, and an observed individual (C), and their respective sociohistorical event sequences (A and D). As in a conversation, each event or node may be considered as a synthesis of the preceding events to which it is related. Events to the right are later in time,

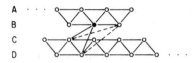

Figure 1. A system of relationships; A refers to the observer's sociohistorical context; B, the observer's event sequence; C, the observed individual; and D, the observed sociohistorical context.

but the temporal relation between the observer's event sequences (A, B) and those of the observed individual (C, D) is arbitrary; that is, the former may be temporally ahead of, simultaneous with, or behind the latter. For example, Figure 1 may represent Dr. Seldon considering the actions of an individual at some point in the future, or a developmentalist such as Elder (Elder, 1979; Elder, Liker, Jaworski, Chapter 8, this volume; Rockwell & Elder, 1982) considering individuals during and after the Great Depression. In each case, the general problem is the same, namely, to understand the relations from which individual (C) and historical (D) changes are derived.

The system of relations presented in Figure 1 is reflective, that is, the observer may consider not only another individual, but also him- or herself as a part of the system. This feature will be explored in a later section (see "The Observer Is Part of the System") of this chapter, and in a subsequent section (see "The Observed Individual's Reflections on History") will be extended to observed individuals. In the very next section, however, reflectivity will be disregarded; the observer considers him- or herself to be outside the observed system of relations.

THE OBSERVER OUTSIDE THE OBSERVED SYSTEM

The Individual versus History

Social scientists, as observers of sociohistorical and individual life-span changes, have tended to hold themselves outside the observed system of changes, which is thereby reduced in its descriptive form to the sequence of changes for the individual (C) and for the sociohistorical context (D). Not infrequently, changes in one of these sequences have been overemphasized to the neglect of changes in the other. Thus the developmental psychologist interested in normative age-graded (ontogenetic) influences on behavior and development seeks to know what these might be in the absence of potentially confounding history-graded influences. The historian, on the other hand, seeks to understand the broad sweep of historical changes without being deceived by particular cases, for example, of well-known individuals.

These differences in emphasis have given rise to futile debate over whether individual destinies are determined by the course of history or whether the course of history is determined by the actions of individuals.

The present volume provides recognition of the need to emphasize changes in both the individual and the sociohistorical event sequences. Nevertheless, this recognition of the need for balance between descriptions of the individual's life span and the social context in which the individual lives, and of the difficulties in achieving and maintaining such a balance, is hardly new. For example, the humanist philosopher and historian Dilthey (1833–1911) wrote of the need for biographies to reflect not only the individual as a focal point but also the general historical horizon (1962, p. 91). More recently, the French historian Braudel (1980/1969) has commented on the need to remain sensitive to both individual history and social history "at one and the same time and, fired with enthusiasm for one, not to lose sight of the other" (p. 20). Yet the social sciences have continued to remain schizophrenic, giving alternating emphasis to the individual and to the sociohistorical context, only occasionally attempting to bring these isolated event sequences into relationship one with the other.

A contrasting solution to the previously mentioned perspectives—C, D, or both C and D—is neither C nor D. Rather than attempt to bring the individual (C) and the sociohistorical context (D) into relationship, one can emphasize the relationships themselves and explore how changes in both the individual and the sociohistorical context are dependent upon these relations. This perspective seems implied by Dilthey most clearly in his statement that "the task of all history is to grasp the systems of interactions" (1962, p. 89) in which the individual both is moved by historical factors such as the structure of the state, religion, and law and at the same time is affected by these. In terms of the framework introduced within the present chapter, the individual is a consumer of history while simultaneously a producer of historical change. (One might say that the individual is a product of the sociohistorical context—indeed, this phrasing may be more familiar to many developmental psychologists. The latter phrasing, however, connotes a less active role for the individual than does the former.)

The Nature of Historical Changes

Despite what has just been said regarding the need to emphasize the relationships from which changes in individuals (C) and sociohistorical contexts (D) are derived, many developmental psychologists will be tempted to construct detailed descriptions of sequences of historical events, expecting that at some later time these descriptions can then be related to sequences of changes for individuals. Certainly, they might argue, historical events can be reliably identified, their features and durations measured, their temporal and causal relations noted, and the whole lot organized along multiple intersecting dimensions, and so forth, yielding numerous new and not-yet-investigated independent variables that ought to predict changes for individuals. Nevertheless, just as each new domain of knowledge appears most simple from the perspective of relative ignorance and increasingly complex the more one learns (Meacham, 1983), so there is much in the preceding sentence that becomes uncertain under closer examination, especially in light of the experiences of historians themselves.

The positivist philosophy of the developmental psychologists in the preceding paragraph has not been popular among historians (Walsh, 1967, p. 18); indeed, much of late nineteenth-century philosophy of history may be understood as a reaction to, although in some cases a transcendence of, early nineteenth-century positivism. Certainly positivism stimulated the collection and organization of historical records, texts, and so forth; and for a time, some were eager to move forward with the task announced by the German historian Ranke (1795–1886), to describe history precisely as it occurred. Despite early expectations, however, historians have not employed descriptions of history as a base from which to deduce more general laws paralleling those of the natural sciences.

Instead, the task more traditionally taken up by historians, in response to what Walsh (1967, pp. 119, 144) described as the morally outrageous notion that history has no rhyme or reason, has been to search for meaning and purpose in the sequence of historical events. Early speculation on the meaning of history centered on the influence of divine providence and, particularly during the Enlightenment, the idea of continual progress. The Italian philosopher Vico (1668–1774), whose work was not widely read until the early nineteenth century, suggested that cultures and societies pass through cycles. This idea is also expressed in more recent histories such as Spengler's *Decline of the West,* published following World War I, in which history is conceived as an overlapping of cycles of growth and decay of independent civilizations, and Toynbee's comparative study of civilizations, which achieved a certain popularity following publication of the condensed version after World War II. Also influential in the eighteenth century was the German writer Herder (1744–1803), who maintained a view of progress toward a more complete humanity. He emphasized the need to consider not only the human spirit but also the particular external circumstances of geography, climate, and so forth. Other meanings were advanced by Hegel (1770–1831), for whom history was the dialectical unfolding of absolute spirit, and Marx (1818–1883), for whom history was a reflection of material, economic relations.

Speculative philosophy of history did not extend, for the most part, beyond the close of the nineteenth century, as the task for historians came to be seen as less one of finding the meaning *in* history and more one of understanding in a critical, analytical manner how it is that historians attribute meaning *to* history. What is significant in the shift from speculative to critical philosophy of history is that, at a time when psychologists were embracing positivism in order to have an objective science in which they as observers had no relationship to the individuals observed, historians had already rejected both the extreme positivism as exemplified by Ranke as well as the speculative philosophies of history of the eighteenth and nineteenth centuries. Thus, for developmental psychologists to embark on the task of describing historical changes in the manner set forth previously in this section would be to begin roughly a century behind historians. Further, for developmental psychologists to attempt to bring together the hitherto relatively isolated event sequence of the changing individual (C)—a sequence that Kitchener (1983) argued continues to be investigated with a positivist philosophy abandoned by other sciences early in this century— with the sociohistorical event sequence (D) investigated by historians who fully acknowledge their participation as observers within the system being observed, would require ignoring rather obvious differences in epistemology. Certainly in order to make his predictions, Dr. Seldon would have needed to understand not only the relationships between the individual and sociohistorical event sequences, but also the relationships between himself as observer (B) and these observed sequences.

THE OBSERVER IS PART OF THE SYSTEM

Can There Be Objective History?

To include the observer—Dr. Seldon or a developmental psychologist—within the system of relations presented in Figure 1 is to raise the question of the extent to which the sociohistorical sequence, as well as the individual sequence, can be known objectively, that is, in isolation from the observer's own perspective. The question cannot be avoided for it appears widely accepted that all histories are constructed from a particular, even moral, perspective and can be understood from only that perspective (Walsh, 1967, pp. 97, 182). The question has two aspects: first, the problem of bias between the observer and the observed event sequences, and second, changes of perspective within the observer's own event sequence (B).

BIAS

As the choices of the supermarket consumer are limited by the decisions of the manager regarding which items to stock and how these should be displayed, so interpretations of the historian as consumer are limited by the evidence that remains from the past and that happens to catch the historian's attention; as the consumer's choices are guided by personal preferences and needs and by beliefs regarding nutritional value, deceptive marketing practices, and so forth, so the observer is guided by personal preferences and practical necessity to emphasize certain events while ignoring others. Walsh (1967, pp. 99–106) listed four problems that may impede the attainment of an objective history. The first three of these, which Walsh did not regard as serious for historians, continue to receive considerable attention from psychologists concerned with methodology: (1) Personal bias for or against particular historical figures or ideas can be corrected, according to Walsh, by recognizing our biases and being on guard against them. (2) Prejudices and assumptions regarding particular groups, such as social classes, can be confronted and overcome, in principle, through rational thinking. (3) Conflicting theories of historical interpretation, for example, regarding the importance of various causal factors, can be tested against the empirical evidence.

The fourth and most serious problem, one that is sufficient to weaken the possibility for an objective history and that has received, in contrast to the other three, relatively little consideration by psychologists, is (4) underlying philosophical conflicts. The observer's philosophical perspective, including judgments of value and beliefs about what is reasonable in human behavior, is implicit throughout the observer's event sequence and is always integrated through constructive relations into particular events of the sociohistorical and individual sequences. The observer by constructing interpretations and giving meaning to past sequences of events is thus a producer of history, and the sociohistorical sequence is a product of the relationship with the historian.

Yet, one might argue, there is agreement that certain events did actually occur, for example, the Great Depression. Nevertheless, an agreed upon and objective sequence of events that could presumably stand alone as "History" would be at a level of abstraction that does not relate to the lives of individuals and so lacks utility for developmentalists. Instead, the sociohistorical event sequence is of interest only as these events are related to the lives of individuals and as these events reflect the meanings that have been given to them by individuals. The American Revolution, for example, was a different event for Thomas Paine, whose pamphlet "Common Sense" argued for independence from Britain, than for the 60,000 loyalists who took refuge in Canada at the conclusion of the war. The use of young boys from the Virginia Military Institute to defend Confederate lines during the Civil War Battle of New Market in 1864 is portrayed in the North as a shameful act by Southern leaders, in the South as an act of valor. Alternative interpretations may be given to other historical events, including the Industrial Revolution, the Great Depression, and so forth. Is any one of these interpretations more valid than another? On what basis could one argue for this? One might attempt to discover the objective events by coordinating the interpretations attained from all the different perspectives, hoping to find "truth" at the intersection, that is, in what remains in common among the various interpretations. Nevertheless, such an attempt rests on the assumption that the common core at the intersection can have any meaning when it is separated from the interpretive actions and the perspectives of the individual observers. The history that ought to be of interest to life-span developmentalists is a social phenomenon constructed in relation to individuals.

CHANGES IN THE OBSERVER'S PERSPECTIVE

The first aspect of the preceding question of objective history concerned the problem of bias stemming from the observer's philosophical perspective. The second, and the more interesting, aspect concerns changes of perspective within the observer's own event sequence. This sequence includes all the events in the observer's life, including those related to personal development, family life, and career, as well as the sequence of conceptual or philosophical perspectives that have been employed. In Figure 1 the critical node or synthesis represents a particular understanding on the part of the observer of the relationship of individuals and history. This understanding is particular and not general because it is based in the immediately preceding events in the observer's sequence (B), for example, a particular philosophical perspective or particular motivations for making the observations. Thus, we can expect interpretations of historical changes in family structure to differ from before to after the observer's divorce, of aging to differ from before to after the observer's retirement, and so forth.

Within the system of relations of Figure 1, there are two primary reasons for changes in the observer's perspective. First, events in the observer's event sequence (B) continually reflect relationships with the sociohistorical (D) and individual (C) event sequences. Any interpretation of these sequences by the observer eventually can be reintegrated within the observer's own event sequence, changing the observer's perspective, preparing the way for a new interpretation, and so forth. The broken lines in Figure 1, therefore, may represent both a second interpretation by the observer of an individual within a sociohistorical context as well as a change within the observer's interpretive perspective. Of course, in practice, the situation is far more complex, for historians continually read and are influenced by each other's interpretations of particular historical events. The second reason for changes in the observer's perspective, hitherto not discussed, derives from the fact that the observer's event sequence reflects relationships not only with the observed sequences, but also with the observer's own sociohistorical context, event sequence A (Meacham, 1978; Riegel, 1976b). Thus the syntheses at each node for the observer reflect the cultural values, the social structure, and the historical events that are significant in his or her own life. For example, our interpretations of the impact of the Great Depression (D) are no doubt colored by current economic uncertainties (A), interpretations of early nineteenth-century family life are contrasted with contemporary high divorce rates, and so forth. The observer's relationships with his or her own historical context will be considered in the subsequent section.

The Observer's Relationships with History

The observer, while studying the relationships of individuals with sociohistorical contexts, is at the same time an individual in relationship with his or her own sociohistorical context. A problem that must have arisen for Dr. Seldon, and so for contemporary developmentalists, is that of the observer's perspective, interpretations, and predictions being unduly influenced by—and perhaps even wrong because of—the observer's relationships with the past sequence of interpretations and the contemporary sociohistorical context. Dr. Seldon would have needed to be confident in making his predictions that his interpretations were not invalidated in some manner by their relationship to events in his own personal life or the political context in which he was working. Similarly, as developmentalists we would like to be confident that our interpretations do not reflect, to an exaggerated extent, our personal motivations and political commitments, our position as young adults, middle age, and so forth within the course of life, our being embedded within a particular social or class structure and living within a particular segment of the stream of history, and so forth. For example, the significance that we attribute to Elder's (Elder, 1979; Elder, Liker, Jaworski, Chapter 8, this volume; Rockwell & Elder, 1982) findings on the relationship between individual development and the historical circumstances of the Great Depression may depend on whether or not we consider ourselves to be at the brink of another economic catastrophe.

The solution to this problem is not to attempt to sever these relationships with our own personal and historical contexts and in so doing to strive to attain an "objective" perspective. Rather, the solution is to understand the relationships themselves and to guard against any exaggerated influence. A portion of the observer's task, therefore, is to understand the processes or relationships that have given rise both to his or her own life

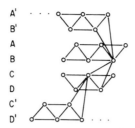

Figure 2. Autobiographical reflections.

course and to the contemporary historical context. Understanding the relationships between him- or herself and the historical context, between event
sequences B and A, is little different from the initial task set for the observer,
to understand the relationships between an observed individual (C) and an
observed context (D). The observer's event sequence B now includes, among
the various relationships, the observer's autobiographical reflections on
these relationships. Although we could let C and D represent these autobiographical reflections, the system of relations will shortly be extended to
include as well the autobiographical reflections of the observed individual
(C). Thus in Figure 2 the observer's autobiographical reflections on him- or
herself (B') and on the contemporary context (A') are indicated with primes.

The expanded system of relations shown in Figure 2 is now sufficient to
represent the actions of Dr. Seldon, the psychohistorian and observer (B).
Dr. Seldon's understanding of the relationships between individuals (C) and
their sociohistorical context (D) provided the basis for subsequent projec-
tion of his own situation many years into the future (A', B'). These predictions provided support for his actions within the current political context
(A), setting in motion the events that would lead to the establishment of the
foundation and the preservation of scientific knowledge. In summary to this
point, the individual in event sequence B—Dr. Seldon, an historian, a developmental psychologist, and so forth—has been seen to be both a consumer
and a producer of historical change. These aspects emerge at each node or
event, which represents both a synthesis of relationships with other event
sequences and the basis for future relationships. Dr. Seldon consumed and
was a product of his previous interpretations and his own sociohistorical
context, and he produced through his interpretations and his actions a
changed sequence of future events. It would be as correct to say that Dr.
Seldon's interpretations and predictions were consumed by or incorporated
within subsequent history, although the apparent attribution of cause may
be somewhat less. It is the relationships themselves, however, that are primary or causal, for the essential action was the *relating* of Dr. Seldon's
interpretations to the sociohistorical context.

The Observed Individual's Reflections
on History

As the observer—Dr. Seldon or a developmental psychologist—may reflect upon the relationships between him- or herself and history, so may the individuals who are being observed. These autobiographical reflections are represented in Figure 2 as C' and D'. The potential content of these reflections may include all the topics of the social sciences, including not only memories of past relationships but also hopes and expectations of future relationships, such as whether the state of the economy is likely to improve (see Klineberg, Chapter 6, this volume). The actual content for a particular individual may be far more limited, however.

To bring the expanded system of relations together with some typical life-span research, let me refer to the classic work of Neugarten (Neugarten & Datan, 1973; Neugarten, Moore, & Lowe, 1965) and others (Atchley 1975) on social norms, in particular, age norms. Respondents were asked to indicate on a questionnaire the ages they regarded as appropriate for certain behaviors, such as getting married, settling on a career, and so forth. The results demonstrate an aspect of the socialization process in which shared norms (D) are a basis for evaluation and guidance of individuals' (C) behaviors. Nevertheless, additional questions can be raised beyond the fact of these individuals' knowledge of age norms. In particular, do they reflect on the relations between these age norms and their own actions and on changes in these norms over the course of history? Certainly social scientists know that these norms are changing, but we rarely consider whether the individuals whom we are observing know this as well. In more general terms, the question concerns the extent to which individuals reflect on relationships between social structure (D') and changes in their own lives (C'). This question will be explored in the present section, with the presentation of three different levels of reflectivity and an examination of the validity of autobiographical memories.

Levels of Autobiographical Reflectivity

That individuals may not always engage in the expanded system of relations presented in Figure 2 has been implied in the preceding discussion. In the present section, three partial forms of this system of relations are presented, corresponding to hypothesized levels of autobiographical reflectivity with regard to one's relating with the sociohistorical context. (The term levels has been used deliberately so as not to make a commitment that these partial forms are developmental stages, although they may be. On the

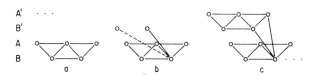

Figure 3. Levels of reflectivity: a, lack of reflectivity; b, recognition of alternative perspectives; c, historical perspective.

other hand, an individual at one level may function at that level and at all the lower levels at different times or in different domains. See Glasersfeld and Kelley, 1982, for further discussion.) The three partial forms or levels are shown in Figure 3, for the case of the observer. The forms for the observed individual would be identical but have not been shown in order to simplify later discussion.

First, consider Figure 3a. This limited set of relations between the individual and the sociohistorical context, omitting the autobiographical reflections on event sequences A' and B', represents a lack of understanding that there may be alternative conceptual and philosophical perspectives. This *lack of reflectivity* may be illustrated by the alienated adolescent who lacks a feeling of relationship with the sociohistorical context, or by the foreclosed adolescent, who has settled on a career or role in society without confronting and evaluating a range of alternative roles to which a commitment might be made during identity achievement (Meacham & Santilli, 1982). Figure 3a also represents an individual at the third level of Labouvie-Vief's (1982) neo-Piagetian structural model of development, the intrasystemic level (formal realism). The individual fails to recognize that the current perspective is only one of many possible perspectives.

Figure 3b represents a more complex set of relations, in which the individual recognizes that there are *many alternative,* equally viable *perspectives.* The choice among these is arbitrary, and one might consider this level as analogous to that of identity achievement in Erikson's (1963) theory, in which the action of making a commitment to one of the alternatives serves to validate that alternative as the appropriate choice. Perry (1970), who has outlined a sequence of stages of intellectual and ethical development for college students, describes a similar stage of contextual relativism (Perry's stage 5), in which some alternatives are considered to be better than others despite the fact that none are seen to be context-free. This also parallels the fourth level of Labouvie-Vief's model, the intersystemic level.

Figure 3c represents a subsequent level, in which the individual who previously was unable to apprehend the relationship between any two perspectives of level b, now is able to consider these perspectives from an *historical perspective,* taking into consideration their relationship with each other. In terms of Perry's stages, the individual is able to understand the adoption of a perspective as "an ongoing, unfolding activity" (Perry, 1970, p. 10). This level also corresponds with what Labouvie-Vief (1982) has termed the autonomous level, in which "systems are reexamined from the aspect of their historical construction" (p. 183). The third level of reflectivity is illustrated by the older adult who has attained ego integrity, who feels a oneness with the stream of history that has paralleled his or her life, who knows "that an individual life is the accidental coincidence of but one life cycle with but one segment of history" (Erikson, 1963, p. 268), and who develops "the particular style of integrity suggested by its historical place" (p. 269).

We can also consider the case of individuals born in the baby boom of 1960 and so now subject to the impact of that historical event, for example, in the limiting of occupational opportunities. Whereas only a few years ago this might have been understood in terms of relationships between the individual and sociohistorical event sequences, now—due in part to the actions of social scientists plus intensive media attention to the "fact" of the baby boom and its consequences—one must also include consideration of young peoples' autobiographical reflections upon their position within the changing demographic structure, and the potential for reduction of expectations for the future, increased or decreased striving for achievement, reduced commitment to the reward structure of society, and so forth.

The extent to which observers will have to consider observed individuals as being at levels b or c, in order to have a complete understanding of the relationships between individuals and the sociohistorical context, is likely an empirical question. What aspects of individuals' development are related to their reflections upon their own life histories? And what aspects of their development are related to *their* understanding of their own relationship with history, bringing in the relationship between the autobiographical self and one's conception of the contemporary sociohistorical context? Such concepts as nationalism, oppression, liberation, and so forth no doubt merit discussion in this context.

Validity of Autobiographical Memories

An issue implied in the preceding discussion of reflectivity concerns the sources of knowledge regarding past relationships, and the validity of that knowledge. In more familiar terms, the issue is one of the validity of autobiographical memories. Autobiographical and biographical methods have not yet had a major impact in the study of human development. The use of autobiographical remembering as a methodology and as a source of data has, unfortunately, been tainted by the association with idiographic case-study methodologies and has been evaluated only by the validity criteria appropriate for the study of learning and remembering as basic cognitive processes.

The distinction between idiographic and nomothetic approaches was introduced by Windelband (1848–1915) in 1894 and later extended by Allport (1937). These terms denote methodologies that are at first glance contrasting: Nomothetic approaches, utilizing data averaged for groups of individuals, are consistent with the assumption that it is reasonable to search for general laws; idiographic approaches, utilizing primarily individual or case studies, provide evidence for the uniqueness of individuals. Nevertheless, Marceil (1977) has argued that Allport is often misunderstood (see also Riegel, 1969, 1976b). Rather than as contrasting methodologies, nomothesis and idiography ought to be understood as "overlapping and contributing to one another" (Allport, 1937, p. 22). We have needlessly believed that the theoretical assumption of general laws had to be pursued with a nomothetic methodology and that the assumption of individual uniqueness had to be pursued with idiographic approaches. Rather, Marceil argued, general laws may also be confirmed by studying a few individuals intensively (as do Skinnerians), instead of a large number of individuals rather superficially. Indeed, there is a danger in the latter method, for generalizations to all individuals may be unwarranted. Developmental functions based on averages of scores from a large number of individuals may obscure important information about how specific individuals within the group are changing (Wohlwill, 1973, p. 124). Thus, idiographical approaches—autobiographical remembering—can be important, both in confirming general laws of development and in revealing important individual differences.

The issue of the validity of autobiographical memories may be considered by describing the process of autobiographical remembering in somewhat greater detail. A transactional perspective on remembering (Meacham, 1977b, pp. 276–278) will be employed, in which remembering is viewed not as an intraindividual process, but as a social, communicative process. Memories are viewed as the constructed products of this process. The transactional process includes and gives meaning not only to the memories, but also to the individual rememberer and to the social context, which in turn includes other individuals who participate in the validation of shared memories. Thus memories reflect both the original events in which they are based and the context in which they are remembered (see also Kvale, 1977).

Some of the relationships implied in an individual's remembering are shown in Figure 4 for an individual B (a parallel figure could be presented for C). The event to be remembered is E_1, which of course reflects prior

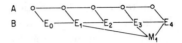

Figure 4. Relations in remembering; E refers to the event, M to the memory.

events E_0 as well as the sociohistorical context A. Remembering is a claim to know something from personal experiences in the past without just having learned or inferred it (Meacham, 1977a). That is, at least one event E_2 intervening between E_1 and the remembering of E_1 is necessary in order to suit the definition of remembering (without the intervening event, one would have merely sustained duration of E_1). The constructed memory M_1 is a synthesis of the event E_1 with the current state of the individual remem-berer E_3, which in turn reflects the current sociohistorical context of the individual. Consistent with the transactional or constructive perspective on remembering, memories of a particular event will vary as the context of remembering changes—the memory of E_1 in the context of E_2 may be quite different from the memory of E_1 in the context of E_3. (For example, Piaget's [Liben, 1977; Piaget & Inhelder, 1973] research on remembering consists essentially of contrasting the memories of children within two different conceptual contexts, the preoperational and the concrete operational struc-tures.) Subsequent to the production of a memory, the memory may then be incorporated within the ongoing stream of events to yield E_4, as shown in Figure 4.

What does it mean to say that an autobiographical memory is a valid memory? Two quite different meanings may be distinguished. In the study of learning and remembering as basic cognitive processes, the question of validity or accuracy of memories has been a matter of whether or not the memory M_1 corresponds with the initial event E_1. For reference, let us refer to this type of validity as *memory correspondence*. Typically, the researcher is present at the initial event or otherwise is able to establish, independently of the memory, the nature of the initial event. Although memory correspon-dence may be an important aspect of validity for some limited questions about the nature of remembering processes, including autobiographical re-membering (e.g., Squire & Slater, 1975; Warrington & Sanders, 1971), for more general purposes it is clear from this transactional perspective that memory correspondence should not be expected, because memories depend not only upon the initial event but also on the current context of remember-ing—and the latter is continually changing. The lack of memory correspon-dence is not simply a matter of decreased correspondence as a function of increased retention interval. Piaget's (Piaget & Inhelder, 1973) research on remembering illustrated *increased* correspondence with increased retention interval, due to changes in the context of remembering. A similar observation was made by Wenar (1961): "Change does not have to be in the direction of repression, distortion, and defensiveness, but it can be in the direction of greater clarity and understanding. Having more children, for example, can make a mother realize that her first born was not as fretful and demanding as she had thought" (p. 495).

The second sense in which autobiographical memories may be valid memories is in terms of their coherence within the current context of remembering. Is the memory M_1 a coherent synthesis of the initial event (E_1), the context of remembering (E_3), including the sociohistorical context (A), and memories of other related events? The type of validity that will be referred to as *memory coherence,* then, concerns the relationship of the memory to present motivations, values, and so forth. The distinction between memory correspondence and memory coherence is illustrated in research by Woodruff and Birren (1972). Longitudinal data in the researchers' files showed that the personalities of the observed individuals had not changed over the course of 25 years. Nevertheless, these same individuals reported that they had changed in positive ways from how they remembered their personalities to be 25 years earlier. These individuals' memories were not valid in the sense of memory correspondence for their memories did not correspond with the initial events as recorded by the researchers. Yet their memories were valid in the sense of memory coherence for there was a successful synthesis of these individuals' autobiographical memory traces with their current view of self.

It may be that one of the reasons such embarrassingly low correlations are obtained in much antecedent–consequent research on, for example, personality development is that we typically attempt to include as the antecedent the initial event, the "objective fact," and not the event as subsequently remembered and reinterpreted by the individual. For example, consider physical punishment of children during childhood and its possible later influences on delinquency during adolescence. Is it the event of physical punishment that is essential, or is it how the adolescent at age 16 years understands the earlier punishment in the context of present interpersonal relationships? These later memories or interpretations may also lack stability, as Reiff and Sheerer (1959) nicely illustrated: "Each time, the event is placed into a different structured personal frame of reference of an ever-growing autobiography, which in turn affects the respective remembering in a different way. A girl who married at twenty may at thirty remember chiefly the dress she wore at her wedding; at forty, the food consumed at the wedding breakfast; at fifty, the fact that her uncle sent a stingy present" (p. 39).

Not only does the construction of memories depend on the current context, but the memories in turn have a reciprocal relationship with current functioning. From the point of view of the individual rememberer, memories are valid not because they correspond with past events, but because they are coherent, appropriate, and useful within the context of present personality and social conditions (Meacham, 1977b). The concepts introduced in this section, including the distinction between memory correspondence and memory coherence, and the view that the function of remembering is to serve the present and not the past, as well as the framework of three levels of autobiographical reflectivity, have prepared the way for an evaluation of our discipline in the following section.

Evaluating Our Discipline against the System of Relationships

Lack of a Historical Perspective

In summary to this point, the argument has been that if we consider as a goal for our discipline being able to make valid predictions on the order of what Dr. Seldon was able to do, then we will need to be able to take into consideration simultaneously the multitude of relations outlined so far (and shown in Figure 2). Because no real Dr. Seldon has yet appeared, it seems that the procedures of our discipline of life-span developmental psychology do not at present conform to the system of relations. The next step, therefore, is to evaluate our discipline—the observer—against the various partial forms of the system of relations, as shown in Figure 3. This West Virginia Life-Span Developmental Psychology Conference is evidence that at least some observers within the discipline are thinking at level a, that is, seeking to understand individual and historical development in their mutual relationships. At this level, however, the observer remains unaware that his or her present conceptual or philosophical perspective is only one of many possibilities.

The efforts of Reese and Overton (Reese & Overton, 1970; Overton, in press) in calling attention to contrasting philosophical perspectives (mechanistic, organismic) within developmental psychology, and setting forth the conceptual and methodological implications of each, no doubt have been instrumental in moving many developmentalists from level a to b. It is not essential that anyone's perspective change, merely that the observer recognize that alternative perspectives such as Pepper's (1970/1942) world hypotheses exist. The observer at level b recognizes the existence of alternative perspectives yet remains troubled by the apparent lack of criteria for choosing among these, perhaps decrying the apparently random shifts of the discipline from one fad to the next and perhaps despairing of the lack of cumulation of knowledge (see Meacham, 1981, p. 469, for further discussion of reactions at this level).

A description of our discipline in terms of the historical perspective of level c is not warranted, however, for by and large we fail to reflect upon and discuss the relationships between our perspective as researchers (B') and the social, historical, and political contexts within which we work, despite the fact that previously there have been numerous attempts to call attention to this failure. Notable among these attempts has been Habermas's (1971) call for theory that is aware both of its origins in the sociohistorical context and of its role in changing that context. In the framework of the present chapter, the observer must recognize both the retrospective and the prospective relationships, as consumer and producer, of the perspective itself (B') with the sociohistorical context (A'). Other calls for greater attention to the relationships between the discipline of developmental psychology and developmental theory, on the one hand, and the contemporary sociohistorical context, on the other, have been put forth by Broughton (1981), Gergen (1980), Meacham (1981, pp. 468–470), and Youniss (1983), among others. Youniss (1983), among others.

Although there has been increasing scholarship on the relationships of *observed* individuals to their sociohistorical contexts (that is, relationships between C and D), there have been too few responses to the call for investigation of the relationships between *ourselves* as observers and our contemporary sociohistorical context (B' and A'). One such attempt, not yet extended to present times, is Riegel's (1972) analysis of the influence of economic and political ideologies, in capitalist England and mercantilist Continental Europe, upon the development of the mechanistic and organismic perspectives in developmental psychology. Riegel's analysis illustrated his dialectical perspective, not because the apparent contradictions between the mechanistic and organismic perspectives were resolved, but because each perspective when examined within its appropriate sociohistorical context could be seen as coherent and appropriate. This examination necessarily is from a level of abstraction above the level of Pepper's (1970/1942) world hypotheses (one might refer to this level as metacontextualism). The dialectical perspective is, among other aspects, fundamentally an historical perspective (Meacham, 1978) and entirely consistent with the description of relationships at level c (and so it is not surprising that the psychohistorians of the second foundation made use of the Rigellian integral).

Other attempts to examine the relationships between ourselves as observers and our own sociohistorical context include Buck-Morss's (1975) critique of Piaget's theory as reflecting an ideology of abstract exchange, and Sampson's (1981) critique of the same theory for reflecting merely contemporary values and interests, in particular in the adoption of technical knowledge as a model for all human knowledge. These attempts, although a step in the right direction, nevertheless have been too easily and readily criticized (see Broughton, 1981, and Youniss, 1983, respectively). Other descriptions of relationships between the sociohistorical context and developmental theory include Meacham's (1981, pp. 463–468) brief consideration of the societal functions supported by maintenance of the heredity–environment dichotomy, excluding the role in development of the individual's own actions, and Parke's (see Parke & Tinsley, Chapter 9, this volume) review of the influence of changing social conditions upon investigation of the role of fathers in children's development. Much more might be written regarding the influence of the relative affluence of the 1960s, civil rights legislation, changing demographic structure (children, older adults), and so forth upon contemporary developmental theory (see, e.g., Kuhn & Meacham, 1983).

To summarize this evaluation of our discipline in terms of the system of relations, we are now striving for an understanding of the relationships between individuals and the sociohistorical context (C, D) but have far to go in terms of understanding the reflections of observed individuals on their relationship with history (C', D'), as well as our own relationship with history (B', A'). In order for the discipline to advance to the historical perspective of level c, a more rigorous and constructive level of self-criticism must be achieved. Broughton (1981, pp. 394–398) has provided a list of criteria that a successful critique ought to meet. First among these criteria is specificity of the level of analysis that is being critiqued. For example, is it the theory of moral stages, the child's structures of judgment, or Kohlberg the theorist that is related to the sociohistorical context? Second, the types and directions of causality should be clarified. Third, when a causal relation between sociohistorical contexts and the development of the discipline and its theories is implied, then concrete evidence for the relation should be provided. Fourth, there should be a clear specification of which ideology is being critiqued. Fifth, critiques should be capable of discriminating among theories that are derived from incompatible ideologies and even formulated as critiques of each other. Broughton cites two critiques that fail this criterion because Piaget, Freud, Chomsky, and gestalt psychology are grouped together in the first case, and structuralist, humanist, and neo-Freudian theories of development are grouped in the second. Sixth, a successful critique should attempt to conform to a consistent epistemological position. As Broughton notes, "Without grounding itself in some way, an ideology-critique invites the accusation that it is itself ideological. It could perhaps even derive from the same ideology that it criticizes" (p. 397). The task ahead for the discipline of life-course developmental psychology will not be easy.

Looking to the Future

Looking to the future, do we want our discipline to develop so that it corresponds with the system of relations within which Dr. Seldon was presumably working? This question may be answered by raising another, namely, what are the aims of our discipline? Dr. Seldon's aim was clearly the prediction and control of future historical events. For his predictions to hold, however, he had to assume that people in general would not learn key details of his plan to alter the course of history; for if they did, they might act, not according to the statistical principles of psychohistory, but in reaction to their knowledge of the plan, perhaps in a way that had not been predicted. In other words, although Dr. Seldon permitted himself as observer to function with the historical perspective of level c, he assumed that observed individuals would not reflect on their own relationships with history, and so would function at a lower level. Such an assumption, although necessary to permit prediction and control, is represented by only a partial form of the system of relations, with the observed individuals' reflective event sequences C' and D' omitted. More important, the limitation of access to information regarding the plan would violate both the principle of participatory government and the concept of science based on unrestricted access to and exchange of knowledge (Meacham, 1983). Thus Dr. Seldon's aims of prediction and control (historicism) ought to be rejected as aims for our discipline (see also Gergen, 1980).

If our aim as a discipline is not the prediction and control of the future, then perhaps it is to validate our interpretations of the past. That is—by extension from the preceding discussion of autobiographical remembering—is there a correspondence of particular interpretations of the past with actual past events? Yet, as discussed here previously, the answer must generally be no, for the interpretations reflect an effort toward coherence with present conditions, motivations, and so forth, and these are continually changing. Further, there appears to be no certain way of establishing correspondence of interpretations with the actual past, short of having a better record of the events, in which case the interpretation becomes redundant. So our aim is not to validate our interpretations of the past.

The future and the past having been ruled out, it must be the case that the aim of our discipline is to better understand relations between event sequences in the present. Because of the bidirectionality of the relations described in this chapter, not only are interpretations of past events validated through their coherence with present conditions, but also *our under-standing of the present is continually validated through constructing relations with the past.* Support for this conclusion may be found in the words of historians: Braudel (1980/1969, p. 69) wrote that history is a dialectic of the time span, a study of the past and equally of the present of society. And Walsh (1967) commented that "human beings . . . feel a need to form some picture of the past for the sake of their own present activities . . . . history throws light not on 'objective' events, but on the persons who write it; *it illustrates not the past, but the present.* And that is no doubt why each generation finds it necessary to write its histories afresh" (p. 109, emphasis added; see also pp. 173, 187).

The fundamental contrast between the second and third levels of reflectivity outlined previously is that at the second level the individual recognizes the alternatives but is snared in the trap of choosing among them, whereas at the third level the individual is able to consider these alternative interpretations as themselves embedded within an historical context. The third level, the historical perspective, is consistent with contemporary thought in history: "The fundamental movement of history today is not one of choosing between this or that path, or different point of view, but of accepting and absorbing all the successive definitions in which, one after another, there have been attempts to confine it" (Braudel, 1980/1969, p. 66). "The only error," in Braudel's view, "would be to choose one of these histories to the exclusion of all others. That was, and always will be, the cardinal error of historicizing. It will not be easy, we know, to convince all historians of the truth of this. Still less, to convince all the social sciences, with their burning desire to get us back to history as we used to know it yesterday" (1980/1969, p. 34).

CONCLUSION

The problem for life-course developmental psychology is not merely to understand the impact of past historical events upon the development of individuals. Rather, the general problem is to understand the processes or relationships from which sequences of both sociohistorical changes and individual life-course changes are derived, giving equal balance to social history and to individual history. Individuals are not merely products of their sociohistorical contexts; they are consumers of interpretations of past historical change, which give meaning to their present condition, and they are producers of historical change through their construction of historical interpretations and their actions in the present. In this chapter, three levels of reflectivity are described: (a) lack of reflectivity; (b) recognition of alternative perspectives; and (c) the dialectical or historical perspective. In order for our discipline of life-course developmental psychology to advance to this third level, a more rigorous and constructive level of self-criticism must be achieved, and the positivist search for "objective facts" of history must be abandoned. We need not, after all, be too much concerned with historical events in the past, for the aim of our discipline is not to understand the past, nor to predict and control the future, but—as in autobiographical remembering—to better understand the present.

REFERENCES

Allport, G. W. (1937). *Personality: A psychological interpretation*. New York: Holt.

Asimov, I. (1951). *Foundation*. New York: Avon.

Asimov, I. (1952). *Foundation and empire*. New York: Avon.

Asimov, I. (1953). *Second foundation*. New York: Avon.

Atchley, R. C. (1975). The life course, age grading, and age-linked demands for decision making. In N. Datan & L. H. Ginsberg (Eds.), *Life-span developmental psychology: Normative life crises*. New York: Academic Press.

Baltes, P. B., Reese, H. W., & Lipsitt, L. P. (1980). Life-span developmental psychology. *Annual Review of Psychology, 31*, 65–110.

Braudel, F. (1980). *On history* (S. Matthews, Trans.). Chicago: University of Chicago Press. (Originally published, 1969.)

Broughton, J. M. (1981). Piaget's structural developmental psychology: V. Ideology-critique and the possibility of a critical developmental theory. *Human Development, 24*, 382–411.

Buck-Morss, S. (1975). Socio-economic bias in Piaget's theory and its implications for cross-cultural study. *Human Development, 18*, 35–49.

Dilthey, W. (1962). *Pattern and meaning in history* (H. P. Rickman, Ed.). New York: Harper.

Elder, G. H., Jr. (1979). Historical change in life patterns and personality. In P. B. Baltes & O. G. Brim, Jr. (Eds.),*Life-span development and behavior* (Vol. 2). New York: Academic Press.

Erikson, E. H. (1963). *Childhood and society* (2nd ed.). New York: Norton.

Gergen, K. J. (1980). The emerging crisis in life-span developmental theory. In P. B. Baltes & O. G. Brim, Jr. (Eds.), *Life-span development and behavior* (Vol. 3). New York: Academic Press.

Glasersfeld, E. von, & Kelley, M. F. (1982). On the concepts of period, phase, stage, and level. *Human Development, 25*, 152–160.

Habermas, J. (1971). *Knowledge and human interests* (J. J. Shapiro, Trans.). Boston: Beacon.

Kitchener, R. F. (1983). Changing conceptions of the philosophy of science and the foundations of developmental psychology. In D. Kuhn & J. A. Meacham (Eds.), *On the development of developmental psychology*. Basel: Karger.

Kuhn, D., & Meacham, J. A. (Eds.). (1983). *On the development of developmental psychology*. Basel: Karger.

Kvale, S. (1977). Dialectics and research on remembering. In N. Datan & H. W. Reese (Eds.), *Life-span developmental psychology: Dialectical perspectives on experimental research*. New York: Academic.

Labouvie-Vief, G. (1982) Dynamic development and mature autonomy: A theoretical pro-
logue. *Human Development, 25,* 161–191.
Liben, L. S. (1977). Memory in the context of cognitive development: The Piagetian approach.
In R. V. Kail, Jr. & J. W. Hagen (Eds.), *Perspectives on the development of memory and
cognition.* Hillsdale, NJ: Earlbaum.
Marceil, J. C. (1977). Implicit dimensions of idiography and nomothesis: A reformulation.
American Psychologist, 32, 1046–1055.
Meacham, J. A. (1977a). Soviet investigations of memory development. In R. V. Kail, Jr. & J.
W. Hagen (Eds.), *Perspectives on the development of memory and cognition.* Hillsdale,
NJ: Earlbaum.
Meacham, J. A. (1977b). A transactional model of remembering. In N. Datan & H. W. Reese
(Eds.), *Life-span developmental psychology: Dialectical perspectives on experimental re-
search.* New York: Academic Press.
Meacham, J. A. (1978). History and developmental psychology. *Human Development, 21,*
363–369.
Meacham, J. A. (1981). Political values, conceptual models, and research. In R. M. Lerner &
N. A. Busch-Rossnagel (Eds.), *Individuals as producers of their own development.* New
York: Academic Press.
Meacham, J. A. (1983). Wisdom and the context of knowledge: Knowing that one doesn't
know. In D. Kuhn & J. A. Meacham (Eds.), *On the development of developmental
psychology.* Basel: Karger.
Meacham, J. A., & Santilli, N. R. (1982). Interstage relationships in Erikson's theory: Identity
and intimacy. *Child Development, 53,* 1461–1467.
Neugarten, B. L., & Datan, N. (1973). Sociological perspectives on the life cycle. In P. B. Baltes
& K. W. Schaie (Eds.), *Life-span developmental psychology: Personality and socialization.* New York: Academic Press.
Neugarten, B. L., Moore, J. W., & Lowe, J. C. (1965). Age norms, age constraints, and adult
socialization. *American Journal of Sociology, 1965, 70,* 710–717. (Also in B. L. Neu-
garten, Ed., *Middle age and aging.* Chicago: University of Chicago Press, 1968.)
Overton, W. F. Historical and contemporary perspectives of development. In I. Sigel & D.
Brodzinsky (Eds.), *Developmental psychology.* New York: Holt, Rinehart & Winston, in
press.
Pepper, S. C. *World hypotheses.* Berkeley: University of California Press, 1970. (Originally
published, 1942)
Perry, W. I. *Forms of intellectual and ethical development in the college years.* New York:
Holt, Rinehart & Winston, 1970.
Piaget, J., & Inhelder, B. *Memory and intelligence* (A. J. Pomerans, trans). New York: Basic
Books, 1973.
Prisco, S., III. Psychohistory can help to explain the "why" of human experience. *Chronicle of
Higher Education,* June 9, 1982, p. 27.
Reese, H. W., & Overton, W. F. Models of development and theories of development. In L. R.
Goulet & P. B. Baltes (Eds.), *Life-span developmental psychology: Research and theory.*
New York: Academic Press. 1970.
Reiff, R., & Sheerer, M. *Memory and hypnotic age regression.* New York: International
Universities Press.
Riegel, K. F. (1969). History as a nomothetic science: Some generalizations from theories and
research in developmental psychology. *Journal of Social Issues, 25,* 99–127.
Riegel, K. F. (1972). The influence of economic and political ideologies upon the development
of developmental psychology. *Psychological Bulletin, 78,* 129–144.
Riegel, K. F. (1975). Adult life crises: A dialectic interpretation of development. In N. Datan &

L. H. Ginsberg (Eds.), *Life-span developmental psychology: Normative life crises.* New York: Academic Press.

Riegel, K. F. (1976a). From traits and equilibrium toward developmental dialectics. In W. J. Arnold (Ed.), *1975 Nebraska Symposium on Motivation.* Lincoln: University of Nebraska Press.

Riegel, K. F. (1976b). *The psychology of development and history.* New York: Plenum.

Riegel, K. F. (1977). The dialectics of time. In N. Datan & H. W. Reese (Eds.), *Life-span developmental psychology: Dialectical perspectives on experimental research.* New York: Academic Press.

Riegel, K. F. (1979). *Foundations of dialectical psychology.* New York: Academic Press. (Also Stuttgart: Klett-Cotta Verlag, 1980.)

Riegel, K. F., & Meacham, J. A. (1978). Dialectics, transaction, and Piaget's theory. In L. A. Pervin & M. Lewis (Eds.), *Perspectives in interactional psychology.* New York: Plenum.

Rockwell, R. C., & Elder, G. H., Jr. (1982). Economic deprivation and problem behavior: Childhood and adolescence in the Great Depression. *Human Development, 25,* 57–64.

Sampson, E. E. (1981). Cognitive psychology as ideology. *American Psychologist, 36,* 730–743.

Squire, L. R., & Slater, P. C. (1975). Forgetting in very long-term memory as assessed by an improved questionnaire technique. *Journal of Experimental Psychology: Human Learning and Memory, 104,* 50–54.

Walsh, W. H. (1967). *Philosophy of history: An introduction.* New York: Harper & Row.

Warrington, E. K., & Sanders, H. I. (1971). The fate of old memories. *Quarterly Journal of Experimental Psychology, 21,* 432–442.

Wenar, C. (1961). The reliability of mothers' histories. *Child Development, 32,* 491–500.

Wohlwill, J. F. (1973). *The study of behavioral development.* New York: Academic Press.

Woodruff, D. S., & Birren, J. E. (1972). Age changes and cohort differences in personality. *Developmental Psychology, 6,* 252–259.

Youniss, J. (1983). Beyond ideology to the universals of development. In D. Kuhn & J. A. Meacham (Eds.), *On the development of developmental psychology.* Basel: Karger.

CHAPTER 4

Simulation of Cultural Change by Cross-Cultural Research: Some Metamethodological Considerations

LUTZ H. ECKENSBERGER
BERND KREWER
ELISABETH KASPER

It is the dilemma of psychology to deal as a natural science with an object that creates history.

BOESCH, 1971, P. 9

INTRODUCTION

Baltes, Reese, and Lipsitt (1980) distinguish three types of influence on the individual: normative[1] age-graded, normative historical (evolutionary), and nonnormative influences, "which, mediated through the developing individual, act and interact to produce life-span development" (p. 75). The inclusion of history-graded (evolutionary) influences, defined as biological and environmental determinants associated with historical time and historical contexts related to cohort explicitly demands investigation of "the developing individual in a changing world" (Riegel & Meacham, 1976, p. 75). That is, one should explicitly include sociohistorical change in experimental designs within life-span developmental psychology. Previous investigators

---

[1]In anthropology, Leach (1968) distinguished between normative and normal events. Whereas the latter refers to the empirical distribution of events, the first implies an *ideal*-norm of customs. According to this terminology, in life-span developmental psychology *normal* events are clearly meant.

LIFE-SPAN DEVELOPMENTAL PSYCHOLOGY
HISTORICAL AND GENERATIONAL EFFECTS

73

Copyright © 1984 by Academic Press, Inc.
All rights of reproduction in any form reserved.
ISBN 0-12-482420-X

attempted retrospective analyses of historical processes and/or events (see Elias, 1979; Rabb & Rotberg, 1971; Ziehe, 1975) that affect different cohorts at different ages (see Schaie, Chapter 1, this volume). However, although retrospective historical analysis is a prerequisite for the inclusion of concurrent historical (sociohistorical) change processes in experimental designs within life-span development psychology, this latter procedure is itself very difficult to handle because the selection of concurrent historical processes at the outset requires a theory that allows these processes to be linked with ontogeny. Second, aside from a few circumscribed historical events like earthquakes, wars, or economic depressions (see Elder, 1974; Janney, Masuda, & Holmes, 1977), the *continuously* changing historical context represents long-term processes that are difficult to handle within the life span of a researcher or a developmental project.

It is therefore very reasonable and indeed urgent to ask whether these phenomena can be simulated by imitating exactly those conditions which cannot (or can only with difficulty) be investigated directly. The purpose of such a simulation then would be to clarify or explain the underlying mechanism involved that relates these conditions to the observed processes or events.

Within this broader framework of a life-span perspective in developmental psychology and the practical problems given, it is challenging to discuss the limitations and possibilities of interpreting cross-cultural differences (determined at a given point of historical time) as a simulation of sociohistorical or cultural change, that is, as indicants of the same mechanisms that also underlie social–cultural change.

As a starting point to this discussion it may be helpful to realize that the underlying rationale is analogous to the idea of interpreting age differences determined in cross-sectional designs as simulation of age changes in longitudinal designs.[2] Consequently, one might suppose that an answer could be found in the bulk of literature on longitudinal, cross-sectional, and sequential designs since the late 1960s. However, the first step into this field is already the last one simply because the age variable, which serves as a comfortable (although only descriptive; see Schaie, Chapter 1, this volume) index for change and development on the individual level, does not exist in the same way on the cultural, social, or aggregate level. This fact leads to the conclusion that some other criteria are necessary to justify interpreting cross-cultural differences as a simulation of cultural change: namely, a substantial universal developmental dimension, which could serve the same function on the cultural level as the age variable on the individual level. If

---

[2]It is terminologically interesting that at least in German sociology a cross-sectional design is sometimes labeled a *simulated panel*.

one appeals to cross-cultural research for an answer to this question, it becomes apparent that the idea of interpreting cross-cultural differences as a simulation of cultural change is not mentioned in modern discussions of the general purpose of cross-cultural research in psychology (see Brislin, Lonner, & Thorndike, 1973; Dasen, Berry, & Witkin, 1979; Eckensberger, 1973; Jahoda, 1980).

But it is interesting to note that now and then in cross-cultural psychology the opposite of our question has been proposed, namely, that studies of social or cultural change, as well as studies of acculturation (both of which represent the analysis of change and/or development of sociocultural systems during longer time periods), should (and can) be used to support the interpretation of data from cross-cultural research (see Eckensberger, 1973; Gutman, 1977). In addition to the absence of this idea (interpreting cross-cultural differences as change processes) in theoretical discussions, this strategy is also practically nonexistent in empirical studies. Besides sociological studies such as that of Lupri, who investigated the structural "change" of families during the industrialization "process" by a cross-cultural comparison of nations that differed in their societal "stage" of development (Lupri, 1965, p. 62), the authors know of only one psychological study that approximates the design in question: This is Edelstein's (1979) attempt to simulate the intracultural economic change of Iceland by a purposive selection of samples from different areas within the Icelandic culture representing different economic developmental states. Edelstein was aware of the problems involved in this simulation and was very cautious in identifying cross-sample comparisons as change. The data have not yet been published under this specific aspect.

Interestingly, however, this argument arose earlier and in other subdisciplines that are based on cross-cultural comparisons. Klineberg's (1980) and Orlove's (1980) analyses of the history of a cross-cultural perspective show that the interpretation of cross-cultural differences between individuals (determined at one point in time) in terms of sociocultural change was predominant in anthropology of the nineteenth century evolutionism of Morgan and Tyler, who shared the "assumption that all cultures could be placed on a small number of stages and that cultures tended to move through these states in a relatively fixed sequence" (Orlove, 1980, p. 236). This assumption is one presupposition for the interpretation of cross-cultural differences as cultural change. Consequently, differences between Western and non-Western cultural groups have been interpreted as representing a cultural lag of the latter: They were assumed to be more "primitive," less developed. It is implied that this perspective went hand in hand with an "almost universal ethnocentrism" (Klineberg, 1980, p. 34), a tendency that became, however, increasingly unacceptable after Boas (1911) "asked for an understanding of other cultures as *different* rather than as inferior, as *qualitatively* varied rather than as early groupings in a process of evolution leading up to our own 'higher civilization'" (Klineberg, 1980, p. 37). This perspective finally led to the claim of a cultural relativism as represented in the work of Sapir, Benedict, Mead, Herskovits, and others. And it is obvious that under the assumption that every culture and its development is to be understood in its own terms, a descriptive or theoretical universal developmental dimension that theoretically allows for an interpretation of cultural differences (at one given point of time) as indicants of a general process of cultural evolution is difficult to formulate. Whether or not this perspective dominates cross-cultural research within psychology today (see Berry, 1972), it is perhaps one reason why the idea of interpreting cultural differences as simulations of cultural change is not elaborated in this field.

It is also true, however, that the idea of cultural evolutionism is not completely obsolete; this is partly because it is necessary on the individual as well as on the aggregate level to formulate some aspects or dimensions that are common to all cultures and human beings, that is, to formulate *cultural universals*. Second, a closer look at various theories of psychology reveals that some theories are built more upon the assumption of universal developmental processes than others. Although the present authors are not trained in anthropology or sociology, they have the impression that this is also true for some present-day anthropological theories.

In fact, the often found distinction between a *synchronic* and a *diachronic* analysis of culture exactly addresses our problem: Some anthropologists try to keep these aspects strictly apart (Clignet, 1970, pp. 610ff.); others, however, intentionally try to interpret synchronically collected data (structural or functional descriptions of cultures at one given time period) as if they also represent diachronic (historical or evolutionary) processes (see Carneiro, 1970). They thereby do exactly what we are looking for: They interpret cross-cultural differences as sociocultural change. Still others try to integrate synchronic and diachronic processes in cultural evolution via the distinction of different cultural aspects (domains) that are assumed to be differently affected by the diachronic or synchronic factors (cf. the concept of a cultural type proposed by Steward, 1955).

Up to this point, one might conclude that the treatment of our question with reference to the aggregate level could be solved solely by looking at theories of sociocultural change that allow for identification of those variables and/or conditions (including their underlying mechanisms) that (1) can be simulated by cross-cultural comparisons and (2) can serve as antecedent conditions within developmental designs (see Eckensberger, 1973; Schaie, Chapter 1, this volume).

Unfortunately, the problem becomes more complicated if one takes into consideration that the concept of development as well as the assumptions about the kind of relationship between the aggregate level and the individual level (the relationship between sociocultural and individual change) is quite different in different approaches of social science.

Although these introductory notes necessarily have been kept rather sketchy, they nevertheless lead to the following considerations about how to handle the present topic:

1. Since the influential work of Reese & Overton (1970), it seems to be broadly accepted that the concept of development as well as the relationship between the environment and the subject is quite different in different theory-families. Because a substantial developmental dimension is needed that allows for an interpretation of cross-cultural differences as a simulation of sociocultural change and because the simulations also aim at clarifying the underlying mechanisms involved, it seems to be fruitful, if not necessary, to discuss our question in the framework of different paradigms existing in cross-cultural and/or life-span developmental psychology.

2. Five paradigms are distinguished. They are based upon the previously mentioned work of Reese & Overton (1970) and Looft (1973) but have been expanded by the senior author (Eckensberger, 1979), under the specific aspect of the relationship between the individual and the environment (culture). A *paradigm* in psychology and/or anthropology and sociology is understood as a summary of a whole scientific approach consisting of (a) a metaphysical model or analogy of humans and their functioning, (b) the associated family of theories, and (c) the methodological implications. The five paradigms have been selected primarily for heuristic reasons; it is not claimed that they cover all psychological approaches. Their methodological implications, especially under a cross-cultural perspective, are discussed by Eckensberger and Burgard (1983).

The following paradigms have been distinguished: (a) The paradigm of *quantification* (only), which includes the model of multitude and extent, and which does not have any specific substantive (psychological–anthropological) theory associated with it; (b) the *mechanistic* paradigm, based upon the engine analogy; (c) the *organismic* paradigm built upon the analogy of the living organism; (d) the *ecobehavioral* paradigm based upon organism–environment systems and most often linked to sociobiological and ecological theories; and (e) the *self-reflexive* paradigm, which is based upon the reflexive human being and usually connected with action theories.

3. Space limitation does not permit an extensive elaboration of all five paradigms. The reader who is interested in a more detailed discussion of these paradigms within psychology is referred to Eckensberger (1979). This discussion will be expanded, however, in three directions: (a) An attempt

will be made to demonstrate that these paradigms can also be distinguished on the aggregate level, although this argument is made very cautiously. (b) The basic distinction between a desirable and an undesirable eclecticism, proposed by Reese & Overton (1970, p. 123), is expanded inasmuch as it is argued that if theories of social and individual change are to be linked, this should be done only within the same theory-family, that is, not across paradigms. (c) Because the mechanistic and organismic paradigms are well known within the scientific community of life-span developmentalists (see the publications of the preceding life-span conferences), their description will be treated rather parsimoniously, and more attention will be focused on the fifth paradigm.

The following aspects of paradigms are relevant to the present discussion: the status of development; the specific type of relationship between the individual and the environment; and assumptions about the underlying developmental mechanisms.

4. An evaluation of the five paradigms (in terms of their fruitfulness) will be undertaken under two aspects: (a) under the aspect of the task proper, namely the analysis of possibilities and limitations of interpreting cross-cultural differences as indicants of social change, and (b) within the broader framework of a life-span developmental perspective.

Because the senior author argued (Eckensberger, 1983) that the life-span perspective and the cross-cultural perspective in psychology are confocal, some evaluative arguments on the paradigms will be taken from a previous discussion that was limited to cross-cultural research (Eckensberger, 1979). Two criteria are applied that are part of both the life-span developmental and the cross-cultural perspective: If it is the general aim in both approaches to interpret the changing individual in a changing world, then ideally an interactionistic theory is advocated to reach that goal (Looft, 1973). This would require, however, the construction of transformatory constructs (Klausner, 1973) that in principle would explain both cultural–social and individual change, as well as their interrelationship. Therefore, this possibility will be used as the first criterion to evaluate the different paradigms. The second criterion is quite different: Not only in cross-cultural research (see Eckensberger, 1979; Munroe & Munroe, 1980) but also in a life-span perspective (see Filipp, 1981), the contextual and subjective meanings of processes and events become more and more crucial. Although we realize that this problem is one of the most difficult to be solved within psychology (Lewin, 1930), we nevertheless will try to use it as a second evaluative criterion for the paradigms. We will ask whether any theory (family) allows the determination of general laws and concepts and still retains the uniqueness of single concrete events, processes, persons, objects, time, and space for single subjects (Looft, 1973; Schütz, 1960). This dichotomy is characterized as emic versus etic on the cultural level (see Berry, 1969, p. 125).

CROSS-CULTURAL SIMULATION OF SOCIOCULTURAL CHANGE WITHIN LIFE-SPAN DEVELOPMENTAL PSYCHOLOGY

Table 1 outlines some of the defining and differentiating features of the five paradigms. Table 2 demonstrates that (1) the aim in using cross-cultural strategies for simulation of sociohistorical change is quite different in the various approaches, as is the rationale for doing so. Also the strategic consequences are different. (2) The table also shows that apart from this narrower concern, the five paradigms realize the previously defined criteria of lifespan and cross-cultural perspectives to varying degrees.

The Quantification Paradigm

As mentioned elsewhere (Eckensberger, 1979), this paradigm is based upon a very basic ideal of scientific work, approaching reality in terms of "multitude and extent" (p. 261). Although it seems to the authors that this psychologically "empty" paradigm is rather obsolete in modern research, it may be useful to point out that any approach that primarily relies on statistical procedures is in danger following this paradigm as long as it does not relate statistically defined regularities to a substantive theory. This is true for the interpretation of cohort effects within sequential designs in terms of social change when they are defined only in parts of variance (Baltes, 1968) and when they are not explicitly linked to sociocultural conditions that are explicitly included in the designs (Eckensberger, 1973).

An example that follows this paradigm rather closely on the aggregate level and that explicitly interprets cross-cultural data as cultural change seems to be represented in the work of Carneiro (1970) on *cultural complexity,* which is primarily determined by the statistical procedure of scalogram analysis. Within this approach "a society's 'level of complexity' and its 'degree of evolution' can be said to be the same thing looked at in different ways. The first of these expressions focuses on a society as a structural end-product; the second focuses on the process which gave rise to that end-product" (Carneiro, 1970, p. 835). Because cultural complexity is defined by a scalogram analysis of cultures and cultural traits, this logic is also applied to the result of this method. "The evolutionary explanation of a

TABLE 1

Summary of Five Paradigms: Conceptualizations of the Relationship
between the Environment and the Individual

Paradigm	Metaphysical model	Theory–family	Type of relationship to environment	Type of reconstruction of processes–events
I. Quantification	Multitude and extent	No explicit substantive theories	Descriptive; statistical interaction	Taxonomy
II. Mechanistic	Engine	Learning theories; environmental determinists	Causal; statistical interaction	Explanation
III. Organismic	Living organism	Cognitive development and structural–functional theories	Teleological (functional) interdependency	Explanation
IV. Ecobehavioral	Ecosystem	Sociobiology; cultural ecology	Teleonomic (functional) inter- and intrasystemic relationships	Explanation
V. Self-reflexive	Human being	Action theories	Dialectical transaction	Understanding reconstruction

scalogram analysis is as follows: the order in which the traits are arranged, from bottom to top, is the order in which the societies have evolved them" (p. 837) and "scale analysis" of "synchronic cultural data can be made to yield a diachronic sequence of traits. . . . In a very real sense, then, we are wringing history out of ethnography" (p. 839.) It is the logic of scalogram analysis (as a conjunctive method) and not a theory of social change that makes the assumption of accumulation and retention of cultural traits necessary.

Within such an approach the status of development is purely descriptive change. Consequently, no specific preconditions to or results from change processes exist (see Table 1); also the interaction between variables

TABLE 1 (*Continued*)

Logical status of development	Assumptions about development		
	Preconditions	Process	Result
Descriptive (change)	Nonspecific	Description of change	Nonspecific
Explanandum	Circumscribed environmental condition or state	Association formation	Continuous accumulation of associations
Explanans	Contradiction (within and between organic systems)	Equilibration	Discontinuous successive states of equilibrium
Descriptive (change) explanandum	Environmental stress; state of system	Adaptation, selection, mutation, succession	Environmental fit; alternative states of intrasystemic dynamic equilibrium
Explanans; explanandum	Crisis, obstacles, barriers, facilities	Reorganization of internal and external field of action	Reification of actions (→culture); objectivations (→cognitive schemata); idealized ego-environment relationships (→affective schemata)

is not only reduced to a purely statistical term but additionally the variables themselves cannot be identified as antecedents or consequences. Therefore, aside from being rather obsolete in developmental psychology and anthropology, it is important in the present context to note that such approaches by definition do not permit a simulation of cultural change by cross-cultural differences because they contain no theoretically justified mechanism that is to be clarified. As noted in the beginning of this chapter, this aspect is part of our definition of simulation.

In conclusion it can be said that within this descriptive approach neither the reconstruction and interrelationship of individual and social change nor the definition of a unique context of behavior is possible; that is, neither

TABLE 2

Evaluation of the Five Paradigms

	Fruitfulness for life-span perspective	
Paradigm	Reconstruction of individual and social change	Context maintained
I. Quantification	Not available	Descriptive categories
II. Mechanistic	Either individual or social change	S = abstract categories (class)
III. Organismic	Either individual or social change	Abstract categories (schemata, structures)
IV. Ecobehavioral	Phylogenesis; social change (ultimate and proximate cause kept apart)	Superindividual categories
V. Self-reflexive	Actual genesis; ontogenesis; cultural change	General conceptions of reality; concrete field of action

the concern of a life-span developmental perspective nor the interest of cross-cultural psychology is realized.

The Mechanistic Paradigm

The complete set of hidden assumptions made in this paradigm need not be delineated and summarized here (see Looft, 1973; Reese & Overton,

TABLE 2 (*Continued*)

Fruitfulness for simulations of cultural change by CCR		
Aim in using CCR as simulation for sociohistorical change	Criteria for selection of cultures (cultural groups/conditions)	Rationale to simulate cultural changes by cultural change differences
No explicit aim (generalization studies)	Not available	Not available (no equivalent for age variable)
Determination of antecedent conditions for developmental consequences	Realization of specific antecedent conditions (single or many)	Independence of empirical laws (nomothetical) of space and time; identity of relations between causes and effects
Determination of incitement (inhibitory) conditions for stage transitions (stage-stagnation)	Realization of specific incitement or inhibitory conditions	Universality of structures; universal developmental logic
1. Description of stability of eco-behavioral systems (carrying capacity);	1. Ecological stability indexes (e.g., diversity, liability);	1. Not available;
2. Developmental trends in systems (succession);	2. Types of compositions of species analogies (ethnic subgroups);	2. Developmental state of systems controversial;
3. Change and differentiation (evolution)	3. Realization of a maximum variation of culture types as conditions that moderate human/nature relationship	3. Phylogenetic development on cultural level not available
1. Analysis of actions in their contexts (subject–object mergence);	1. No systematic criteria (cultural contexts = casuistic examples);	1. Question does not make sense;
2. See organismic paradigm (III)	2. See organismic paradigm (III)	2. See organismic paradigm (III)

1970). However, some aspects relevant in the present context may be mentioned (see Table 1). First, within the theories that follow this approach, the type of relationship between culture (environment) and the individual is assumed to be a causal one. If the concept of interaction is used (Baltes & Willis, 1977), then it is defined statistically as an interaction between independent variables (Buss, 1979). Change or developmental processes are explained within the Hempel–Oppenheim scheme, wherein development is the phenomenon to be explained (*explanandum*). This explanation is done by the formation of associations built up by circumscribed environmental conditions (association between different stimuli [S–S] or between discriminative stimuli [S^D] and consequences). The result of this process is assumed to be a continuous accumulation of these associations. Classical and modern learning theories are prominent examples of this paradigm in psychology (Looft, 1973; Reese & Overton, 1970). Although the kind of underlying mechanisms that relate environment and environmental (sociocultural) change to behavior are not always as explicit as one would wish in life-span developmental psychology, the methodological work of Baltes (1968) follows this paradigm (Buss, 1979) in principle. Also much developmental work done under an ecological perspective remains within this paradigm. This is true, for instance, of Bronfenbrenner's (1979) approach. Although he expands the environmental conditions to several interlocking system layers, the assumed causal chain to the behavior is unidirectional.

On the aggregate level the position of the environmental determinists seems best to fit the mechanistic model. Originating in early (rather taxonomic) conceptions about the relationships between the ecological environment and cultures (Wissler, 1926), a rather strong environmental determination point of view was held by Coon (1948), who claimed, "Differences in environment . . . are the chief if not the only reason why historical change has proceeded at different rates in different places, and why more complicated systems have not diffused rapidly from centers of development" (p. 614). This point of view was later weakened, primarily by Meggers when she found that the environment determines only a negative boundary for development. She formulated a "moderate environmentalism" in saying that "the level to which a culture can develop is dependent upon the agricultural potentiality of the environment it occupies" (Meggers, 1966, p. 136). This position still seems to follow a mechanistic world view, and it is interesting to note that efforts of Steward (1955) to integrate these positions with cultural evolutionism led to a system perspective that on the aggregate level is related to the fourth paradigm (see the following paragraph).

Within the mechanistic paradigm the rationale for a simulation of cultural change by cross-cultural differences is stringent because nomothetically defined laws are by definition independent of space and time. Identical (causal) relationships are assumed between environmental causes and behavioral effects, or between ecological conditions and cultural effects. Whether they are defined synchronically or diachronically, they are assumed to represent *empirical universals* (Eckensberger & Burgard, 1983). Hence, the aim of both the analysis of social change and the determination of cross-cultural differences would seem to be the same: to determine antecedents of change and to define consequences as change. Therefore, both strategies would be equivalent in principle and could theoretically be substituted for each other. Consequently, any design that explicitly includes certain sociocultural conditions (whether they are measured repeatedly within one culture or varied across cultures) would be feasible (Eckensberger, 1973).

From a cross-cultural perspective in psychology, the concept of *cultural complexity* would be especially advocated as a meaningful cultural antecedent as long as its theoretical basis follows a mechanistic perspective so that no cross-paradigmatic linkages between the individual and cultural level are involved. Although this concept does not yet seem to be important in lifespan developmental psychology, it is becoming increasingly meaningful in cross-cultural research (see Triandis, 1980). It is a concept used in Berry's (see Witkin & Berry, 1975) ecological model to relate cultural complexity to psychological (affective, cognitive, and social) differentation (among other aspects), and it is one of the main aspects of culture used by the Whitings (Whiting & Whiting, 1975) as an antecedent condition for interactional variables (dependency/dominance vs. nurturant/intimate behavior) in individuals. Although the transformatory processes are not yet clear in Berry's system (1975), the Whitings explicitly use learning environments as "transformation concepts" (Klausner, 1973, p. 74) to link cultural complexity to individual behavior.

However, if we try to evaluate this paradigm with reference to the preceding criteria, then it becomes evident that even if theories on the aggregate level are included, either sociohistorical change or ontogeny is explained but no interactionistic mechanism is entailed that allows for a transformatory concept to explain both. Second, the concreteness of events or processes is not maintained; the antecedents—as environmental conditions for cultures or stimulus conditions for behavior—are abstract classes (Eckensberger, 1979).

Finally, it is worthwhile mentioning that, on the individual as well as the aggregate level, this model seems to be fruitful primarily below a certain level of development (Berry & Annis, 1974; Kohlberg, 1971; Steward, 1955).

The Organismic Paradigm

On the individual level the following aspects of this paradigm are important (for a more detailed discussion consult Looft, 1973; Reese & Overton, 1970): First, the type of relationship between culture (environment) and individual is *teleological* inasmuch as there is a final end state toward which development strives; it is *functional* in that the developmental states of an organism result from its functionality and lead to an increase in its functionality. Environmental variables are not antecedents but incitement conditions that may or may not facilitate development. The type of interaction between the individual and the environment seems best to be characterized as interdependency between psychic structures (e.g., schemes) and environmental conditions. It is explained by the underlying mechanism of equilibration. Development is not only a discontinuous process but also a phenomenon necessary for explaining the specific state of an organism. This means that development not only is to be explained but also is primarily something that explains (*explanans*). This model is best represented in the theories of Piaget, Kohlberg, and Werner (see Reese & Overton, 1970).

It is our opinion that on the aggregate level the functionalistic theories of Malinowski, Radcliffe-Brown, and Parsons follow the same world view. As Strasser (1974) put it, "It is the idea of an 'organismic' system assumed by functionalism that makes it distinct from other forms of explanations in sociology. . . . Functional explanation also implies the assumption that systems of relations between human actors, in their own right, are capable of exercising a determining influence upon the behavior. It is this form of holism derived from physiology that became so central to the structural–functional approach" (pp. 68f.).

Radcliffe-Brown based his functional concept mainly on the analogy and comparison between organic and social structures (Rüegg, 1969). "To turn from organic life to social life . . . we can recognize the existence of a social structure. Individual human beings, the essential units in this instance, are connected by a definite set of social relations into an integrated whole" (Radcliffe-Brown, 1935, p. 396). He viewed the social system as a unit to whose inner harmony all parts contribute. The structure's continuity is contained in the process of social life, which he defined as the functioning of social structure. Radcliffe-Brown saw "evolution as a process by which stable integrations at a higher level are substituted for or replaced by integrations at a lower level" (Radcliffe-Brown, 1930, quoted by Dole, 1973, p. 247).

Malinowski, in contrast, emphasized the "constantly increasing institutional crystallization of activities" (Malinowski, 1942, in Dole, 1973, p. 247). His conception of culture as the instrumental reality for satisfying basic needs is also characterized by its fundamental holistic idea: "Culture appears as a closed system, a network of inter-working variables dependent upon each other which can and must be studied separately, but which do not allow themselves to be taken out of their structural context" (Rüegg, 1969, p. 62, translated by the authors). Whereas Radcliffe-Brown and Malinowski emphasized the functionalistic aspect, the structural–analytic approach is based on works by Weber and Durkheim (Dreitzel, 1972) and had its main effect on sociological and anthropological theories in France (e.g., Levi-Strauss's structural anthropology).

The functionalistic and structural analytic tradition appears finally in a systematic form in Parsons's integrated structural–functional approach. In his early work, Parsons emphasized the synchronic analysis of society and viewed social systems as "a plurality of individual actors interacting with each other in a situation which has at least a physical or environmental aspect, actors who are motivated in terms of a tendency to the optimization of gratification and whose relations to their situations, including each other, is defined and mediated in terms of a system of culturally structured and shared symbols" (Parsons, quoted by Lauer, 1973, p. 77). Society is regarded as an equilibrium system in which each element is constantly adapting to all the others and which, as a whole, is itself in reciprocal conformity with other equivalent and higher-order social systems (Dreitzel, 1972). In more recent works (Parsons, 1960, 1966), Parsons took up the criticism of the conservative, change-antipathetic position of the structural–functionalistic theory and incorporated the evolutionary idea into his theory. Bee (1974) accordingly divided the functional theories into static functionalism (implying a nearly perfect state of equilibrium in which the component parts are mutually adjusted into a working whole) and dynamic functionalism (which implies a relative equilibrium, constantly subject to certain intrasystemic tensions and strains). Parsons replaced the general function concept with four kinds of processes (Lauer, 1973) that already exist, at least in analog form, on the individual level in organismic theories (e.g., Piaget, 1970): (1) *equilibrium:* a process that serves to maintain the boundaries of the system (this idea is equivalent to Piaget's concept of assimilation); (2) *structural change:* change in the system's normative culture (similar to the concept of accommodation in Piaget's theory); (3) *structural differentiation:* alterations in the subsystems but not in the system's overall structure (this concept seems to be equivalent to the idea of a horizontal decalage in Piaget's theory); and (4) the evolution of society's *enhancement of adaptive capacity* (a concept that enters several aspects of Piaget's theory that is implied in the increasing reversibility of structures).

Consequently, Parsons (Lauer, 1973) also ended up with evolutionary stages of cultural development (primitive, intermediate, and modern) which he assumed follow from sequentially ordered evolutionary universals (communication, kinship organization, religion, and technology).

Thus, structural–functional theories (Parsons, Moore, 1963; Wilson & Wilson, 1945) are characterized on the aggregate level by the holistic view of society and emphasize the analysis of structure–function relationships. Insofar as they portray diachronic development as dynamic equilibrium theories, they describe a developmental direction (Parsons: enhancement of adaptive capacity; Moore: perfect control of man's environment; the Wilsons: increase in scale, see Bee, 1974). The cause of development is localized intrinsically for the most part as either intrasystemic tension and breaks (e.g., Parsons, Moore, the Wilsons) or as the unforeseen consequences of social actions (Merton, 1972). As in Piaget's accommodation–assimilation process, integrative achievements are also possible in the structural–functional equilibration theories (Parsons: equilibrium process; Wilsons: ordinary opposition), as well as resolution by structural changes (Parsons: structural change; Wilsons: radical opposition). The distinguishability of developmentally related structures implies developmental models with qualitatively different stages, as demonstrated by the theories of Parsons and the Wilsons.

If we now turn to our task proper, discussing the possibilities and limitations of using cross-cultural differences as indicants of sociohistorical change processes, we come to the conclusion that this strategy would be justifiable, but for quite different reasons from the previous paradigm. The most important argument would be the assumption of a universal developmental logic of structure that has a mental existence and is not the result of a social situation. The aim of such a simulation procedure would be to clarify the role of specific incitement or inhibitory conditions for development in order to elaborate the underlying mechanism in stage transitions. Because of the existence of the aforementioned developmental logic that implies an invariant sequence of development states (Piaget, 1970), it would be rather unimportant whether these conditions are realized in different cultures at the same time (cross-cultural research) or in the same culture at different times (sociohistorical change). They have only to be realized purposively within a design.

However, if this paradigm is evaluated with reference to the two criteria derived from the cross-cultural and life-span perspectives, difficulties arise. Although the assumption of a structural isomorphy of parallelism between ontogeny and social change can be derived from various statements (see Kohlberg, 1971) and from Piaget's and Parsons's underlying interests,[3] an explicit integration of both theory–systems does not yet exist.

Broughton (1981) stated, in a similar context, "It does not seem impossible that some synthesis may fruitfully be attempted. For example, Piaget surely needs an anthropological dimension to his theory, while French structuralism conspicuously lacks the cognitive and developmental aspects" (p. 105–106). Although as yet only social change or individual change is explained within this paradigm, it is of central importance that *action* (or

---

[3]Piaget justified his focus on ontogeny by his interest in history (see Broughton, 1981), and Parsons justified his analysis of cultural change in terms of structure and function by referring to biology (Strasser, 1974).

better, activity) is a core concept of the theory levels of both Piaget and Parsons. This concept would probably best serve as a transformation construct (Eckensberger, 1976). Nevertheless, the central feature of any human action—self-reflexivity—seems not to be realized in either theory; in Parsons's and in Piaget's theories, action is interpreted primarily as a biological activity. In Parsons' theory it is reduced to the maximization of gratification by consuming the resources of a system (i.e., it is not a creative act; see Haferkamp, 1972). In Piaget's theory the acting self is either a biological person or an epistemic subject (something common to all subjects; see Broughton, 1981). And it is the same aspect in Piaget's theory that leads to a biogenetic reduction of history and a naturalization of culture. These parameters therefore are also responsible for the fact that the individual subjective substance of processes and/or events is not maintained within these theories: The structures are abstractions from any specific content. The critique of Piaget's theory, especially under the cross-cultural perspective recently formulated by Buck-Morss (1975), goes even further than that. She asserted that the frequently obtained finding that children of non-Western societies show a time lag in developmental stages and often do not reach formal–logical thinking is not only a problem of varying incitement conditions, but also an indication that the structures postulated by Piaget as universals are actually the results of sociohistorical development.

The Ecobehavioral Paradigm

This model includes only those system approaches that follow either directly or analogically the idea of an *ecosystem,* which contains the relationship of living organisms with each other and with their nonliving environment (see Ricklefs, 1973). They are

conceptualized as (a) dynamic networks containing biotic and abiotic elements which are assumed to be interrelated and in a "state of balance." (b) The state of balance provides an evaluative underpinning—a system may be more or less stable, and hence better or worse for a species living in the system. (c) The interrelationship between organism and the environment is *explained* as adaptation of the *species* to the environment, but also as active modification of the environment by the organism. The organisms may "create" particular conditions which improves their chances to survive. Since certain antecedents lead to certain consequences which are more or less advantageous for a species, causal and functional relationships between the organism and the environment are assumed. (d) Different aspects of ecosystems can be studied, such as circulation, transformation, accumulation, and application of matter, energy and information within the system; their entry into, their distribution within and their departure from the system. One can also focus on different kinds of organisms and their distribution within a particular system. (e) Ecosystems can be ordered hierarchically since the input and output of systems of lower order can be interpreted as circulation within systems on a higher level. (f) All species are treated identically within a system—this is also true for *homo sapiens*. (Eckensberger, 1979, pp. 267f.)

The applications of this model in social sciences vary in immediacy inasmuch as it is sometimes used only as a rather weak analogy (see the "unified theory of biocultural evolution;" Ruyle, 1973, p. 201) and sometimes as an explicit explanatory principle (Bischof, 1975). Applications also vary, however, in comprehensiveness, that is, with reference to the number of elements contained in a system. It may contain only a dyad, as in the case of the mother–child dyad in the system approach to the development of anxiety and attachment (Bischof, 1975); it may entail many more subjects (groups), as in the case of the behavior setting (Barker, 1969); and it may be applied to whole settlements (Burgard, 1978) or to whole cultures (Rappaport, 1971; Steward, 1955).

Let us examine briefly some examples of this model in psychology and anthropology, first turning our attention to the system interpretation of attachment. Studies influenced by models of animal ecology explain attachment as the process by which mother and child mutually regulate each other to maintain an optimal spatial distance necessary for preserving the growing individual and thereby the species. The complementary processes (attachment and need for nurture) that maintain the optimal distance are regarded as instinctive (Ainsworth, 1973). (For more examples, see Eckensberger, 1978.)

We turn next to the explicit aggregate-level theories. In sociology the Chicago school of Park, Burgess, McKenzie, and others were the pioneers for an ecological orientation. As in plant and animal ecology, the human community was studied with respect to its adaptation to conditions of the physical environment. Afterwards, human ecology was the attempt to study processes that maintain biotic balance and social equilibrium or cause transition to a new order. The main subject of research for this early human ecology was the regional diffusion of social phenomena caused by competition in human members of the community. Change was registered in concepts such as succession, expansion, and invasion. Although the ecosystem model enables the formulation of theories of *cultural development* (culture as a system of adaptation to natural and man-made environment) by analyzing the human–environment interaction, the validity of such aggregate-level theories seems to be limited to so-called natural populations. Highly developed, complex industrial societies in which humans have achieved great ecological flexibility—particularly through technology and transport systems so that direct interaction with his habitat is less likely—apparently can be analyzed with this model only with supplementary postulates. This is especially clear in

Rappaport (1971), who attempted a direct application of the ecological model and its related concepts within neofunctional ecological cultural anthropology. For him the ecological perspective in anthropology consists of asking to what extent cultural behavior contributes to the survival and well-being of the society's members. He distinguished between "the '*cognized*' model [italics added], which contains culture-specific ideas about the functioning of nature, and the '*operational*' model [italics added] as 'a description of the same ecological system' (including the people) in accordance with the assumptions and methods of the science of ecology" (p. 247). Taking as an example the rituals of the Tsembaga, a Maring-speaking tribe in New Guinea, he was able to show how these rituals could be interpreted according to ecological and cybernetic principles, even though they are not so interpreted by the Tsembaga themselves, who view them as service to the spirit world. Actions originating in the cognized model (pig offerings as thanks for divine help in the last war), however, stabilize the ecosystem (fewer pigs mean less work for the women).

The question of what an ecological model based on a biological viewpoint can contribute to the illumination of cultural phenomena is a relatively old one. Whereas for Levi-Strauss (1969) culture is subject to its own laws and cannot be explained by laws governing physical processes, Steward (1955) saw cultures as participating in ecological systems separate from the organisms that compose them. His cultural ecology nevertheless includes modern technological industrial societies in its analysis. Steward's concept of *cultural type* is based on two frames of reference: cultural features derived from synchronic, functional, and ecological factors; and cultural features represented by a particular diachronic or developmental level (successive levels of sociocultural integration). The primary method of *cultural ecology* is to explore the cultural core, the constellations of features most closely related to subsistence activities and economic arrangements; it focuses mainly on those features that empirical analysis shows to be most closely involved in the utilization of environment in culturally prescribed ways.

In trying to evaluate this paradigm for life-span developmental psychology, which includes social change processes, it would be advantageous to use the same theoretical language on all levels of comprehensiveness so that aggregate- and individual-level theories can be linked within one model of thinking simply by interconnecting different systems. There is, however, one serious limitation to this paradigm in psychology: Explanations are restricted to *ultimate causes* (Wilson, 1975), that is, causes that ultimately originate in phylogeny and selective mechanism. *Proximate causes*—that is, mechanisms of learning, cultural impact, and so forth—are not part of this model (Wilson, 1975). The methodological dilemma is that the kinds of explanation have to be kept strictly separate. This means that if a given behavior is ultimately explained with reference to the survival of the whole system and if the same behavior is proximately explained with reference to certain psychological conditions, then it does not follow that these psychological conditions also can be explained ultimately with reference to the survival value of the system, although they indirectly (via behavior) contribute to the survival of the system (Eckensberger & Burgard, 1983).

Thus, even Rappaport must admit that "how structures such as Maring cosmology develop remains a problem for which no satisfactory solution can yet be offered" (p. 261). Ruyle (1973) did, however, attempt to describe cultural development as selection of ideas, by drawing close parallels between biological and cognitive–social components; those ideas predominate that promise most satisfaction to the individual, just as those genes predominate that have proved to be best in the struggle for survival. Similar mechanisms have also been postulated in more recent sociobiological approaches (e.g., Cavalli-Sforza & Feldman, 1981; Lumsden & Wilson, 1981).

Aside from the fact that such a purely functionalist approach is very controversial in the social sciences, it contributes nothing to our problem of joining cultural development and ontogeny simply because this approach is limited to ultimate causes.

This epistemological problem of explanation implies that ontogeny itself is not explained psychologically within this system. Hence, although the model allows for the definition of true interaction between organisms and environment, it seems to be of rather limited value for psychology because neither an adequate set of transformation constructs that explain ontogeny and social change can be developed within this approach, nor can the uniqueness of processes and events be maintained (see Eckensberger, 1978; Eckensberger & Burgard, 1976).

If we then try to answer whether it makes sense to interpret cross-cultural (cross-system) differences as simulations of social change (system change), we also come up with a rather negative answer. This is partly because the development of systems is in general not a true part of the ecological perspective (see Ambrose, 1977) and partly because the ecosystem model seems to be restricted to rather simple systems. This seems to be true both for the individual level (the mother–child dyad is described in these terms only until the child is 18 months old and then cognitive variables seem to change the whole phenomenon; see Kornadt, Eckensberger, & Emminghaus, 1980) and for the aggregate level in which ecosystem analogies are usually restricted to subsistence-level societies (see Rappaport, 1971).

Despite the fact that this model entails the assumption of "natural universals" (Eckensberger & Burgard, 1983, p. 472), which seem to allow the comparison of systems in principle, this comparison seems to be very difficult with respect to a substantive developmental dimension that is the prerequisite for answering our question because systems that vary in their degree of complexity at a given time cannot easily be interpreted as if they represent different developmental states.

One could apply a system parameter such as stability as a criterion for comparison; this might at first seem paradoxical, just as the assumption of an equilibrium state seems at first glance to contradict developmental thought. However, another look at general ecology reveals the concept of *ecological succession* in the development of an ecosystem, by which is understood "an orderly process of community development that involves changes in species structure and community processes with time [and] results from modification of the physical environment by the community" (Odum, 1971, p. 251). "It involves a sequence of community types from pioneer stages to mature or climax stages" (Southwick, 1972, p. 254).

There is, apparently, no agreement even in general ecology on the question of whether this process is predictable. Odum (1971) drew up a list of ecosystem attributes that could distinguish between developmental and mature stages. In a direct analogy the Chicago school employed the concept of succession, which they defined as the stepwise (and caused by competition) interchange of a city area in the population. Caution should be taken, however, in comparing cultures that have developed in different places. Ellenberg (1973) wrote that even for nonhuman ecosystems "not all ecosystems that can be ordered according to increasing or decreasing complexity or other characteristics are connected with each other by succession. It is often simply the case of a spatial proximity of ecosystems which have always been different and under no condition merge into each other" (p. 17). The fact that mature ecosystems are characterized by a well-organized community structure as well as by higher stability makes transfer to human cultures even more difficult. Experiences suggest that complex modern industrial societies, with their high organizational structure (usually considered to be highly developed), are about to fall out of equilibrium, for "some aspects of what we have called progress or evolutionary advance are, in fact, pathological or maladaptive" (Rappaport, 1971, p. 264).

Therefore, we conclude that at present a rationale does not yet exist that allows for a systematic interpretation of cross-cultural differences as a simulation of social change, as long as we interpret cultures as analogous to ecosystems.

The Self-Reflexiveness Paradigm

We assume that this last model of man underlies several counter-cultures in psychology of the last decades, the hermeneutic–interpretive, the

dialectical, the critical, and the ethogenic movements, as they are enumer-
ated and characterized for instance by Gergen & Morawski (1980). Although for heuristic reasons the authors think that it is at present preferable
to speak explicitly of a different paradigm, they also realize that it is still an
open question whether these approaches are really following an alternative
model of man, or whether they are finally integrative, synthesizing attempts
(Frese, 1981). The authors also feel that this model of man is in principle
affiliated with the family of action theories in social science, a theory–
family that is in itself not homogeneous with regard to all its detailed
aspects.

These theories range from rather cybernetic process models, through
dynamic action theories, to what is called symbolic action theories (see
Eckensberger, 1978, 1979; Eckensberger & Emminghaus, 1981). Consequently, not all theories that are now called action theories are necessarily
built upon the assumption of self-reflexivity. Before the minimum features
of action theories are summarized, it would be useful to state that the term
action is used on quite different logical levels in social science literature,
although these levels are not totally independent. It is especially important
that the use of action as an empirical unit is based upon its use as an
analytical unit in philosophy. The methodological implications of this approach cannot be treated here in detail, and only those methodological
aspects that are relevant in the present context are discussed. Some others
are treated by Eckensberger and Burgard (1983).

Although the action theory does not at present exist (see Kaminski,
1979; Werbik, 1978), the following features are thought to be necessary
aspects of an *action theory:*

1. *Actions* are considered to be future-oriented, intentional, and goal-
directed mental activities of which the actor is potentially (i.e., not necessarily in every concrete execution) fully conscious.

2. *Mental activities* are generally the intended use of one's own action
means or the intended exploitation of others' action means, as well as the
intended exploitation of causally determined events or processes. It follows
that one can speak of an action even if a person did not change events or
processes by his/her own doing but only allowed things to happen because
they correspond with that person's goal.

3. *Concrete actions* can be structured according to at least three aspects from a psychological viewpoint: (1) They have a course that can be
divided into three action phases: beginning, course, and end. These phases
can all be considered under an affective, a structural, and an energetic aspect
(see Table 3). (2) They have a certain degree of complexity, which refers to
the internal structure of the action goals, means, results, and consequences.

TABLE 3

Affective, Structural, and Energetic Aspects of Action Phases[a]

Phase	Affective[b]	Structural	Energetic
Beginning	Strength of goal valence course valence result valence Boredom Depression	Anticipations (fantasies) Trial actions Specification of goal and course ideas (action plan) Perceptive sensitization	Mobilization of action energy (activation) Preparation for action Increase in attraction strength of the goal ideas
Course	Function pleasure Function displeasure Anger Fury Fatigue Anxiety Aggression Passion	Guiding the proceeding action Progressive reduction of distance to goal Coordination with other anticipated actions Directional regulations Constancy-maintaining regulations Deviation tolerance Complementary actions	Increased exertion (action intensification) Marshalling reserves Balancing monotony/avoidance of hurrying (optimal activation level)
End	Triumph feelings Function satisfaction Dissatisfaction Guilt Sadness Pride Contentment	Evaluation of the action's effects Integration into the self-image Terminating actions Completing actions Transitions (integration into further actions)	Rest Recovery

[a]Adopted from Kasper & Krewer, 1982.

[b]The affects described in the various phases are not phase-specific in the sense that they occur solely in beginning, course, and end phases; rather, they are typical affective accompaniments to the particular phase.

Action can be incorporated hierarchically: that is, every goal of an action X can be the means of an action Y. Action Y is then the higher action, action X the lower. Action means are applied arbitrarily by a person in order to attain a goal. (Only if this condition is met can we say that a person acts.) The arbitrary choice of means implies the presence of alternatives (i.e., equifinality of action means is given), or vice versa, that a specific means does not necessarily follow from a given goal. Actions have results and consequences (von Wright, 1974). Use of an action means leads first to a result. This can have many different consequences that must be weighed in an action—they can be brought about (by the action), avoided, or accepted. It follows that the actor is responsible for the consequences of her or his own actions or can be made to be. (3) They are related to certain objects or persons, that is, they take place in a certain situation.

4. *Reality* (concrete objects, other persons, etc.) has a symbolic meaning within an action. According to Boesch (1976), this can be situational, functional, or analogical. That is, reality receives a psychological meaning only through its action relationship (see the following definition). This is also true of the self. These different meanings can interact and support each other in the individual case.

5. *Culture*, in contrast to nature, is interpreted as an objectification, or an objective realization of actions (Eckensberger, 1979). This objectification is not only a consequence of new actions, but also the possibility and limitation of new actions, so that—primarily in materialistic activity theories (Vygotsky, Leontyev, Rubinshteyn, Galperin, Luria, etc.; see Becker, 1980)—action is always regarded as being embedded in sociohistorical relationships.

> "Embedded in social relationships" means, first, that the environment encountered by the actor and its conditions are decisively influenced by the social development of the person; secondly, the forms of action available to the person have their origin in the social development of mankind, and the individual actor has adopted them in the course of his own development. With his action—mainly in his work—the individual adds his share to the development of human society, he contributes to the maintenance and further development of its living conditions. (Oesterreich, 1981, p. 7, translated by authors)

In the following, we discuss Western action theories; the pioneers in this field are Lewin (1963) and Miller, Galanter, and Pribram (1960). Whereas Lewin, with his concept of *Lebensraum*, concentrated on the representation of the situation in which the actor finds himself or herself, the *TOTE model* of Miller *et al.* emphasizes the action process, its course over time.

As examples of action theories in psychology that focus on the individual actor, we want to mention those of Oerter (1979, 1982) and Boesch (1976). Both are still speculative for the most part. Oerter (1979, 1982), whose approach is based partially on Soviet activity psychology, chose action as a unit of analysis. It can be used as a monistic principle for further derivations; and it generates materialism and idealism and therefore would seem to be a solution to the problem of translating two different levels of reality (environmental and intellectual). At the center of his definition of action he placed its objectivity, as it is composed of the process of objectification (construction of the environment's and the actor's reality), the object references in existing objects, and the societal aspects of actions resulting from the objectivity. As a result of the objectification, both the *objective structure* (the environment produced by societal action) and the *subjective structure* (ordering of the individual's concrete action pos-

sibilities) are formed. Subjective and objective structures tend to iso-
morphism, which in the end determines the developmental direction of the
individual and society. Both structures can be described by a common level
of object reference, which can be regarded as a reality level in which specific
reality constructs can be found.

In another psychological action theory, Boesch (1976) focused less on
the objectification of action than on the balance in the relationship between
ego and environment. His approach is based on Lewin's field theory,
Piaget's theories of cognitive development, psychoanalytic concepts, and
Janet's dynamic action theory (Schwartz, 1951). Only those features of the
theory relevant in the present context can be touched upon here. The reader
who is looking for more detailed information should consult Boesch (1976).
The focus of the theory is the action itself. Because it takes place in a specific
situation and because it is performed by a unique subject, both are contained in the action, although the action can be interpreted as the true unit
of analysis. The situation is understood as an external field of action within
which all elements get their substantial—instrumental meaning as well as
their symbolic meaning. In general, the action field represents limitations as
well as possibilities for actions. The subject or ego is understood as a higher-
order rule system that acts upon the environment, and thereby changes the
environment, but is itself also changed by this process. Hence, the relation
between the subject and the environment can be called "transactional" and
the developmental process can be interpreted as a reorganization of the
internal and external action field (see Table 1).

The present authors maintain that Boesch's (1976) theory offers at least
theoretically the possibility of interrelating the three main levels of the
concept of development within the same theoretical language: the actual
genesis (microprocess), the ontogeny, and the historiogenesis; that is, it
allows linking historical change to individual change substantially, although
this aspect is not especially elaborated by Boesch himself. With reference to
the *actual genesis,* the analytical distinction between three action phases (see
preceding discussion)—the beginning, course, and end—is especially fruitful as well as the distinction of structural, affective, and energetic processes
within each phase.

In the beginning phase, the structural aspect of an action is represented
in the emergence of goals, their factual consciousness and their (psychological) distance, the organization of means—end relationships, choice of means,
and so forth, becomes relevant. In the affective aspect the emotional and
need states that lead to goals are essential as well as the evaluation of
environmental conditions that get their value (valence) in accordance with
their symbolization of goal aspects as well as with their potential facilitation
or inhibition of action plans. During energetic processes the mobilization of

energy is looked at, as well as the anticipation of costs and benefits of the action—to mention but a few aspects of the beginning phase.

The *course of the action phase* is that part of the action that can be best seen from the outside. It is characterized primarily by regulatory processes (although certain regulations are also assumed to happen in the beginning and end of an action) which are sometimes also called secondary actions. Here especially, the regulatory functions of emotions are crucial (function pleasure, anxiety, fatigue, etc.), but also the structural and energetic regulations are of utmost importance: the goal-directional regulations, the coordinations of different action tendencies, continuous evaluations of means–end adequacies, the intensification or reduction of energy input, the balancing of monotony, maintenance of an optimal activation level, and so forth.

The *end phase,* finally, is characterized structurally by the process of evaluations of action consequences in relationship to the original goals (external aspect) by the integration of instrumental aspects of success or failure into the self (internal aspect), the termination of the action, its integration into higher order actions, and so forth. The affective aspects of the end phase is characterized by the evaluations of the expenditure of the action course and its results and consequences by the awareness of emotional processes like pride, guilt, and so forth. As consciously experienced phenomena, emotions represent a valuable diagnostic approach to possibly unconscious goals and normative orientations (see Eckensberger & Emminghaus, 1982; Kasper & Krewer, 1982). Energetically, in the end phase the necessity for a recovery or an energy surplus is handled.

Within the beginning phase of the actual genesis, the "clutch" of the ego and the environment is particularly clear: On one hand, the preferred strategies, the concretization of goal–means relationships are chosen in accordance with the possibilities and limitations of the situation as well as with anticipations from ego-derived goal–ideals. On the other hand, these schematizations as well as the symbolic meaning of situational aspects are formed from action experiences in the ontogeny (see subsequent paragraph), they determine to a large extent the perception of the concrete situation as an action field as well as the intended reorganization of it. The transactive connection between ego and environment is also evident, however, in the course of the action: The ego may activate or generate further alternative action possibilities, partly independent from and partly in accordance with the emergence of facilitating action qualities or barriers. Also, the whole context of the action may be changed rather drastically by the course of the action itself. Thereby all these phenomena have constant repercussions upon the goal anticipations and the subjective evaluation of the course itself.

With regard to *ontogeny,* two parallel processes can be distinguished:

increasing objectivity, which is largely completed by adolescence, and secondary subjectification, which extends over the entire life span. (Secondary subjectification must be distinguished from Piaget's egocentrism concept, which can be depicted as primary subjectification.) The objectification process, in analogy to Piaget's epistemological development theory, is accomplished by increased decentering, which has its beginning in early childhood egocentrism. In active confrontation with objects, schemes for objects and related concepts are formed through assimilation and accommodation. Gradually, object concepts with constant object characteristics are formed, and rational causality ideas are constructed. This objectivation process is motivated by the desire for consistent communication and organization of one's own experience. Running parallel in the course of ontogeny, however, through individual experience with objects, subjective action experiences are obtained that appear in the personal object relationships. This process of subjectification of the environment consists of a development of the symbolic meaning of objects and/or events already referred to above.

Boesch (1979) distinguished between *contiguity symbols* and *analog symbols*. The former originate when objects are related to certain situations (situation symbolic) or to certain functions or functional experience (functional symbolic) in past actions; the latter are suggested by similarities in formal object qualities. Also, these experiences can be systematized in stages of development, they represent types of ego–environment relationships, which imply connections of the acting subject with the objects of his or her own activity. These relationships are involved with situation references; thus, more and more differentiated functional action schemes are constructed. These schemes form the basis for anticipations; and as such, they are organized into optimizing ideas of ego–environment relationships; this is why they are called subjective–functional schemes, or *fantasms* (Boesch, 1976). In this sense, fantasms are complex anticipations and rule systems possessing motivational power because they specify both the action meaning (valence) of the environment and the action potential (functional potentiality) of the subject.

Cultural change can be interpreted as objectification, as materialistic and idealistic expression of actions. Actions result in material changes of the environment on the one hand—this is why culture is sometimes understood as "the man-made part of the environment" (Herskovits, 1948), and they result in the development of cognitive and affective schemes in the subject on the other hand. Both processes are preconditions, which are contextual conditions for future acts. It is this dialectical interrelational process between material and ideal action contexts that is the key to understanding cultural change. And it is interesting that this same idea is elaborated by Berger and Luckmann (1966) within sociology.

Berger and Luckmann (1966), writing about the sociology of knowledge, which focuses on the existential limitation of thought, have proposed a dialectical model of reality construction. They hypothesized that anthropological constants such as world-openness or the plasticity of the instinct apparatus make possible man's sociocultural creations and at the same time limit them; however, the stamp of human individuality is determined by these same cultural creations, that is, humans create themselves. In a society's beginning, three stages can be distinguished: (1) Every human act is subject to habituation and each action solidifies into a model; (2) this habituation of actions is standardized reciprocally in the fundamental dyadic face-to-face situation with two actors; (3) if this standardization is communicated to a third member (e.g., socialization), this makes it possible to distinguish types of actors as well as types of action and this in turn results in the formation of institutions. Thus, institutions have a history, which creates them. The dialectical relationship between person as producer and the social world as his or her product is reflected in the processes of externalization, objectification, and internalization: Through *externalization,* society is a human product and becomes objective reality through objectification in the process of institutionalization; humans become social products through *internalization.* Knowledge stands in the center of the fundamental dialectic of society because it represents a realization in two senses—through knowledge the objectified social reality is perceived. Knowledge itself causes the continual production of this very reality because the reflecting consciousness superimposes its own logic on the institutional order. The logic of institutions does not consist in its external functionality, but rather consists in the way it is reflected by their participants. In this sense knowledge is a social product and a factor of social change.

From the perspective of the interactive relationship between individual development and social change, the dialectical and historical materialism of Marxist theory seems to be relevant, particularly because of its emphasis on the dialectical concept of development within natural and social sciences (see Ogburn, 1972; Riegel, 1978, 1980): All natural occurrences are viewed in context and in their interactional dependency; nature and its manifestations find themselves in constant flux, change, and development. The developmental process is (1) an outward development from lower to higher and (2) an uneven development, in which at certain crucial points sudden jumps can occur—gradual quantitative changes cause sudden qualitative changes (dialectic leaps). The Marxist dialectic regards the developmental process as the "struggle of opposites" that can be recognized as internal contradictions in all natural occurrences.

Following this rather extensive description of action theories, we turn now to their evaluation, first from the viewpoint of their fruitfulness for a life-span perspective. It is apparent, at least theoretically, that they offer a reference system that (1) allows integration of ontogeny and social change, and (2) leads not only to general regularities but also widely preserves the individual case, the subject side (see Eckensberger, 1978, 1979; Oerter, 1982). For the integration of individual and aggregate-level theories, the concept action is offered as an ideal transformatory construct (Klausner, 1973), even though the individual social sciences that use this concept sometimes put more weight on the objectification or institutionalization of actions in society and culture, and on the intrasubjective action traces, that is, in cognitive structures.

With its emphasis on symbolic processes and elaboration of the connotation net, Boesch's (1976, 1979) theory makes it possible to retain the individual meaning of situations, at least theoretically. In Berger and Luckmann's (1966) theory the particular relevance of historical context is stressed, in that every generation can and must reinterpret the enduring results of actions. To this extent, then, both theories—especially the points they have in common—represent an important frame of reference for approaching life-span developmental psychology.

This theoretical advantage is gained, however, at the cost of a methodological disadvantage and a renouncement of prediction as well as of a law-like interpretation of cultural change and history. Both aspects follow from the assumption that under structural aspects, actions entail not only causal and logical (implicative) relationships but also final ones (see preceding description). Methodologically, this implies that actions cannot be analyzed solely by means of an analytical nomothetical methodology but require also hermeneutic idiographic procedures. Space does not permit a discussion of whether hermeneutic methods can even be called scientific (see Weinberger & Weinberger, 1979) or to what extent methods from the natural sciences are appropriate for human studies (see Stegmüller, 1979, pp. 495f.). What *is* relevant in this context, however, is that hermeneutic procedures are useful for interpreting and understanding the individual case, rather than formulating general laws. Already from this, it follows that the simulation of such individual cases in *another context* is not legitimate. Because intentionality and the choice of alternative (equifinal) action means are assumed within this model, history can be analyzed only partly as a causal or organismic process. Another part has to be interpreted as a unique process that could have taken a different course if different action alternatives had been chosen. It is because of this possibility that human beings have to choose different causal paths (means–consequence relationships) that historians claim that history does not repeat itself and cannot be predicted. Hence, the question itself, that is, whether sociocultural change can be simulated by cross-cultural comparisons, makes no sense within this paradigm, and no rationale is available within this paradigm for any such question.

CONCLUSION

The inclusion of sociohistorical contexts in life-span developmental psychology, especially with regard to the question of the extent to which these diachronic processes can be simulated by different synchronic states, reaches out to the boundaries of the content and methodological self-under-standing of psychology. Even though our line of reasoning might have seemed lengthy at times, it has become apparent to us that the more a particular theoretical approach is oriented toward the natural sciences (physics or biology), the more likely it is that the simulation of sociohistori-cal change by cultural comparison can be legitimized; the change itself is not comprehended in the individual case, however, as historical change but rather is comprehended as a change to be explained in systems. The more social and/or cultural change is conceived as history, the more improbable is its explanation and simulation. For this reason, this new perspective of life-span developmental psychology demands a rethinking about the theoretical and methodological basis of this field. It appears difficult to have both the inclusion of historical processes and the strict adherence to methods from the natural sciences. That this is less alarming than it seems is evidenced by writers such as Sinnot (1981), who stated that, since Einstein, one cannot argue as strictly in physics (which generally serves in this respect as a para-gon for psychology), as many are still trying to do in large areas of psychology.

ACKNOWLEDGMENT

The authors want to express their thanks to Martha Keating for her valuable help in writing an English version of this chapter and to Helga Munz, who coped with the typing.

REFERENCES

Ainsworth, M. D. S. (1973). The development of infant–mother-attachment. In B. M. Caldwell & H. Ricciuti (Eds.), *Review of child development research* (Vol. 3). Chicago: University of Chicago Press.

Ambrose, J. A. (1977). The ecological perspective in developmental psychology. In H. McGurk (Ed.), *Ecological factors in human development*. Amsterdam: North-Holland.

Baltes, P. B. (1968). Longitudinal and cross-sectional sequences in the study of age and generation effects. *Human Development, 2,* 145–171.

Baltes, P. B., Reese, H. W., & Lipsitt, L. P. (1980). Life-span developmental psychology. *Annual Review of Psychology, 31,* 65–110.

Baltes, P. B., & Willis, S. L. (1977). Toward psychological theories of aging and development. In J. E. Birren & K. W. Schaie (Eds.), *Handbook of the psychology of aging.* New York: Van Nostrand Reinhold.

Barker, R. G. (1969). Wanted: An eco-behavioral science. In E. P. Willems & H. L. Raush (Eds.), *Naturalistic viewpoints in psychological research.* New York: Holt.

Becker, M. (1980). *Die Perspektiven des kulturvergleichenden Psychologen und die Theorie der Tätigkeit.* [The perspectives of the cross-cultural psychologist and the theory of activity.] Saarbrücken: Universität des Saarlandes, Unpublished dipl. thesis.

Bee, R. L. (1974). *Patterns and processes: An introduction to anthropological strategies for the study of sociocultural change.* New York: Free Press.

Berger, P. L., & Luckmann, T. (1966). *The social construction of reality.* New York: Doubleday.

Berry, J. W. (1969). On cross-cultural comparability. *International Journal of Psychology, 4,* 119–128.

Berry, J. W. (1972). Radical cultural relativism and the concept of intelligence. In L. J. Cronbach & P. J. D. Drenth (Eds.), *Mental tests and cultural adaptation.* The Hague: Mouton.

Berry, J. W., & Annis, R. C. (1974). Ecology, culture and psychological differentiation. *International Journal of Psychology, 9,* 173–193.

Bischof, N. (1975). A system approach toward the functional connections of attachment and fear. *Child Development, 46,* 801–817.

Brislin, R. W., Lonner, W. J., & Thorndike, R. M. (1973). *Cross-cultural research methods.* New York: Wiley.

Boas, F. (1911). *The mind of primitive man.* New York: Macmillan.

Boesch, E. E. (1976). *Psychopathologie des Alltags.* [Psychopathology of daily life.] Bern: Huber.

Boesch, E. E. (1979). *Kultur und Handlung.* [Culture and action.] Bern: Huber.

Bronfenbrenner, U. (1979). *The ecology of human development.* Cambridge: Harvard University Press.

Broughton, J. M. (1981). Piaget's structural developmental psychology. *Human Development, 24,* 2–6.

Buck-Morss, S. (1975). Socio-economic bias in Piaget's theory and its implications for cross-cultural studies. *Human Development, 18,* 35–49.

Buss, A. R. (1979). *A dialectical psychology.* New York: Irvington.

Carneiro, R. L. (1970). Scale analysis, evolutionary sequences, and the rating of cultures. In R. Narrol & R. Cohen (Eds.), *A handbook of method in cultural anthropology.* New York: Natural History Press.

Cavalli-Sforza, L. L., & Feldman, M. W. (1981). *Cultural transmission and evolution: A quantitative approach.* Princeton: Princeton University Press.

Clignet, R. (1970). A critical evaluation of concomitant variation studies. In R. Narrol & R. Cohen (Eds.), *A handbook of method in cultural anthropology.* New York: Natural History Press.

Coon, C. S. (1948). *A reader in general anthropology.* New York: Harper.

Dasen, P. R., Berry, J. W., & Witkin, H. A. (1979). The use of development theories cross-culturally. In L. H. Eckensberger, W. Lonner, & Y. H. Poortinga (Eds.), *Cross-cultural contributions to psychology.* Amsterdam: Swets & Zeitlinger.

Dole, G. E. (1973). Foundations of contemporary evolutionism. In R. Narrol & F. Narrol (Eds.), *Main currents in cultural anthropology.* New York: Appleton.

Dreitzel, H. P. (1972). *Sozialer Wandel.* [Social change.] Berlin: Luchterhand.

Eckensberger, L. H. (1973). Methodological issues of cross-cultural research in developmental psychology. In J. R. Nesselroade & H. W. Reese (Eds.), *Life-span-developmental psychology: Methodological issues.* New York: Academic Press.

Eckensberger, L. H. (1976). Der Beitrag kulturvergleichender Forschung zur Fragestellung der Umweltpsychologie. [The contribution of cross-cultural research to the concern of an environmental psychology.] In G. Kaminski (Ed.), *Umweltpsychologie.* Stuttgart: Klett.

Eckensberger, L. H. (1978). Die Grenzen des ökologischen Ansatzes in der Psychologie. [Limits of an ecological approach in psychology.] In C. F. Graumann (Ed.), *Ökologische Perspektiven in der Psychologie.* Bern: Huber.

Eckensberger, L. H. (1979). A metamethodological evaluation of psychological theories from a cross-cultural perspective. In L. H. Eckensberger, W. J. Lonner, & Y. H. Poortinga (Eds.), *Cross-cultural contributions to psychology.* Lisse: Swets & Zeitlinger.

Eckensberger, L. H. (1983). Interkulturelle Vergleiche. [Interculture comparisons.] In R. K. Silbereisen & L. Montada (Eds.), *Entwicklungspsychologie: Ein Handbuch in Schlüsselbegriffen* (p. 1). [Developmental psychology: A handbook in key words.] München: Urban & Schwarzenberg.

Eckensberger, L. H., & Burgard, P. (1976). *Ökosysteme in interdisziplinärer Sicht.* Bericht über ein DFG-Symposion in Reisenburg 1976 (p. 49). Saarbrücken: Universität des Saarlandes, Arbeiten der Fachrichtung Psychologie.

Eckensberger, L. H., & Burgard, P. (1983). The cross-cultural assessment of normative concepts: Some considerations on the affinity between methodological approaches and preferred theories. In S. H. Irvine & J. W. Berry (Eds.), *Human assessment and cultural factors.* New York: Plenum.

Eckensberger, L. H. & Emminghaus, W. B. (1982). Aggression und Moral: Zur Systematisierung und Präzisierung des Aggressionskonzeptes sowie einiger empirischer Befunde. In R. Hilke & W. Kempf (Eds.) Aggression: Naturwissenschaftliche und kulturwissenschaftliche Perspektiven der Aggressionsforschung. Bern: Huber. [Aggression and Morality: A contribution to the systematization and specification of the concept of aggression and of some empirical results. Aggression: Science and cultural science perspectives of aggressive research.]

Edelstein, W. (1979, May). *Project child development and social structure.* Paper presented at the Congress of the Scandinavian Association of Psychology, Reykjawik.

Elder, G. H., Jr. (1974). *Children of the great depression.* Chicago: University of Chicago Press.

Elias, N. (1969). *Über den Prozess der Zivilisation.* [The process of civilization.] (2 vols.). Bern: Franke.

Ellenberg, H. (1973). *Ökosystemforschung.* [Ecosystem research.] Berlin: Springer.

Filipp, S.-H. (1981). Ein allgemeines Modell für die Analyse kritischer Lebensereignisse. [A general model for the analysis of critical life-events.] In S.-H. Filipp (Ed.), *Kritische Lebensereignisse.* [Critical Life Events.] München: Urban & Schwarzenberg.

Frese, M. (1981, August). *Skill learning as a concept in life-span developmental psychology.* Paper presented at the meeting of the International Society for the Study of Behavioral Development, Toronto.

Gergen, K. J., & Morawski, J. (1980). An alternative metatheory for social psychology. In L. Wheeler (Ed.), *Review of personality and social psychology.* New York: Sage.

Gutman, D. (1977). The cross-cultural perspective: Notes toward a comparative psychology of aging. In J. E. Birren & K. W. Schaie (Eds.), *Handbook of the psychology of aging.* New York: Van Nostrand-Reinhold.

Haferkamp, H. (1972). *Soziologie als Handlungstheorie.* [Sociology as action theory.] Opladen: Westdeutscher Verlag.

Herskovits, M. J. (1948). *Man and his works.* New York: Knopf.

Jahoda, G. (1980). Theoretical and systematic approaches in cross-cultural psychology. In H. C. Triandis & W. W. Lambert (Eds.), *Handbook of cross-cultural psychology: Perspectives* (Vol. 1). Boston: Allyn & Bacon.

Janney, J. G., Masuda, M., & Holmes, T. H. (1977). Impact of a natural catastrophe on life-events. *Journal of Human Stress, 3,* 22–34.

Kaminski, G. (1979). Die Bedeutung von Handlungskonzepten für die Interpretation sport-pädagogischer Prozesse. [The relevance of action concepts for the interpretation of educational processes in sports.] *Sportwissenschaften, 1,* 9–28.

Kasper, E., & Krewer, B. (1982). *Die handlungstheoretische Rekonstruktion von Mensch-Umwelt-Beziehungen am Beispiel subjektiv erlebter Umweltgüte junger und alter Menschen in der Stadt Saarbrücken.* [An action theoretical reconstruction of man–environment relationships. The example of subjectively experienced environmental quality by young and old subjects from Saarbrücken.] Unpublished dipl. thesis, Universität des Saarlandes, Saarbrücken.

Klausner, S. Z. (1973). Life-span environmental psychology: Methodological issues. In P. B. Baltes & K. W. Schaie (Eds.), *Life-span developmental psychology. Personality and socialization.* New York: Academic Press.

Klineberg, O. (1980). Historical perspectives: Cross-cultural psychology before 1960. In H. C. Triandis & W. W. Lambert (Eds.), *Handbook of cross-cultural psychology: Perspectives* (Vol. 1). Boston: Allyn & Bacon.

Kohlberg, L. (1971). From is to ought: How to commit the naturalistic fallacy and get away with it in the study of moral development. In T. Mischel (Ed.), *Cognitive development and epistemology.* New York: Academic Press.

Kornadt, H. J., Eckensberger, L. H., & Emminghaus, W. B. (1980). Cross-cultural research on motivation and its contribution to a general theory of motivation. In H. C. Triandis & W. Lonner (Eds.), *Handbook of cross-cultural psychology: Basic processes* (Vol. 3). Boston: Allyn & Bacon.

Lauer, R. H. (1973). *Perspectives on social change.* Boston: Allyn & Bacon.

Leach, E. R. (1968). The comparative method in anthropology. In D. L. Shills (Ed.), *International encyclopedia of the social sciences* (Vol. 1). New York: Macmillan.

Levi-Strauss, C. (1969). *The elementary structures of kinship.* London: Eyre & Spottiswoode.

Lewin, K. (1930). Der Übergang von der aristotelischen zur galileischen Denkweise in Biologie und Psychologie. [The transition from an Aristotelicen to a Galilean kind of thinking in biology and psychology.] *Erkenntnis, 1,* 421–460.

Lewin, K. (1963). *Feldtheorie in den Sozialwissenschaften.* [Field theory in social sciences.] Bern: Huber.

Looft, W. R. (1973). Socialization and personality throughout the life-span: An examination of contemporary psychological approaches. In P. B. Baltes & K. W. Schaie (Eds.), *Life-span developmental psychology: Personality and socialization.* New York: Academic Press.

Lumsden, C. J., & Wilson, E. O. (1981). *Genes, mind and culture: The coevolutionary process.* Cambridge: Harvard University Press.

Lupri, E. (1965). Industrialisierung und Strukturwandlungen in der Familie: Ein interkultureller Vergleich. [Industrialization and structural change in the family: An intercultural comparison.] *Sociologica Ruralis, 5*(1), 57–76.

Malinowski, B. (1942). A new instrument for the interpretation of law—especially primitive. *Yale Law Journal, 51,* 1237–1254.

Meggers, B. J. (1966). Environmental limitations on the development of culture. In J. B. Bressler (Ed.), *Human ecology: Collected readings.* Reading, MA: Addison-Wesley.

Merton, R. K. (1972). Die unvorhergesehenen Folgen zielgerichteter sozialer Handlungen. [The unexpected consequences of goaloriented social actions.] In H. P. Dreitzel (Ed.), *Sozialer Wandel.* [Social change.] Berlin: Luchterhand.

Miller, G. A., Galanter, E., & Pribram, K. H. (1960). *Plans and the structure of behavior.* New York: Holt.

Moore, W. E. (1963). *Social change.* Englewood Cliffs, NJ: Prentice Hall.

Munroe, R. L., & Munroe, R. H. (1980). Perspectives suggested by anthropological data. In H. C. Triandis & W. W. Lambert (Eds.), *Handbook of cross-cultural psychology: Perspectives* (Vol. 1). Boston: Allyn & Bacon.

Odum, E. P. (1971). *Fundamentals of ecology* (3rd ed.). Philadelphia: Saunders.

Oerter, R. (1979). Ein ökologisches Modell kognitiver Sozialisation. [An ecological model of cognitive socialization.] In H. Walter & R. Oerter (Eds.), *Ökologi und Entwicklung.* [Ecology and development.] Donauwörth: Auer.

Oerter, R. (1982). Interaktion als Individuum-Umwelt-Bezug. [Interaction as individual–environment relation.] In E. D. Lantermann (Ed.), *Wechselwirkungen.* [Interactions.] Göttingen: Hogrefe.

Oesterreich, R. (1981). *Handlungsregulation und Kontrolle.* [Action, regulation, and control.] München: Urban & Schwarzenberg.

Ogburn, W. F. (1972). Die Theorie des "Cultural Lag." In H. P. Dreitzel (Ed.), *Sozialer Wandel.* Berlin: Luchterhand.

Orlove, B. S. (1980). Ecological anthropology. *Annual Review of Anthropology, 9,* 235–273.

Parsons, T. (1960). *Structure and process in modern societies.* New York: Free Press.

Parsons, T. (1966). *Societies: Evolutionary and comparative perspectives.* Englewood Cliffs, NJ: Prentice Hall.

Piaget, J. (1970). Piaget's theory. In P. H. Mussen (Ed.), *Carmichael's Manual of child psychology* (3rd ed.). New York: Wiley.

Rabb, T. K., & Rotberg, R. I. (Eds.). (1971). *The family in history: Interdisciplinary essays.* New York: Harper & Row.

Radcliffe-Brown, A. R. (1930). The social organization of Australian tribes. *Oceania, 1,* 34–63.

Radcliffe-Brown, A. R. (1935). On the concept of function in social science. *American Anthropologist, N.S. 37,* 394–402.

Rappaport, R. A. (1971). Nature, culture and ecological anthropology. In H. C. Shapiro (Ed.), *Man, culture and society.* Oxford: Oxford University Press.

Reese, H. W., & Overton, W. F. (1970). Models of development and theories of development. In L. R. Goulet & P. B. Baltes (Eds.), *Life-span developmental psychology: Research and theory.* New York: Academic Press.

Ricklefs, R. E. (1973). *Ecology.* London: Nelson.

Riegel, K. F. (Ed.). (1978). *Zur Ontogenese dialektischer Operationen.* [The development of dialectical operations.] Frankfurt: Suhrkamp.

Riegel, K. F. (1980). *Grundlagen der dialektischen Psychologie.* [Foundations of dialectical psychology.] Stuttgart: Klett.

Riegel, K. F., & Meacham, J. A. (Eds.). (1976). *The developing individual in a changing world* (2 vols.). The Hague: Mouton.

Rüegg, W. (1969). *Soziologie.* Frankfurt: Fischer.

Ruyle, E. E. (1973). Genetic and cultural pools: Some suggestions for a unified theory of bio-cultural evolution. *Human Ecology, 1,* 201–215.

Schütz, A. (1960). *Der sinnhafte Aufbau der sozialen Welt.* [The meaningful construction of the world.] Wien: Springer.

Schwartz, L. (1951). *Die Neurosen und die dynamische Psychologie Pierre Janet's.* [Neuroses and the dynamic psychology of Pierre Janet.] Basel: Schwalbe.

Sinnot, J. D. (1981). The theory of relativity: A metatheory for development? *Human Development, 24,* 293–311.

Southwick, C. H. (1972). *Ecology and the quality of our environment*. New York: Van Nostrand-Reinhold.

Stegmüller, W. (1979). *Hauptströmungen der Gegenwartsphilosophie*. [Mainstreams of present philosophy.] (Vol. 2). Stuttgart: Alfred Kröner.

Steward, J. H. (1955). *Theory of social change*. Chicago: University of Illinois Press.

Strasser, H. (1974). *Introduction to theories of social change*. Wien: Institute for Advanced Studies.

Triandis, H. C. (1980). Introduction to handbook of cross-cultural psychology. In H. C. Triandis & W. W. Lambert (Eds.), *Handbook of cross-cultural psychology: Perspectives* (Vol. 1). Boston: Allyn & Bacon.

von Wright, G. H. (1974). *Erklären und Verstehen*. [Explanation and understanding.] Frankfurt: Fischer Athenäum.

Weinberger, C., & Weinberger, O. (1979). *Logik, Semantik, Hermeneutik*. [Logic, semantic, and hermeneutics.] München: Beck.

Werbik, H. (1978). *Handlungstheorien*. [Action theories.] Stuttgart: Kohlhammer.

Whiting, B. B., & Whiting, J. W. M. (1975). *Children of six cultures: A psychocultural analysis*. Cambridge, MA: Harvard University Press.

Wilson, E. O. (1975). *Sociobiology*. Cambridge: Belknap.

Wilson, G., & Wilson, M. H. (1945). *The analysis of social change*. Cambridge: Cambridge University Press.

Wissler, C. (1926). *The relation of nature to man in aboriginal North America*. New York: Oxford University Press.

Witkin, H. A., & Berry, J. W. (1975). Psychological differentiation in cross-cultural perspective. *Journal of Cross-Cultural Psychology, 6,* 4–87.

Ziehe, T. (1975). *Pubertät und Narzissmus*. [Puberty and narcism.] Frankfurt: Europäische Verlagsanstalt.

CHAPTER 5

Culture, Language, and Mature Rationality*

GISELA LABOUVIE-VIEF

INTRODUCTION

The relationship between culture and individual cognitive development is a bidirectional one. On the one hand, culture provides schemata and interpretive frameworks that channel individual experience into communicable patterns, thereby serving as a template that shapes the potentialities of individual thinking. But on the other hand, individuals are not merely reactive to such shaping. In the confrontation with such interpretive frameworks, the individual also must create a system of integrated action and thought in the face of such pluralism. It is the latter direction of the culture–cognition equation with which I am concerned in this chapter.

Of course, to be concerned with either direction of this exchange process is a rather recent endeavor in the study of culture and cognitive development. Thus my collaboration with Schaie (Chapter 1, this volume) convinced me a number of years ago that to talk about adulthood changes in cognition as an abstraction from a cultural context was theoretically meaningless and methodologically problematic. In my own subsequent research I have been motivated, however, to swing back from a position of cultural relativism to a concern with what appeared to be more robust patterns of individual development. Like the research participants I studied and the writers whose thoughts I reflected upon, I was gripped by a slow conviction

*Preparation of this essay was supported by Research Career Development Award NIA 5 KO4 AG00018, and by funds provided by the Wayne State University—University of Michigan Institute of Gerontology.

Copyright © 1984 by Academic Press, Inc.
All rights of reproduction in any form reserved.
ISBN 0-12-482420-X

that the specialization and differentiation of cognitive repertories produced by culture were supplanted in mature adulthood by a new language that was at once more differentiated and more integrated. It was a language, I believed, in which individuals grapple with the fact that culture not only has sustained their cognitive productions but also has constrained them, stunted them, and provided only a partial vocabulary for the interpretation of their experience. It appeared as if by thus differentiating their own experience from the interpretive molds provided by culture, adults felt driven to reinterpret and readjust what until then had seemed a compelling and exhaustive view of the structure of reality. It was, I suspected, a new language of cognitive maturity, and one that supersedes a youthful language of certainty.

If research into the cultural constraints on cognitive development has exposed the deficiency of this youthful language of certainty, it has not yet provided us with a new view by which to structure the new language of adult maturity. Major theories of development still signal maturity by the acquisition of hypotheticodeductive thought, of rational certainty provided by a controlling ego, of individual independence from one's cultural matrix.

It is, we may surmise, no accident that the emergence of these competencies is chronologically identified with youth rather than with mature adulthood. On this backdrop, the language of doubt and even toleration of middle-aged adults often appears regressive, deficient, overly pragmatic, and too much embedded in the concrete; scientific interpretation still acquires an attitude of apology vis-à-vis those labels, attempting to correlate them with less-than-optimal stimulation, education, and so forth. But here, I argue that another interpretation is possible; one that reflects, indeed, a language of advanced abstraction, objectivity, and rationality. I pursue this argument from three different but parallel perspectives: first, the interpretation of research on culture and cognition; second, some recent developments in epistemology; and third, some structural parallels of postadolescent cognition.

THE RELATIVIZATION OF COGNITIVE MATURITY

The two areas to which this attempts to provide an interface—the study of culture and cognition on the one hand, and that of adulthood and cognition on the other —share a common concern: Both are likely to reveal the fact that our conceptions of psychological maturity are too narrowly defined. Take, as an example, the following observation from Bloom's (1981) study on *The Linguistic Shaping of Thought:*

In 1972–1973, while I was in Hong Kong working on the development of a questionnaire designed to measure levels of abstraction in political thinking, I happened to ask Chinese-speaking subjects questions of the form, "If the Hong Kong government were to pass a law requiring that all citizens born outside of Hong Kong make weekly reports of their activities to the police, how would you react?"; or "If the Hong Kong government had passed such a law, how would you have reacted?" Rather unexpectedly and consistently, subjects responded "But the government hasn't;" "It can't;" or "It won't." I attempted to press them a little by explaining, for instance, that "I know the government hasn't and won't, but let us imagine that it does or did . . ." Yet such attempts to lead the subjects to reason about things that they knew could not be the case only served to frustrate them and tended to give rise to such exclamations and "We don't speak/think that way;" "It's unnatural;" "It's unChinese." Some subjects with substantial exposure to Western languages and culture even branded these questions and the logic they imply as prime examples of "Western thinking." By contrast, American and French subjects, responding to similar questions in their native languages, never seemed to find anything unnatural about them and in fact readily indulged in the counter-factual hypothesizing they were designed to elicit. (p. 13)

As a result, the thought of non-Western adults, like that of adults aging in our culture (see Botwinick, 1978), often appears highly inflexible, tied to the concrete, deficient in the ability to abstract. The interpretive framework for this deficit-focused conclusion has a long heritage in Western culture, probably dating back to Plato and his definition of rationality as cognitive maturity. Rationality, Plato (1921) believed, rises above the animal spirit, which is the lowest, childlike, and most immature layer of the soul. It thus transcends those ties that bind us to the organic world and sensory impressions; it frees us from our sensuous heritage, from the passions of the lower body which "[fill] us full of love, and lusts, and fears, and fancies of all kinds, and endless foolery, and . . . [take] away the power of thinking at all" (p. 450). Reason, Plato believed, is not of the body but of the mind; it is divine and certain and *real;* it has knowledge of the ideas; and it is focused on that which is lasting, universal, and immortal.

Plato's spatial metaphor of mature reason and childlike passion has left to the Western world a profound schism. Development has come to be conceptualized as progressing along a number of related polarities. Such dualisms as body *versus* mind, emotion *versus* reason, biology *versus* culture, content *versus* form, context-boundedness *versus* context independence, and action *versus* thought all have connoted the move from lower, less differentiated forms of development to higher, more complex ones. As a result, variation in cognitive structure, whether ordered by culture or by age, has been seen as ordered along this same unilinear scheme with its de-emphasis on individual variability.

Such definitions were not conducive to incorporating the complexities of culturally and subculturally varying meanings of adaptability. Indeed, a deliberate attempt was made to bracket culture and varied individual experience out of the definition of intelligence and cognition. Ebbinghaus's (1913/1885) approach to the study of memory is a good example. He was conscious, of course, of the complexity introduced by the historicalness and individuality of subjects' memories. He decided, however, to table this problem by removing the issue of meaning from his studies. Thus subjects were given material devoid of cultural meaning (that is, nonsense syllables) and were examined under rigidly controlled laboratory conditions. This procedure, Ebbinghaus believed, offered "a possibility of indirectly approaching the problem . . . in a small and definitely limited sphere and, by means of keeping aloof for a while from any theory, perhaps of constructing one" (Ebbinghaus, 1913/1885, p. 65).

The hope, then, was to construct a theory upon the initial study of "pure" processes that might universally hold. Eventually, such pure processes might be reembedded into the contexts of individual activities and meanings that characterize everyday cognition. However, this recontextualization proved problematic as long as it was based upon the assumption of the logically subordinate status of individual and contextual variation.

This is because inevitably there arises a duality in the interpretation of the role of cultural variation. The unilinear Platonic model will inevitably assign primacy to decontextualized thought and construe it as gain but fail to consider that this process of decontextualization entails dangers of an unreflected kind of context dependence just the same.

This duality is well demonstrated by the different interpretations Plato and Socrates held about the role of culture (specifically, literacy) in the development of abstract reason (see Scribner & Cole, 1981). Plato, on the one hand, held that the written mode of information transmission was superior. The oral mode with its emphasis on memorization and recitation appealed to the emotions, not the higher faculties; it was thus seen to undermine the exercise of reason. Socrates, in turn, emphasized that the written mode might weaken the use of reason as the reader became more dependent on external aids.

It was Plato's interpretation that won in this debate and that provided the model of how to interpret cultural variation in cognition. Thus education and literacy were said to foster the development of critical attitude (e.g., Havelock, 1978), the analysis of relationships and logical thought (e.g., Goody & Watt, 1968), and the ability to utilize abstract categories and to adopt an attitude of self-reflection (e.g., Luria, 1976).

Several authors, however, have grown doubtful of this simple hierarchical model of cultural variation. Scribner and Cole (1981), for example, were able to separate the effects of formal education and literacy in their study of the Vai people, a population of Liberia which possesses a script but shows wide variability in exposure to formal education. These authors argued that it is difficult to align a simple inferior–superior continuum with the differences found among their various groups. Rather, performance across a range of tasks appeared to be closely related to specific socially patterned activities that were associated with the process of education, formal or informal, in the different groups.

Scribner and Cole (1981) thus felt critical of attempts to order either antecedents (cultural progress) or consequents (cognitive behavior) on one single hierarchical continuum. Instead, they found that the notion of practice-based skills, which are highly contextualized and defined by specific patterns of experience, offers a better methodological avenue for the study of culture and cognition.

In a similar vein, Bloom (1981) showed that the presence or absence of specific linguistic grammatical forms in speakers' native language constrains their ability to engage in the counterfactual hypothetical. In the Chinese language, these forms are much more closely tied to action contexts, and in such contexts they are readily handled by the Chinese. English, in contrast, tends to separate grammatical forms from action contexts: In the sentence "John hit Mary," for example, the English speaker (one might add, at least in the context of a grammar lesson) thus is less likely to respond with statements about the distasteful nature of such aggressive acts, but rather with grammatical transformations under which the sentence meaning remains invariant.

But, of course, even in English there are limits to the adoption of this transformational form of thought. It is not insignificant, we may surmise, that most demonstrations of such thinking derive from rather formal tasks in which there may be little investment in the bolstering of a premise and thus minimal resistance to adopting the counterfactual. It is well documented, however, that adults, when confronted with evidence that contradicts their cognitive world views, will vigorously resist reasoning upon it in a counterfactual mode—however vital and correct it may be (Janis & Mann, 1979; Zajonc, 1980). Neimark (1982), similarly, has shown that formal reasoning may characterize but a small proportion of adolescent thinking in natural contexts; thus the role of reexamining contextual variation becomes vital in our culture as well, if we wish to further a more analytical theoretical understanding of the relationship between culture and abstract thought.

This issue is of further methodological importance as it teaches us to be wary, when doing research, not to drown research subjects raised in different contexts of language and social activity in our own assumptive frameworks. Rather, the task often is one of an interaction of competing assumptive frameworks, each with context-limited abstract categories but also each with different constraints that define what kind of excursions in the counterfactual realm are permissible, desirable, or even thinkable. Unless these assumptive frameworks are carefully differentiated, one easily creates egocentric distortions of the thought of research subjects.

The resulting ambiguity of interpretation is well reflected in Luria's (1976) study of the effects of schooling in Central Asia. Consider the following excerpt of three subjects who were first shown a picture of a saw, an ax, and a hammer, and then asked if a "log" belonged to the same category (i.e., tools):

> Experimenter (E):   Would you say these things are tools?
> All three subjects: Yes
> E: What about a log?
> S-1:   It also belongs with these. We make all sorts of things out of logs—handles, doors, and the handles of tools.
> S-2:   We say a log is a tool because it works with tools to make things.
> E: But one man said a log isn't a tool since it can't saw or chop.
> S-3:   Yes you can—you can make handles out of it! . . .
> E: Name all the tools used to produce things . . .
> S-1:   We have a saying: take a look in the fields and you'll see tools.
>   (Luria, 1976, pp. 94–85)

If presented with the same task, city-educated subjects will almost inevitably exclude *log* from the category *tools*, and from this fact Luria (1976) argued that the uneducated display a deficit in classificatory behavior. Yet one also senses here a different dimension; these Uzbekistan peasants appear engaged in a bantering argument about the proper definition of *tool*, rejecting any one concrete definition and arguing for a more flexible and even creative stance. And indeed, although the experimenter attempts to guide the subjects toward a "correct" definition of tools, one is hard put to judge who is more rigid or concrete—the subjecs or the experimenter!

The issue, here, is not to deny important structural differences arising from variations of cultural experience. But the important point is that when evaluating notions of cognitive deficit, one must carefully calibrate one's standard according to the modes—often linguistic—that a culture, subculture, or even the individual has developed in order to deal with and to encode complex information. This approach was, in fact, propounded by Bartlett (1932) long ago. Bartlett viewed memory and cognition as processes that are in principle personalized and contextualized and that arise from the schematizing and generalizing activities that individuals apply to their experience.

Without belaboring the issue any further, let me then come to the moral. We have, a bit overenthusiastically and naively, and not unlike the adolescents I shall report on shortly, overgeneralized our own *contexts* of abstract and rational thought when examining other cultures. Now, from our more seasoned perspectives, we are finding there is no such thing as the abstract in the abstract but that, as Whitehead (1938) said, "Everything is something" and must have a reference to the concrete, or to the content. Thus we must confront the concrete boundaries of our own abstractions as well.

Philosophy and the Crisis of the Personal

Are we committed, therefore, to sheer relativism? I believe not, and here, conveniently, we find that the crisis alluded to is of almost universal proportions. It is mirrored, among other fields (see Habermas, 1981), in a crisis in the philosophy of science and of epistemology of this century, and it is captured by nothing more poignantly than the individual development some of the major thinkers of this century have themselves evidenced in their thinking. Whitehead and Wittgenstein, for example, both set out in their young manhood to erect logical systems that once and for all would exclude individual sources of error, by a rigorously axiomatized system of logic. Both men, however, doubted the wisdom of such a strategy in their more mature adulthood. Thus Whitehead (1938) asserted that "an abstraction is nothing more than the omission of part of the truth" (p. 189); Wittgenstein (1968) warned that we must resist "the contemptuous attitude towards the particular case" (p. 18). Piaget (e.g., Bringuier, 1980), similarly, maintained that individuality and affect are not valid epistemological categories; yet when asked, shortly before his death, what was the motor of development, he gave the puzzling answer, "love" (A. Sinclair, 1981, personal communication). If these men are wiser and more abstract in their mature years, what truth then does the youthful model of rationality omit or what is it contemptuous of?

The Western affinity toward equating logic and mature cognition is captured nowhere better than in Piaget's theory. Piaget (e.g., 1971) argued that with the advent of propositional logic in adolescence, cognitive structures achieve closure and self-regulation by their ability to posit zero deviations, thus creating perfectly regulated and rationally controlled homeostatic systems of thought characterized by objectivity, self-reflectiveness, and the conscious pursuit of consistency and coherence. This view of logic is, of course, an important ingredient of Western intellectual tradition and anticipated in Socrates's metaphor of logic as a healer: "You will come to no harm if you nobly resign yourself into the healing hand of the argument as to a physician without shrinking" (1937, p. 535, quoted in DeLong, 1970, p. 12).

The ideal of honest inquiry, of pursuing an argument even against one's intuition and self-interest are at the root of Piaget's interest in logic as a tool subserving the pursuit of objectivity. But not always does logic, nor unreflective trust in the physician, guarantee a cure. Consider the following incident between Protagoras, the Sophist, and his student Euathlus who had studied rhetoric with Protagoras so he could become a lawyer. It was agreed that, after an initial payment, the balance of the fee would be paid after Euathlus had won his first case in court. But when he made no attempt at practicing law, Protagoras took him to court and presented his case:

> Euathlus maintains he should not pay me but this is absurd. For suppose he wins this case. Since this is his maiden appearance in court he then ought to pay me because he won his first case. On the other hand, suppose he loses the case. Then he ought to pay me by the judgment of the court. Since he must either win or lose the case he must pay me.

So well had he taught his student, however, that Euathlus countered:

> Protagoras maintains that I should pay him but it is this which is absurd. For suppose he wins this case. Since I will not have won my first case I do not need to pay him according to our agreement. On the other hand, suppose he loses the case. Then I do not have to pay him by judgment of the court. Since he must either win or lose the case I do not have to pay him. (DeLong, 1970, p. 10)

Both were competent logicians and neither, in fact, committed a logical error. Their disagreement, therefore, is not a matter of logical competence; rather, it is a matter of principle and resides in certain structural features of propositional logic. For example, some (nontautological) propositional forms are contingent on the assignment of truth values; thus extrapropositional variables must serve to disambiguate the situation and assign truth values. If Protagoras were to win and Euathlus to lose, for example, is the moral weight of a promise to be overturned by the court? It is on this pragmatic issue, not their respective logical competencies, that the arguments lead to different conclusions.

Since Leibniz' requirement that logic be true in all possible worlds, logical theorists had attempted to construct systems that range over indefinite domains; that are content-free. But inevitably, these attempts raised paradoxes not unlike the preceding one, in which content stubbornly reasserted itself. If originally the hope was to contain such leakage of content by the construction of more complex systems, metalogic now asserts that this hope was *in principle* illusory and that the notion of logical truth is in principle differentiated and system dependent (see DeLong, 1970; Quine, 1981).

Elsewhere (Labouvie-Vief, 1980, 1982) I have argued that such meta-logical developments have profound implications for the limits of purely logical methods in the analysis of adulthood cognitive change. These implications are well pointed out with the help of a brief analysis of the structure of Protagoras's and Euathlus's argument.

This argument highlights an important differentiation between two types of logic at work: an *implicational* and a *representational* logic. The former concerns the formulae by which the relationships between premises and conclusions are described. This aspect is relatively unproblematic. It does not, however, speak to the truth of the conclusion unless the truth of the premises is presupposed. It merely specifies, in other words, the truth value of sentences as formal, abstract structures and does not take into account their specific content. The latter, in contrast, presupposes that the thinker has arrived at the specific formalization after constructing a symbolic representation of the situation:

> Now any actual activity of thinking involves these two processes, or at least their analogues. It involves these two processes, of symbolization, usually in words. This is much more than a mere description; for it involves relevant selection and combination. Secondly, it involves the drawing of inferences, for which the symbolic representation provides the premises. . . . This part of the thinking is a manipulation of symbols according to rules, and with a knowledge of the rules and a suitable symbolic system, it can be accomplished by a machine. But for the selection and combination of the premises no rules can be given. (Macmurray, 1978, p. 93)

Thus a certain concretism must return to thinking after the mastery of abstract rules. If not, the thinker will, like Protagoras or Euathlus, fail to differentiate the form of thinking from the symbolic domain of thought, and in failing to make this differentiation he or she will be highly egocentric and subjective.

Note that this view extends, in fact, a cycle Piaget has emphasized in his childhood research (for discussion see Labouvie-Vief & Lawrence, 1984). Take moral development as an example. Young children exhibit a naive realism in moral thought by which rules are seen as unalterable and immanent. Yet in this illusion of grasping universal laws they are maximally undifferentiated. Their concepts of laws and rules are merely an expression of the accidents of their concrete experience. They confuse, as Piaget says, logical necessity with contingent regularity. In contrast, the more mature moral thinker achieves objective thought by realizing that laws are a result of the intercoordination of multiple perspectives. The thinker, in other words, must relativize abstract concepts so as to take into account different interpersonal perspectives.

Piaget's view on spatial perspective taking similarly stresses this process of concretization at a more abstract level. At first, ordering relationships (e.g., close–far) are elaborated from the viewpoint of the self; and they are egocentrically overgeneralized as universal from that perspective. Mature forms of perspective taking are achieved, in turn, once the child can relativize such relationships according to different spatial and/or interpersonal perspectives.

Note, now, that this view of the formation of knowledge reflects an epistemology quite different from what Piaget has adhered to in his discussions of adolescent logic (e.g., Inhelder & Piaget, 1958). It is a framework, not of truth in stable abstraction, but of social coconstruction in which development is characterized by rhythmic movements between egocentric and heterocentric (Macmurray, 1979) poles. Movements toward the egocentric pole occur when the individual sets himself or herself apart from the communicative matrix, examines the constraints of that matrix on his or her behavior, and eventually construes the system of those constraints in some representational form. In this movement of withdrawal the external regulative system is set, however, in opposition to the self; the process of reflective abstraction, Piaget (1971) stated, is a process of negation, or of withdrawal from action. Through this act of negation, reflective abstraction always carries with it the danger of structural impoverishment. Thus first steps at cognitive advancement are usually characterized by such structural distortions as egocentrism and correlative distortions of the communicative process.

The objectifying swing toward egocentrism, then, must be counterbalanced by opposite swings toward the contexts of communication and action. Genuine structural advancement, Piaget asserted, is achieved when structures are enriched by action (for discussion, see Labouvie-Vief, 1980). Thus the process of reflection becomes one in which the tie with the original matrix is reaffirmed, that is, in which representations are expanded by reembedding them into a new action context.

Traditional logical theory (from which Piaget has borrowed his model of mature logical competence) does not, however, achieve the resulting necessary differentiation between the form of logical thinking and the concrete domain about which the individual thinks. It thereby falls prey to a new and more abstract form of egocentrism in which the self and the other are confused through an illusion of universal transindividual laws. Macmurray (1979) has commented on this "egocentric predicament" of traditional logic and observed:

> Thinking, like other characteristic activities, is problematic. Whenever we think, we run the danger of falling into error. Part of the distinction between truth and

> falsity lies in a reference to other thinkers. . . . If we all think the truth we all
> think the same thing, so that it is a matter of indifference, from the theoretical
> point of view, which particular thinker does the thinking. Consequently, pro-
> vided we are all thinking the truth, we can treat the particularity of the thinker as
> a negligible constant. (1979, p. 21)

Piaget's account of maturity, in effect, gives up this necessary distinction between the self and the other that is so important in his account of
childhood development. The result, however, is a profound structural flaw
because the self and the other are no longer describable by isomorphic
forms. Instead, the relationship of the *self* and the *other* is purely understood as one of subject and object—that is, the other as object is an entity
not endowed with intention, cognition, and activity on his or her own terms
but one cognized about and acted upon by the subject. Thought, therefore,
is unilateral.

Through this structural asymmetry, however, the structural description
of the subject becomes impoverished as well:

> The primary correlation, in which all knowledge rests, is the "you and I" in the
> active relation. How then is it possible for the Other to be known as non-
> personal? Only by a reduction of the concept of other which excludes part of its
> definition; only, that is to say, by a partial negation: only by down-grading the
> "you" in the "you and I" to the status of "it". If we do this, however, we
> necessarily reduce its correlate, the "I" in the same fashion. The non-personal
> other is thus the correlate of the Self as body, that is, as a material object. Now
> what is excluded in this abstraction is intention. The non-personal other is that
> which is active without intention. Its correlate is myself unintentionally active.
> (Macmurray, 1979, p. 80)

The result of such structural asymmetry and logical reduction of the
form of the self and the other is not just the creation of the unbridgeable
dualism of traditional philosophy; it is also an inevitable selective focusing
of attention away from communicative distortions that thus inevitably slip
into language and behavior. Consider, as an example, the following statement by George Boole, whose logic served as a model for Piaget:

> Were, then, the laws of valid reasoning uniformly obeyed, a very close paral-
> lelism would exist between the operations of the intellect and those of external
> Nature. Subjection to laws mathematical in their form and expression, even the
> subjection of an absolute obedience, would stamp upon the two series one com-
> mon character. The reign of necessity over the intellectual and the physical world
> would be alike complete and universal. (Boole, 1958/1854, p. 408)

On the one hand, one may understand this statement (as intended by
Boole) as an ode to the perfect harmony between thought and reality; on the

other hand, one may also discern here a language of dominance and submission, of coersion and obedience, if one is free to broaden one's attentional focus and let go of one's contemptuous attitude toward the particular.

Nozick (1981) has similarly argued that the language of traditional philosophy thus acquires the communicative deficiency of coercive egocentrism. He maintained that philosophy has tended to carefully select and prearrange its premises so as to lead the thinker to the conclusions intended:

> The language of philosophical art is coercive: arguments are *powerful* and best if they are *knockdown,* arguments *force* you to a conclusion, if you believe the premises you *have to* or *must* believe something, whether he wants to believe it or not. A successful philosophical argument, a strong argument, *forces* someone to a belief. (p. 4)

Thus, we discern that notions of abstract thinking that separate form and content are in no way guarantors of objective thought. By dissociating them, instead, thinking is endangered by dissociation as well. This, I suppose, is the lesson we can learn from Whitehead and Wittgenstein, as well as from more recent developments in epistemology (more extensive discussions of those developments are found in Habermas, 1981, and McCarthy, 1979).

THE REINTEGRATION OF INDIVIDUALITY IN MATURITY

If the crisis in philosophy and epistemology can be characterized as a struggle to reconstitute the logical form of the personal (Macmurray, 1978), the same crisis of structural transformation may also characterize the postadolescent development of thought in adults. Indeed, I am proposing that the purported concrete and pragmatic orientation often found in adulthood is, thus, the sign of a structural progression by which earlier modes of logical thought become transformed.

Of course, if adults thus broaden their view of the meanings of logic and truth, it also becomes necessary to expose the function of their youthful meanings in an enlarged context. To do so, we then must change our focus, as we always must when comparing more complex to less complex levels of development: Rather than attempting to show how adolescent logic permits a culmination of mature thought, we must focus on its negative, on what it does not accomplish, on its immaturity rather than maturity.

These immature and reality-distorting aspects of youthful logic have been pointed out in Perry's (1968) landmark study on the conflicts college students encounter as they confront the multiplicity of university life. These youth search for a single perspective on truth and are deeply confused and profoundly troubled by the fact that no one correct view is apparent, whether in academic matters or in personal decisions. The role of authority, in their mind, is to offer correct interpretations; as a result, they display a high dependence on authority, whose role they view as one of removing ambiguity. Their failure to realize that ultimately the thinker must accept responsibility for his or her own thought—with no guarantees for certainty—creates a kind of obsession with finding safe techniques to unveil truth. They simply fail to realize that the pursuit of truth is a cooperative enterprise in which only partially agreeing individuals engage, and which can be understood only in its flawed and risky process rather than in holding on to a safe product.

Perry described this progression as a stagelike movement through a number of positions. At first, the belief in the unitary nature of truth creates a predication of reality (theories, teachers, etc.) into truthful and false statements and authors of statements. In this process of predication, egocentrism emerges as the coordination of truth with *I* or *we* and nontruth with *they*. Only eventually do youth come to realize that multiplicity of beliefs is a valid and inexcapable aspect of thought and reality. This realization, however, ushers in a new confrontation with oneself and one's role in one's thinking. Once truth is no longer legislated by authority, one must confront one's own standpoint vis-à-vis that which one thinks and does. Thus the intermediate position of relativism is resolved through one of commitment in relativism.

Other authors, following Perry's lead, have similarly shown that this progression can be described in terms of a differentiation of epistemological belief systems (Kitchener & King, 1981) or logical levels (Kuhn, Pennington, & Leadbeater, 1983). I believe, however, that—like Piaget's earlier stages of development—they must be interpreted in a broader context as general levels by which logical, communicative, and affective structures are coregulated in fairly integrative *structures d'ensemble* in which thought comes to progressively sustain higher levels of multiplicity, uncertainty, and affective tension.

Elsewhere (Labouvie-Vief, 1982) I have described this movement as a progression from intrasystemic through intersystemic to autonomous thought. In my own research program, I am attempting to describe this progression by examining how adolescents and adults of varying ages integrate information in social and ambiguous contexts. The study was conducted with Julie Hakim-Larson, Cindy Adams, Marilyn Hayden, and Marlene Devoe. In that study we constructed syllogism-like statements that permit multiple interpretations. One of them, for example, talks of a woman (Mary) who threatens to leave her drunkard husband (John) if he comes home drunk one more time, and then it asks what will happen as he indeed comes home drunk again. Subjects were carefully questioned about the rationales for their answers.

As we expected, most adolescents gave purely intrasystemic answers in which the solution was primarily dictated by the linguistic form of the statements. These adolescents were quite unaware of the issue of interpretation; to them, the evidence was obvious and, as most of them stated, "it says so right there." Thus one 11-year old answered, when asked if Mary will leave John, "Yes, she does because she warned him if he got drunk again that she would leave and take the kids with her. And then he ended going to the party to get drunk again so that means she left." When questioned further as to how certain she was of her answer, she replied, "I'm absolutely certain because she warned him that if he got drunk again she'd leave. Then he went ahead and got drunk, so that means she left."

These adolescents were entirely unaware that in thus responding, they had assumed a particular interpretation. Few, indeed, realized that other interpretations exist, with other options for Mary. If they did, however, such options were not at all integrated with the formal structure of the problem; they were merely added as a kind of afterthought as in the following answer of a 10-year-old, "I'm absolutely certain. Because, you know, she warned him that if he got drunk one more time that she would leave him. . . . And that's what he did. He got drunk and so I guess she's gonna go away."

When further, prompted, she added however, "Well, she warned him so that's what usually happens. And, well, maybe she could give him another chance, maybe. Sometimes that happens."

This relativization did not, however, relativize the notion of what the correct answer was, and thus was not an ambiguity of principle. This same intrasystemic focus on unambiguous answers was revealed when, in a further interview, these adolescents were asked about the differences they saw between syllogisms of this ambiguous and social nature as opposed to more traditional formal problems. One 12-year-old, when asked if she realized a difference between different story types answered, "yes, there was. Because sometimes they told you exactly what was happening and sometimes they didn't. They just gave you bits of information. . . . They should give you all the details in the story. That way you can figure it out easily."

Thus ambiguity is not a matter of principle, but rather of lacking detail. Truth, in turn, was seen as exhaustible in principle, given sufficient information. In general, there is a strong belief in the existence of one right answer, and possible individual differences in answering the tasks were attributed to varying levels of competence in finding this right answer. Even though some adolescents asserted that in principle different answers might be valid, they nevertheless then went on to hierarchize such answers in a strictly unilinear right–wrong framework. Thus one 13-year-old, when asked if there is always one right answer, replied, "No, there could have been a lot of different answers. . . . Well, each person's idea of what's happening in the story is a little different in each way, because none of us think alike."

Yet when prompted further about the nature of these differences, she proceeded to reduce them to a single dimension—an ability to disambiguate confusing information:

> Well, people younger than me might've answered them maybe a little more confusing, or if they knew they were really smart they could have answered it really easier than me . . . (And people older than you?) . . . I think they would have answered it easier because they might have had a really confusing story when they were my age and maybe understand it a little more when they got a little older.

This emphasis on certainty and the syncretic identification of formal and content features of the problems contrast sharply with the solution approach of some of the older subjects. Consider the following answer to the John-and-Mary problem given by a 20-year-old chemistry student, Jan.

> I would say no and I would say somewhat certain because it seems that if she stayed with him for so long . . . because it seems like they've been married long since they have children that she would stay with him *even though it was one more time*. Because if she loved him that much to stay with him all these years, she'd probably find other ways than . . . to just up and leave after all the years of staying. It doesn't seem that she'd . . . change so quickly in her actions towards him.

Note, first, that in this mode of problem solving, explicit realization is given of the linguistic constraints of the problem ("one more time"). From this formal constraint, however, subjects attempted to proceed to solutions that extended beyond the information specified in the problem and to search for answers in more deep structural constraints: constraints located in the motivational equipment and tendencies of the protagonists. Different possible solutions, therefore, were no longer a matter of right and wrong logical procedure. Thus the same subject asserted, "There was no right or wrong answer. You could get logically to both answers."

Logic or truthfulness were thus in principle multifaceted, and the process of following a logical procedure was differentiated from the specific conclusions which one derived. Different conclusions may have simply resulted from the fact that different thinkers started from different premises, "It depends on the steps they take to get to their answer. If they base it on what they feel, what they know and they have certain steps and get to an answer, it can be logical."

Individual differences which arose from different knowledge systems and different feelings therefore became valid and a matter of principle. At the same time, logic no longer offered the only decision criterion, but affective variables must enter in, as well. Thus when asked how to decide between different answers, she replied:

> Because sometimes in some of them you could get to answers but to get to *your* answer, you would take what you think is important and your feeling on it and the sentences you think that are the main part of it, and you would take what the main idea out of all of that is to you and you'd get your answer.

Clearly, therefore, truth was no longer solely dictated by adherence to logical procedure. Rather, the individual was seen to engage in processes of symbolization, selection, comparing, weighing, and taking an active, conscious, self-referential posture vis-à-vis information integration.

Indeed, the more youthful predilection toward logical formalism now is reinterpreted as a means by which the real confusion of reality is reduced in a manner later to be exposed as dualistic and distortive. Thus Jan went on to point out that from her (more mature) perspective, her earlier approach to logic appears to have been highly defensive:

> You know, I used to watch Star Trek and I just liked Spock a lot. So I always thought that logic was the best way to go. And as I get older, I don't think that anymore. I'm more open than I used to be. . . . I used to think that logic was everything. It was a lot more important because . . . in my particular situation I was bombarded with emotional traumas all the time during high school—you know, teenage years—and my home wasn't too swift, so it was a lot of emotional things, and I was trying to cut it off. And I feel that that's harmful in the long run because you end up dealing with it sooner or later anyway. So now I tend to think it's a combination of the two—logic and emotion. Like with the chemistry and schoolwork, it's logic and everything but to deal with people you have to be more on an emotional level. You can't always assume that people are going to come out like an equation, that they are going to do this just because they always have.

For this young woman, unusually mature for her age, her redefinition of what is logical then had the function of permitting a broader, more objective look at herself and a deepened understanding of others. Not all subjects, however, handled this transcendence of dualities with the same insight. For some of them, instead, the polarity emerged as a sharp clash. Thus one subject in his 30s responded to the John-and-Mary syllogism:

> The key is "one more time". Mary's simple statement—if she meant it—is weighed off of John's drunkeness. The logic is clear, clean,—if you choose to ignore human dimensions. If A happens, then B will result—a gross simplification

of cause and effect, or event and result—again, again when my creative interpretive urge is suppressed, I can misfire, hear what I want, distort the story
and place a wrong answer firmly convinced that is correct.

In this subject, then, the adolescent struggle described by Jan continued
in a cryptic fashion. Structurally, his answer is suggestive of a struggle
between two antagonistic inner voices, and the content of his protocol
similarly reveals a struggle between an approach he termed logical, correct
though simplistic, and one he felt is creative and human, though threatening
to catch him in a vortex of subjectivity.

The same structural features of carving a superordinate perspective out
of potentially ambiguous information is also revealed in a dissertation by
Blanchard-Fields (1983). In this study, adolescents and adults were given
two accounts told by two different protagonists of the same event. This task
was fashioned after Kuhn's (Kuhn *et al.*, 1983) task of the two Livian Wars
but translated it into a more normative interpersonal setting. In one task, for
example, both the parents and their adolescent son (John) gave somewhat
different accounts of the same event sequence—a family visit to the grandparents. Because these two accounts centered around a conflict, most adolescents identified the event sequence with the son's interpretation; thus the
task became one of assigning right and wrong or victory and defeat to one
party. As one adolescent, Dave, answered when asked who won the
conflict:

> The parent won because John gave in and went with them to the grandparents'
> house. The parents were glad that he decided to go, so John was the loser in this,
> because he was the one that had to give in.

Contrast this answer, now, with that of Linda, a woman 36 years old:

> Well, either neither or both, depending on how you look at it. My first reaction
> would say neither, because I don't think his parents or John really came together.
> They think they came to one kind of decision, and he thinks they came to another
> kind of decision, and in that respect I don't think either of them won, because
> neither one is really aware of what the other meant and had in mind. On the
> other hand, you could say that they both won, in that they have opened an
> avenue to talk. They both mentioned discussions, or decision-making, and that
> kind of thing; but I think that what John meant was that his parents would give
> him freedom to make whatever decisions he wanted without infringing upon that
> at all, and I don't think that's at all what his parents meant, so this seems to me
> that it's going to be a scene that will recur many times, because neither the
> parents or John have come to the point where they realize that there has to be an
> amount of discussion that goes on. (Blanchard-Fields, 1983, personal communi-
> cation)

Note that Linda did not merely transpose Dave's approach to side with
the parents. Rather, she exposed the very problem of siding as a problem

that must be structurally transcended. Thus neither side was right or wrong, but both were wrong to the extent that they failed to establish effective communication.

These differences are parallelled, as well, by differences in the way in which the actions of the two parties were processed. Thus for the adolescents, the parents' actions were interpreted strictly from the vantage point of the son and as opposing those of the son, as shown in Dave's reply to the question of how the accounts are different:

> The parents didn't really see what John was going through, they just saw what they wanted John to be doing. They saw and heard only what they wanted to see and hear, and so they were surprised when he got angry, because they thought, "Well, he's having a good time," even though he was bored. They thought that his good manners were a sign that he was—ah—having fun, when he was really being bored—he was bored. And then John said that he was bored, and that they were sitting there and they were lecturing him, and it was all on his—you know, they were making him do things he didn't want to do, and he was just putting up with it because he was going to be leaving there soon, and he wouldn't have to worry about it after he left, and he was mad because his parents didn't see that he was bored. (Blanchard-Fields, 1983, personal communication)

In contrast, no such antagonistic interdependence was perceived by Linda. In her view, instead, one is dealing here with two different and largely independent interpretations of an event sequence that itself must be distinguished from the protagonists' interpretation of that sequence:

> They agreed that the decision to visit the grandparents had been made well in advance, although John said he had forgotten about it; they do agree that they disagreed about whether or not John should go; they agree that he did go; and they agree that he behaved very well and participated while there. So on the surface there is agreement. Where the disagreement occurred is that in the interpretation, his parents interpret his participation and being in the discussion and looking at the slides, and all that kind of thing, as having a good time. John, on the other hand, interprets them as, "I did what I had to do to avoid the argument. I hated it, I didn't want to do it, I didn't want to be there, but I had to play the role." So, as far as events, they are the same; their feelings and interpretations are different. Linda, then, makes a clear and specific differentiation between event structure on the one hand, and individual differences arising from interpretation, on the other. (Blanchard-Fields, 1983, personal communication)

I suggest that we are observing here the emergence of a more mature mode of reason—one in which, in acknowledging individual differences in representations of reality, the language and structural representation becomes less egocentric and distortive, and more objective. It does so, however, by explicitly embracing the problem of content and individuality in order to differentiate the content boundedness of the self from that of the other.

CONCLUSIONS

What, then, ties these three lines of evidence together? In the mundane resolution of these tasks, I suggest, we see a common sense solution to the problem of rationality that has haunted philosophy since the Greeks. This problem has been defined around a duality, one side affirming rationality as a mode of conduct in which morality, responsibility, respect, mutuality, and the transcendence of egocentrism through self-reflection all have a place, the other side emphasizing, instead, the pursuit of formal knowledge as a path to maturity. As psychologists, we have tended to side with the latter notion but failed to examine how the resulting emphasis on formalism ties in with the former. What our research subjects realize, instead, is that formal thought per se must be decoupled once more from the contexts in which we have elaborated these notions in order to carve an integration between formal correctness and interpersonal mutuality.

The methodological consequences of such a view are profound. Certainly, they suggest that we direct our research approaches away from the still predominant counting the wrinkles (Kastenbaum, 1968) approach to aging. Neither will it be sufficient to attempt to smooth those wrinkles out through training in formal logic. Instead they demand that we relocate the study of adult cognition into the action contexts in which Piaget (1980) has seen childhood cognition as embedded: the contexts of communication and either the tendency to egocentrically distort communicative structures or the ability to balance them symmetrically and equitably.

And, if we do so, we may well find that there is a kind of abstract wisdom in maturity, that permits adults a 'return' to the concrete—a return that is not at all regressive but that consists in the reflection of concreteness onto a higher and more complex level of analysis in which the individual can be reembedded into a complex social context. This post concrete quality may be profoundly different, therefore, from that of the child: For the child, to say "but the emperor does not wear any clothes" takes concreteness *only*, but for the adult, it *may* indicate complex skills of self—other differentiation, of differentiation of self from norms, of knowing why nobody dares to see the obvious, and of having the courage to do so.

REFERENCES

Bartlett, F. C. (1932). *Remembering*. Cambridge, England: University Press.
Blanchard-Fields, F. (1983). *The social integration of logic from adolescence to adulthood*. Unpublished Dissertation, Wayne State University, Detroit, MI.
Bloom, A. (1981). *The linguistic shaping of thought*. Hillsdale, NJ: Erlbaum.

Boole, G. (1958). *The laws of thought.* New York: Dover. (Originally published, 1854.)

Botwinick, J. (1978). *Aging and behavior* (2nd ed.). New York: Springer.

Bringuier, J. C. (1980). *Conversations with Piaget.* Chicago: University of Chicago Press.

DeLong, H. (1970). *A profile of mathematical logic.* Reading, MA: Addison-Wesley.

Ebbinghaus, H. (1913). *Memory.* New York: Teachers College Press. (Originally published, 1885.)

Goody, J., & Watt, I. (1968). The consequences of literacy. In J. Goody (Ed.), *Literacy in traditional societies.* New York: Cambridge University Press.

Habermas, J. (1981). *Theorie des Kommunikativen Handelns.* Frankfurt: Suhrkamp.

Havelock, E. A. (1978). *The Greek concept of justice: From its shadow in Homer to its substance in Plato.* Cambridge, MA: Harvard University Press.

Inhelder, B., & Piaget, J. (1958). *The growth of logical thinking from childhood to adolescence.* New York: Basic Books.

Janis, I. L., & Mann, L. (1977). *Decision making.* New York: Free Press.

Kastenbaum, R. (1968). Perspectives on the development and modification of behavior in the aged: A developmental-field perspective. *Gerontologist, 8,* 280–283.

Kitchener, K. S., & King, P. M. (1981). Reflective judgment: Concepts of justification and their relationship to age and education. *Journal of Applied Developmental Psychology, 2,* 89–116.

Kuhn, D., Pennington, N., & Leadbeater, B. (1983). Adult thinking in developmental perspective. In P. B. Baltes & O. G. Brim, Jr. (Eds.), *Life-span development and behavior* (Vol. 6). New New York: Academic Press.

Labouvie-Vief, G. (1980). Beyond formal operations: Uses and limits and pure logic in life-span development. *Human Development, 23,* 141–161.

Labouvie-Vief, G. (1982). Dynamic development and mature autonomy: A theoretical prologue. *Human Development, 25,* 161–191.

Luria, A. R. (1976). *Cognitive development: Its cultural and social foundations.* Cambridge, MA: Harvard University Press.

McCarthy, T. (1979). *The critical theory of Juergen Habermas.* Cambridge: MIT Press.

Macmurray, J. (1978). *The self as agent.* Atlantic Highlands, NJ: Humanities Press.

Macmurray, J. (1979). *Persons in relation.* Atlantic Highlands, NJ: Humanities Press.

Neimark, E. D. (1982). Cognitive development in adulthood. In T. Fields *et al.* (Eds.), *Review of human development.* New York: Wiley.

Nozick, R. (1981). *Philosophical explanations.* Cambridge, MA: Harvard University Press.

Perry, W. G. (1968). *Forms of intellectual and ethical development in the college years: A scheme.* New York: Holt.

Piaget, J. (1971). *Biology and knowledge.* Chicago: University of Chicago Press.

Piaget, J. (1980). *Experiments in contradiction.* Chicago: University of Chicago Press.

Plato. (1921). *The republic* (B. Jowett, Trans.). Oxford: Clarendon.

Quine, W. V. (1981). *Theories and things.* Cambridge, MA: Harvard University Press.

Scribner, S., & Cole, M. (1981). *The psychology of literacy.* Cambridge, MA: Harvard University Press.

Whitehead, A. N. (1938). *Modes of thought.* New York: Macmillan.

Wittgenstein, L. (1968). *Philosophical investigations.* Oxford: Blackwell.

Zajonc, R. B. (1980). Feeling and thinking: Preferences need no inferences. *American Psychologist, 35,* 151–175.

CHAPTER 6

Social Change, World Views, and Cohort Succession: The United States in the 1980s

STEPHEN L. KLINEBERG

> *As each new generation (or cohort) enters the stream of history, the lives of its members are marked by the imprint of social change and in turn leave their own imprint*
>
> RILEY, 1978

INTRODUCTION

The study of life-span development has been enriched by the renewed attention that is being paid to the complex mechanisms of intersection between the rhythms of social time and the stages of personal growth. The emerging perspective reminds us that each individual experiences any given slice of history at particular moments in that person's passage through the life-course pattern as society defines it (Elder, 1975). Different cohorts are likely to be affected somewhat differently by the same historical event; their experiences mediated by their life-stage at the time. When a society is changing rapidly, when the radically new experiences of one generation become the taken-for-granted expectations of the next, successive cohorts may view the world through different prisms. It is then that the biological succession of generations may become, through its own inherent dynamic, a major vehicle for societal transformation (Jones, 1980). In this chapter, I briefly

LIFE-SPAN DEVELOPMENTAL PSYCHOLOGY
HISTORICAL AND GENERATIONAL EFFECTS

129

Copyright © 1984 by Academic Press, Inc.
All rights of reproduction in any form reserved.
ISBN 0-12-482420-X

explore some empirical examples of this process, first in a third-world country undergoing modernization, then in the United States in the 1980s.

GENERATIONAL DISCONTINUITIES IN TUNISIA

This small North African country undertook an extraordinary program of wholesale social change during the years of optimistic commitment to modernization that followed its independence from the French in 1956. In the words of one observer (Micaud, 1964), the period was dominated by "a massive effort to transform attitudes and values and to reduce psychological and social obstacles to progress."

A survey was conducted in the spring of 1970 among adolescents and their parents randomly chosen from households living in the inner city of Tunis (Klineberg, 1974, 1976). The intergenerational differences painted a striking picture of transition. In the samples, 46% of the fathers and 87% of the mothers had had no formal education whatsoever. All of their children, daughters as well as sons, had gone to school; fully 70% of the adolescents were still in school at the time of the interviews. Whereas 78% of the mothers said they always wore the veil when they went out, 74% reported that their daughters never did.

The two generations were experiencing the same events in different ways and with varying degrees of acceptance or rejection. Even after 14 years of intensive modernization, the perspectives of the parental generation remained firmly anchored in the age-old pattern of separate roles for men and women. The mothers were far less knowledgeable than their husbands about current events and much less likely to have close friends outside the kinship network. Increasing exposure to modernizing influences, instead of bringing the sexes closer together, generated even greater attitudinal differences between husbands and wives. Each group was changing psychologically as a consequence of the social forces they were experiencing, but each remained within a circumscribed realm, the women becoming more open to change primarily in their roles as mothers, the men primarily in their perspectives on the wider society outside the home.

For the adolescent generation, the data suggested that a quite different world view was in the process of emerging. In comparison with their less educated parents, both sons and daughters evidenced more knowledge of current events, a far greater belief in their personal control over the forces that would shape their lives, and a desire for fewer children than their parents said they would recommend. Gender differences among the adolescents, although still present, were far less marked than among their parents.

Nevertheless, the traditional gender-role distinctions in Tunisian society continued decisively to influence the younger generation, for the parents were encouraging their sons far more than their daughters to develop more modern attitudes and aspirations.

Parents evidently regarded the new demands and opportunities available to the younger generation as extensions of masculine role-expectations, but as threats to the traditional roles and responsibilities of women. We conducted a series of regression analyses to test the differential impact of parental perspectives and school attainment on the attitudinal modernity of the adolescents. The data indicated that the views of their parents played an independent role of considerable importance in influencing more modern outlooks in the sons, but they had little direct impact on the attitudinal differences among the daughters. Schooling for the young men reinforced the same values and expectations that their more traditional parents espoused for them. For their sisters, however, school was virtually the only opportunity to develop friendships outside the home and to find support for the new self-images that they were developing. Parents were much less supportive of modern attitudes and aspirations for their daughters, and in their case, educational experience was by far the more powerful modernizing influence. There may thus have been greater conflict between parents and daughters than there was for sons, but the intergenerational discontinuities were striking in both sexes.

The adolescents who were still in school at the time of the interviews were asked how far they expected to be able to continue their education. Over 48% of the girls and 65% of the boys expected to acquire university training. When asked what job they thought they would have at the age of 25 years, over 61% of the boys and 52% of the girls said they would be professionals, such as doctors, lawyers, or college professors; another 30% saw themselves in white-collar positions as school teachers, policemen, secretaries, or nurses. When asked to list all the events they thought would happen to them in the future, only 17% of the girls in school referred to marriage or children, whereas more than 67% of the items they envisioned spoke of educational attainments or occupational success. Such images of the future are particularly striking when it is recalled that all but 13% of their own mothers were illiterate and all but 12% were unemployed.

The interviews left little doubt that these Tunisian adolescents were defining themselves and their futures in ways that contrasted markedly with traditional expectations and parental models. Although 40% of their fathers held unskilled or semiskilled blue-collar jobs, not a single one of the boys in the sample of school attenders expected to follow them into occupations of that sort. Whereas only 10% of the fathers were in high white-collar or professional positions, over 60% of their sons aspired to those types of occupations.

The historical events brought about by independence and the government's commitment to universal education succeeded in releasing the future from its givenness (Berger, Berger, & Kellner, 1973; Mead, 1970), but the new possibilities meant different things to the two generations. More generally, it seems clear that whether one experiences change as an exhilarating opportunity or as a violation of age-old values and expectations, or whether the feeling is one of playing a part in an historical transformation or of being left behind by the winds of change—these are differences in the construction of reality that are mediated by age and generation, as well as by sex and social status. It is also evident from the Tunisian study that these adolescents, as they assume the mantle of adult power and responsibility, will make their own very different imprint on their society for they will have to reconcile the exuberant aspirations and self-conceptions they have developed with the sad realities of economic stagnation.

It is precisely under these sorts of circumstances, when social structural transformations have varying effects on persons of different ages and when the impact of those experiences carry over into their subsequent perspectives and behaviors, that cohort effects are most likely to play an important role in carrying the processes of social change (Ryder, 1965). There are reasons to believe that similar effects may be operating today in the changes that are transforming industrial societies in the 1980s.

THE TRANSFORMATIONS OF INDUSTRIALISM

There was a time when the confident belief prevailed among American social scientists that fundamental change had essentially ended in Western societies. During the 1950s and early 1960s, industrialism was reaching its fulfillment, and ideological divisions seemed to melt into universal approval of the rationally managed society. The dominance of structural-functionalism in sociology and of evolutionism in the study of social change reflected the confident belief that Western modernity was the common future of all humanity. Structural change—the kind that is painful and agonizing and that forces individuals and generations into a sense of radical disjuncture between traditional ways and contemporary realities—would henceforth be confined to developing nations, like Tunisia, transitional societies converging on the single path to Western industrialism.

That set of beliefs reflected an extraordinary period when, as Kumar (1978, p. 185) remarked, "the motor of social change seemed to have come to a stop, idling contentedly in happy contemplation of a spreading world-wide felicity." The quarter century following World War II was a time of unprecedented economic growth, when the stability and legitimacy of institutional structures went largely unquestioned. The procreation ethic and the baby boom it generated were sustained by an economic expansion that brought about the doubling of per capita income between 1950 and 1970. These were the heady years of American optimism, when the visions of young and old alike were firmly hitched to images of a future that promised more of everything in a cornucopia without limits. There were unmistakable intimations in the upheavals of the 1960s that there were problems with that vision of reality. In the 1970s the bubble burst.

The decade just passed marked the ending of a period of prosperity that was fueled by cheap energy and was sustained by American world domination. If the economy faltered during the postwar years, or if protests and violence occasionally threatened the sense of national well-being, they were seen as temporary setbacks on a path of unending progress. If energy (or any other resource) threatened to run short, the solution was to be confidently sought in new discoveries or new technologies. The institutional structures and corporate interests that developed in support of these traditional views persisted through the 1970s; the constructions of reality honed in that extraordinary quarter century of rapid economic growth were still reflected in most newspaper and magazine commentaries, and still safely ensconced between the ears of most businessmen, politicians, and economists. Among the general public, however, the opinion polls appeared to be telling a somewhat different story (Klineberg, 1982a). During that decade, the vision of unlimited abundance gradually came to look like a mirage to many Americans, and the traditional consensus that placed economic growth above virtually all other values began to crumble. The polls revealed a striking transformation in the taken-for-granted assumptive worlds of Americans of different ages, as individuals, engaged in their own developmental trajectories, tried to make sense of the new realities of the preceding 10 years.

A NEW SENSE OF LIMITS

A number of themes emerged from the changes in survey responses that occurred through the 1970s, none more striking than the dramatic turning away from the traditional American faith in an unlimited future. From the late 1940s through the 1960s, the public consistently believed that the present was a better time for the country than the recent past and that the future would inevitably be better still. In 1964, for example, Americans gave the past of the United States ("about five years ago") an average rating of 6.1 on a 10-point scale; they rated the present at 6.5, and the future ("about five years from now") at 7.7. By 1978, that "normal" pattern had completely reversed itself in a general decline that saw the past of the United States at 5.8, the present at 5.4, and the future at 5.3. By February and March of 1979, the comparable figures were 5.7, 4.7, and 4.6 (Yankelovich & Lefkowitz, 1980a). National moods will surely fluctuate from time to time, but the postwar optimism that fueled the exuberant expectations of a generation seemed to have ended, for Americans slowly came to recognize the genuine fragility of the U.S. resource and energy picture.

The evolving public perceptions of energy problems revealed a reluctant learning process. Gallup polls periodically ask the open-ended question, "What is the most important problem facing this country today?" Between 1973 and 1977, energy was never mentioned by more than one-fourth of the public, except at the very height of the Arab oil embargo between December 1973 and February 1974 (Rosa, 1978). Even in 1978, Americans continued to be skeptical about the information that industry spokesmen and government representatives were providing. Most believed that the oil companies, the Organization of Petroleum Exporting Countries (OPEC), and the federal government were powerful, monopolistic, and irresponsible; and they suspected that the shortages were being manipulated by the energy companies in order to enrich themselves at the public's expense, with the full compliance of the government (Schneider, 1979).

The events of 1979, however, made the vulnerability and precariousness of the country's energy situation unmistakable. As Stobaugh and Yergin (1980) showed, 20 years of anticipated change were dramatically telescoped into fewer than that many months:

> From $12–$13 per barrel in late 1978, oil prices had risen to the $30–35 range, a level that many 1978 predictions had not anticipated until the year 2000. And political threats to the world's oil supply that had been discussed as potentially serious 5 or 10 years in the future had become visibly critical in 1979 alone. It was a fateful 18 months. (p. 563)

By August of 1979, 73% of the public were prepared to agree with the view, "The energy crisis is real, and is a clear and present danger to the country" (Harris Survey, 1979).

DISTRUST OF INSTITUTIONAL LEADERSHIP

Reflected in the length of time that it took Americans to reach that conclusion was the public's increasing distrust of those in charge of the major institutions of society. The decline of confidence in government was swift, sharp, and all-encompassing. The belief that "the government can be trusted to do what is right all or most of the time" was held by 40% of the public in 1976, by 35% in 1977, and by 29% in 1979 (Yankelovich & Lefkowitz, 1980a). Between 1964 and 1976, the proportion of Americans agreeing that "the government is pretty much run by a few big interests looking out for themselves" rose from 29 to 66% (Magney, 1979).

The declining confidence in government officials was more than matched by the public's distrust of the country's corporate leadership: Between February 1966 and November 1982, those expressing to Harris pollsters "a great deal of confidence" in the people in charge of running "major companies" dropped by 37 points, from 55 to 18%. During that same period, confidence in the "executive branch of federal government" dropped 21 points, from 41 to 20%, and in "Congress" from 42 to 13% (Harris Survey, 1982). In 1976, 68% of the American people agreed that the federal government "is getting too powerful for the good of the country"; yet concern over the social and environmental costs of uncontrolled business activity was still greater than the fear of big government. In that same poll, 55% believed that the government "should put a limit on the profit companies can make" (up from 28% in 1962), and 63% favored governmental action to "require local businesses to meet job safety standards" (Magney, 1979).

SKEPTICISM ABOUT TECHNOLOGY

Given the plummeting confidence in leaders and experts, it was perhaps inevitable that the American optimism about the promise of science and technology—a belief that was particularly widespread during the 30 years from the Manhattan Project in 1940 to the moon landings in 1969—would also be followed by disillusionment. The 1970s marked the watershed between a time when matters of science and technology could be confidently left to the experts and the new era when the public at large would demand a far greater decision-making role. The applications of science and technology were coming to be viewed as too important to be left to a small coterie of experts. The decade brought accelerating revelations of the long-term and often invisible hazards of new technologies—in the unintended consequences of DDTs and PCBs, and of asbestos and phosphate detergents; and in the potential cumulative effects of burning fossil fuels on levels of sulfuric acid and carbon dioxide in the atmosphere, of fluorocarbons from spray cans on stratospheric ozone, of radioactive waste management on future generations. What was emerging was an increasingly skeptical appraisal of the costs and benefits of a technological society and of the possibilities and limits of scientific inquiry itself (Holton & Morison, 1979).

Public opinion polls nevertheless showed Americans to be remarkably steady supporters of the technological enterprise as a whole. The belief that technology generally brings more benefits than problems was consistently endorsed throughout the 1970s by 81 to 84% of the public (Marshall, 1979). In November 1980, when Americans were asked which one course seemed to them most likely to improve the country's energy situation, only 17% put their faith in "an all-out effort to increase current energy production," and only 28% sought salvation in "a tough program to conserve energy"; but 47% felt that the problem would most likely be improved by "a technological breakthrough that would provide new sources of energy" (Harris, 1980).

By 52%, a majority of Americans in 1978 continued to believe that, "technology will find a way of solving the problem of shortages and natural resources." In reporting this continuing confidence, Yankelovich and Lefkowitz (1980b) took note of a striking division in the views of Americans:

> In virtually all of the other survey findings, reported demographic differences among various subgroups in the population were not of major significance. But when it comes to confidence in technology to solve our national resources problems the country is sharply divided. The 52% level of support masks a deep split in faith in technology. (p. 9)

Many of the transforming events of the 1970s appear to have affected all age groups in largely similar ways. The 10-fold increase in the price of oil, for example, accompanied as it was by years of persistent stagflation, induced almost all Americans to lower their economic expectations and to recognize that resource scarcities were a threat to the continued expansion of industrial economies. Similarly, the period was marked by a series of events that appear to have contributed to political alienation throughout society. The assassination of leaders, the Vietnam conflict, the Watergate scandals, the evidence of governmental impotence in the face of mounting economic problems—all helped to generate increasing distrust of institutional leadership in the population as a whole, in ways that cut across region, gender, social status, or age. The declining economic expectations and the plummeting confidence in institutions might therefore best be interpreted as period effects attributable to the events of the 1970s (Bengtson and Cutler, 1976). There is little evidence to suggest that, on these dimensions, the consequences varied for persons of different ages in ways that would generate further change through cohort succession.

When we come to measures of the traditional faith in technology, however, we get a different impression. Only 29% of Americans between the ages of 18 and 24 who had attended college agreed that resource problems will be solved by technology, whereas this traditional view was held by 69% of the older, less educated, lower-income segments of the population. "Whether it is due to insight or prejudice or both combined," Yankelovich and Lefkowitz (1980b, p. 9) concluded, "skepticism about technology is likely to spread. Almost invariably, the young and well-educated anticipate attitudes that spread to the larger society."

GENERATIONAL SHIFTS IN WORLD VIEWS

Peculiarly related to age and education, this surprising split over the time-honored American faith in technology suggests the more general possibility that a generational shift may be taking place in central aspects of the cultural ethos of industrial society. The dominant social paradigm that informed and legitimated the industrial era was based above all on confidence in the developments of science and technology to perpetuate man's successful dominance over nature and thereby to generate ever-increasing material wealth (Cotgrove, 1982; Harman, 1979; Pirages & Ehrlich, 1974). The data suggest that a quite different world view may now be gradually emerging, carried along by the organic process of cohort succession.

During the mid-1970s, an intergenerational shift in political values among Western publics was reported (Inglehart, 1977). Across Western Europe and the United States, it seemed, the younger age groups, socialized during the postwar period of peace and prosperity, were giving distinctly higher priority than their elders to such postmaterialist goals as freedom of speech or broader participation in political decision making. Older cohorts, whose formative experiences took place in years of depression and world war, gave overwhelmingly greater priority to materialist concerns, such as maintaining domestic order or fighting inflation.

Further research revealed some signs of a life-cycle or aging effect, a slight tendency for individuals to acquire more materialistic values as they grow older and begin to settle down to family responsibilities, but the cohort effects were clearly stronger, for the generational differences appeared to be lasting (Dalton, 1977). Particularly striking in this regard was evidence that the age differences in value preference were most marked in precisely those countries that had experienced the greatest degree of economic development during the previous 50 years and in which the formative experiences of successive cohorts were therefore most dissimilar—countries such as Germany or France, in comparison to Britain or the United States. As Inglehart (1977, p. 37) was able to show, "the amount of value change seems to reflect a given nation's recent history."

The postwar cohorts are now beginning their own period of dominance in the cultural evolution of Western societies. Brought up in affluent, communications-rich, and peaceful times, their value priorities may well be different, on the average, from those of their parents and grandparents. If so, we can expect the traditional world view of industrialism to come under increasing challenge in certain respects, as individuals who emphasized personal and economic security are gradually succeeded by those who are more likely to value self-expression and participation.

Public opinion polls in the United States in the early 1980s seem to reflect a more ambiguous conception of what Americans mean by human progress. We have seen that the benefits of technology are no longer viewed with unquestioning approval, though some of the traditional faith remains. In November 1977, 92% agreed that scientific research and technological development "are necessary to keep the country prosperous"; for 69%, they constituted "the main factors in increasing productivity." On the other hand, 65% of Americans were now prepared to blame the development of science and technology for making "people want to acquire more possessions rather than enjoying non-material experiences," 56% for making "everything bigger and more impersonal," 52% for tending "to over-produce products, and this is wasteful" (Harris, 1978).

As the postwar cohorts now entered into adulthood, they were bringing about a perceptible shift in what Americans seemed to want out of life. Material possessions, economic security, and social mobility remained important, but new motives and concerns made these older aspirations less powerful and more ambiguous than they used to be. In a famous Harris poll taken in April 1979, the public was asked to choose among competing societal goals. By 53 to 40% a majority would reject putting more emphasis on "satisfying our needs for goods and services," and would give instead a higher priority to "learning how to get our pleasures out of non-material 'things'." By 55% they would choose an emphasis on "learning to appreciate human values more than material values" rather than on "finding ways to create more jobs for producing more goods." An impressive 72% would opt for "breaking up big things and getting back to more humanized living" instead of "developing bigger and more efficient ways of doing things" (Harris, 1979).

THE RISE OF ENVIRONMENTALISM

It was in their continuing commitment to environmental protection, in spite of economic stagnation and energy shortages, that the public's new-found transmaterialist concerns were most clearly manifested. The spread of ecological consciousness during the 1970s, with its emphasis on the earth's finite resources and the delicate balance of its biosphere, was among the most rapid and pervasive in the history of novel ideas. Concern for the environment, contrary to the expectations of many in business and industry circles, retained a firm position among the enduring commitments of the American public (Mitchell, 1979).

In early May 1981, 86% of Americans expressed opposition to any weakening of air pollution standards. By 93% they were almost unanimous in opposing any diminution of environmental rules governing water pollution. Pluralities of 40 and 48%, respectively, held that current standards were still not protective enough of the people's health; and 52% of the nationwide sample thought that Congress should make the Clean Water Act stricter (Harris, 1981). Even after 19 additional months of spreading recession, by December 1982 the majority calling for stricter controls had grown to 60% (Harris, 1982).

In a March 1982 survey of adults residing in metropolitan Houston, arguably one of the nations's most business-oriented cities, concern for environmental protection was found to be strikingly unambiguous (Klineberg, 1982b). When asked about federal programs, 46% asserted that the government is spending too little on "improving and protecting our environment," whereas only 6% believed that too much is being spent in that effort. Fully 63% agreed with the seemingly extreme position that "protecting the environment is so important that continuing improvements must be made, regardless of cost." By 60 to 33%, they rejected the assertion that "today's requirements for pollution control cost more than they are worth." The tendency of younger adults to lead the way in expressing environmental concern was also clear in the data. Among the respondents aged 18 to 44 (the postwar cohorts), 71% endorsed the first statement and 67% rejected the second; whereas among those aged 45 to 78, the comparable figures were down to 52 and 58%, respectively. Fifty-six percent of the younger respondents, but only 33% of those in older cohorts, believed that the government was not spending enough on protecting the environment.

In a review of all available studies exploring the public's concern with environmental quality, Van Liere and Dunlap (1980) also reported that age was a remarkably consistent and significant correlate. Almost regardless of the way the level of concern with environmental problems was measured, and no matter where in the nation the population was sampled, the polls in the 1970s provided evidence of a generational shift in environmental concern that paralleled the broader picture Inglehart (1977) painted for Western publics in general. More recent cohorts, reared in affluence and peace, and exposed in their formative years to mounting evidence of environmental deterioration, have become the nation's first ecology-minded generation. When older cohorts confronted that same evidence, they may well have assimilated it into their more extensive experience with putative obstacles to economic growth that proved to be readily overcome throughout the post-war period. They may be less likely therefore to regard these newer problems as signaling the need for major change in the established processes of societal adaptation. Many other factors obviously play a role as well in shaping such responses, but it is not surprising to find that cohort effects loom large in this connection.

Such effects are likely to be present whenever emotion-laden social mores are undergoing rapid change. In 1960, some 70% of all American families consisted of the stay-at-home wife and the bread-winner husband. By 1980, with the accelerating trek of married women into the work force and the rise of singles and single-parent households, that traditional pattern was true of only 12% of all families. The tendency to reject or to embrace such changes will be profoundly and lastingly affected by the observer's position in the life cycle, as it affects his own experienced or anticipated family style. When the respondents in the Houston survey were asked to react to the statement, "It is much more important for a wife to help her husband's career than to have one herself," 52% of the adults aged 45 and older agreed, whereas 74% of the younger respondents disagreed.

In sum, the events of the 1970s do appear to have generated cohort as well as period effects within the American population entering the 1980s. It is often difficult to distinguish among these interdependent processes, and much remains to be disentangled through further exploration and analysis. The research reviewed offers suggestive evidence that a generational shift may be occurring in central aspects of the culture of industrialism. If so, cohort succession is certain to have profound effects upon the future course of American society.

REFERENCES

Bengtson, V. L., & Cutler, N. E. (1976). Generations and intergenerational relations: Perspectives on age groups and social change. In R. H. Binstock & E. Shanas (Eds.), *Handbook of aging and the social sciences* (pp. 130–159). New York: Van Nostrand-Reinhold.

Berger, P., Berger, B., & Kellner, H. (1973). *The homeless mind: Modernization and consciousness.* New York: Random House.

Cotgrove, S. (1982). *Catastrophe or cornucopia: The environment, politics, and the future.* New York: Wiley.

Dalton, R. J. (1977). Was there a revolution? A note on generational versus life cycle explanations of value differences. *Comparative Political Studies, 9,* 459–473.

Elder, G. H., Jr. (1975). Age differentiation and the life course. In A. Inkeles, J. Coleman, & N.

Smelser (Eds.), *Annual review of sociology* (Vol. 1, pp. 165–190). Palo Alto: Annual Reviews Press.

Harman, W. W. (1979). *An incomplete guide to the future.* New York: Norton.

Harris, L. (1978, February 27). Scientific research and technology. *The Harris Survey.*

Harris, L. (1979, May 17). Experiences important to Americans indicate U.S. in post-industrial, non-materialistic era. *ABC News—Harris Survey,* I, No. 60.

Harris, L. (1980, December 8). Americans disenchanted with government. *ABC News—Harris Survey,* II, No. 153.

Harris, L. (1981, June 11). Substantial majorities indicate support for clean air and clean water acts. *The Harris Survey,* No. 47.

Harris, L. (1982, December 16). Americans want strict standards on water pollution. *The Harris Survey,* No. 101.

Harris Survey. (1979). *73 percent of Americans feel energy crisis presents clear and present danger to U.S.* (The Houston Post, 17 August).

Harris Survey (1982). *Americans have little confidence in leaders.* (The Houston Post, 27 November).

Holton, G., & Morison, R. S. (Eds.). (1979). *Limits of scientific inquiry.* New York: Norton.

Inglehart, R. (1977). *The silent revolution: Changing values and political styles among western publics.* Princeton: Princeton University Press.

Jones, L. Y. (1980). *Great expectations: America and the baby boom generation.* New York: Ballantine.

Klineberg, S. L. (1974). Parents, schools, and modernity: An exploratory investigation of sex differences in the attitudinal development of Tunisian adolescents. *International Journal of Comparative Sociology, 14,* 221–224.

Klineberg, S. L. (1976). Intergenerational change: Some psychological consequences of modernization. In R. A. Stone & J. Simmons (Eds.), *Change in Tunisia: Studies in the social sciences* (pp. 289–310). Albany: State University of New York Press.

Klineberg, S. L. (1982a). The near-term outlook for space solar power: Societal trends and technological options in the 1980s. *Space Solar Power Review, 3,* 151–165.

Klineberg, S. L. (1982b, November). The Houston Area Survey—1982. Rice Institute for Policy Analysis. *Action briefs,* No. 2.

Kumar, K. (1978). *Prophecy and progress: The sociology of industrial and post-industrial society.* New York: Penguin.

Magney, J. (1979, May/June). Mountains, molehills, and media hypes: The curious case of the new conservatism. *Working Papers,* pp. 281–285.

Marshall, E. (1979). Public attitudes to technological progress. *Science, 205,* 281–285.

Mead, M. (1970). *Culture and commitment.* Garden City: Doubleday.

Micaud, C. A. (1964). Social and economic change. In C. A. Micaud, L. C. Brown, & C. H. Moore (Eds.), *Tunisia: The politics of modernization* (pp. 131–190). New York: Praeger.

Mitchell, R. C. (1979). Silent spring/solid majorities. *Public Opinion, 55,* 16–20.

Pirages, D. C., & Ehrlich, P. R. (1974). *Ark II: Social responses to environmental imperatives.* San Francisco: Freeman.

Riley, M. W. (1978). Aging, social change and the power of ideas. *Daedalus, 107,* (n4), 39–52.

Rosa, E. (1978). The public and the energy problem. *Bulletin of the Atomic Scientists,* pp. 5–7.

Ryder, N. B. (1965). The cohort as a concept in the study of social change. *American Sociological Review, 30,* 843–861.

Schneider, W. (1979). Why most Americans say the energy crisis is not real. *Politics Today,* pp. 12–14.

Stobaugh, R. T., & Yergin, D. (1980). Energy: An emergency telescoped. *Foreign Affairs, 58,* 563–595.

Van Liere, K. D., & Dunlap, R. E. (1980). The social bases of environmental concern: A review of hypotheses, explanations and empirical evidence. *Public Opinion Quarterly, 44,* 181–197.

Yankelovich, D., & Lefkowitz, B. (1980a). National growth: The question of the 80's. *Public Opinion,* pp. 44–57.

Yankelovich, D., & Lefkowitz, B. (1980b). The new American dream: The U. S. in the 1980s. *The Futurist,* pp. 3–15.

CHAPTER 7

Love, War, and the Life Cycle of the Family

NANCY DATAN
AARON ANTONOVSKY
BENJAMIN MAOZ

. . . there was a war; this war, the last war, any war, it does not matter which war . . . It is strange that their first Latin declension and conjugation should be of love and war."

RUMER GODDEN, *The River*, 1959, p. 4.

INTRODUCTION

The lives of women described in this chapter have been shaped by love and war, as our own lives have been, of course. But the perspective of the individual life-span developmental psychologist is not sufficiently broad nor sufficiently distant to encompass personal experience within the historical context; the historian, like the pathologist, often achieves distance through the study of the dead. In this chapter, we travel across the Atlantic Ocean and the Mediterranean Sea for a glimpse into the histories of middle-aged women from Austria, Hungary, Czechoslovakia, Germany, Turkey, Persia, Morocco, Tunisia, Algeria, and Palestine, in order to see how the family, that most sensitive barometer of social change, is shaped by the social context; how middle age is shaped by youth; and how both are shaped by history.

LIFE-SPAN DEVELOPMENTAL PSYCHOLOGY
HISTORICAL AND GENERATIONAL EFFECTS

143

Copyright © 1984 by Academic Press, Inc.
All rights of reproduction in any form reserved.
ISBN 0-12-482420-X

From the very beginning of Datan's association with the Life-Span Developmental Psychology conferences at West Virginia University, she has tried to muddy the waters of the crystalline cross-sequential methodology with a serious consideration of the influence of history on human development. In 1973, Neugarten and Datan proposed three dimensions of time: *life time,* approximated by chronological age; *social time,* the age-grade system of a society, which governs the age-related expression of biological potential; and *historical time,* which shapes the social system and with it the age-grading of life time. In 1975 Datan resorted to irony and commented that some life-span developmental models seem to emerge by subtraction: that is, some theorists appear to believe that if change over time can be shown to result from historical change or a concomitant social change, it may be eliminated from a developmental model. This notion was first put to the empirical test by the King of Prussia, who reared two infants in isolation to see whether their first spoken language would be Hebrew or Greek. Deprived of a context, the infants perished.

In 1975 Datan suggested a dialectical tension in the human condition between the biological bounds of the individual life cycle and the effort of the individual to transcend them. Those who attended that conference may recall that Datan's remarks were made in response to Riegel's dialectical model of time. We now award him the last word on that debate, for he has forced us to go backward in time in order to reach the present point of departure (Datan, 1975; Neugarten and Datan, 1973; Riegel, 1977).

In this chapter we show the interaction between life time, social time, and historical time as these are reflected in the family life cycle of middle-aged women from Central Europe, Turkey, Persia, and North Africa, who are all Jewish immigrants to Israel; and native-born Moslem Arab women. The research of which I speak was designed to explore the effects of modernization on the transition to middle age, and the subcultures we chose to study represent a quasi continuum from tradition to modernity. All the women in our study were born between the years 1915–1924. This decade brought the First World War to Europe and the beginnings of Ataturk's reforms to Turkey, reforms that would ripple through Persia; the Balfour declaration, encouraging Jewish settlement in Palestine; and the second wave of Jewish immigration, from which would come the founders of the State of Israel. Thus the European women in our study were born between one world war and the next; the Turkish women were born at the start of a process of modernization that would make their generation different from their mothers; the Persian women were born into an ebb and flow of revolution and reaction, which has continued to the present day; the North African women were born into a period which would climax in the years 1952 and 1953 with a rise of anti-Semitism and the expulsion of Jews; and the Moslem Arab village women would see change come slowly to their villages, heralded by nationalized health services for themselves and compulsory public education for their daughters. We are accustomed to seeing history mirrored in the lives of men; this chapter will show how the rhythms of war and social change are refelcted in the lives of women and in the family life cycle.

The research reported here was carried out in the years 1967–1970 in Israel. It was born in response to a modest question: Why was hospitalization for involutional psychosis, a psychiatric diagnostic category of questionable usefulness, referring to unipolar depression appearing for the first time in middle age, almost never seen among traditional women from Near Eastern cultures? The question expanded to a hypothesis advanced by Antonovsky and Maoz that the transitions of middle age were more stressful on modern women from youth-oriented Western cultures in which advancing age means only declining status; whereas, traditional women, who might expect to rise to the status of matriarch in the middle years, would find middle age a blessing.

Datan joined this study as it was commencing and brought a hypothesis favoring the modern woman, arguing that modernity provided a choice of roles inside and outside the home, together with resources gained from earlier transitions; and that the traditional women, whose claim to identity was the bearing of sons, would lose what claim they had with the loss of fertility at menopause.

As it turns out, each was half right: Datan was correct in supposing that the modern European woman would cope successfully with the transitions of middle age; and Antonovsky and Maoz were correct in seeing the strengths of the traditional family. It was the transitional women—the women of Turkey, Persia, and North Africa; daughters of traditional cultures; immigrants to modern Israel—for whom the transitions of middle age compounded the transitions of history and migration and for whom these transitions proved most stressful.

But in the long run we are all in transition; each of us reaches adulthood with what we have learned in childhood and adolescence—earlier years for us and for our cultures. The dilemma of the transitional women of our study highlights the dilemma of the life cycle, and it is not surprising that we had to turn to the histories of the five cultures to understand the responses of five historically distinct cohorts of women born in the same decade. In the five historical sketches that follow, we show how the middle years of women and the family life cycle are shaped by the generations that have come before them.

THE CENTRAL EUROPEANS

The history of the Jews of Europe is a history of periods of exile and persecution alternating with periods of peace and prosperity. The plague that devastated Europe in the fourteenth century left in its wake ghettos walling off Jews from their neighbors—yet one more instance in which the dietary practices and ritual baths of Orthodox Judaism, which may have saved a few lives from disease, left the survivors to face accusations of witchcraft. The ghetto walls or their legal equivalents spread across Europe, dividing Jew from non-Jew until the French revolution. In 1791 the Jews of France were voted free and equal citizens; the Austrian constitution granted Jews equal civil rights in 1849, only to rescind equality 2 years later. The Prussian constitution of 1850 decreed a separation of civil and political rights from religious creed, although religious discrimination did not vanish in practice. In 1871, 80 years after the French emancipation, the empire of Bismark proclaimed full emancipation for its Jews in the German Imperial Constitution.

In 1915, the start or the decade in which the women of our study were born, the Jewish communities of the Austro-Hungarian empire were emancipated and their freedom formally guaranteed. In Hungary, a Jewish population of almost 1 million believed itself legally secure; its prominence in cultural and professional life was equal to any Jewish community in the world. Most of the 175,000 Jews of Austria were part of the advance of the arts and sciences in Vienna. The 360,000 Jews of Czechoslovakia included prominent artists and writers. Although Germany of 1914 was not free of anti-Semitism, its 500,000 Jews were part of the German scholarly communities in literature, science, and philosophy. Thus, though the restrictions of earlier centuries had not entirely disappeared, the Jews of Central Europe had reached a position of distinction in European culture by the start of the twentieth century. But in 1915, just as the first of the women of our study were born, all this was about to change.

The emancipation of the Jews of Central Europe in the nineteenth century was paralleled by an increased emancipation of women and an increase in their participation in cultural life—social changes that foreshadow some of the more recent changes in women's lives, including urbanization and its attendant economic equality for women, beginning with efforts promoting the health and welfare of mothers and children. In 1841 the German Jew Morgenstern began her work in child welfare; by 1896, the International Women's Congress met in Berlin. The women of the Austrian Jewish community came to dominate as hostesses in the growing salon society, bridging the gap between the bourgeoisie and the nobility. Austrian women were also active in a wide range of professions, as doctors, lawyers, delegates to parliament, teachers, writers, and artists.

The third move toward emancipation and assimilation represented, in some ways, an intersection between the emancipation of women and the emancipation of the Jews of Central Europe. This was a movement to reform Jewish religious ritual—much of it discriminatory against women—which began in Germany. The Reform movement in Judaism reflected, on the one hand, the spirit of the Enlightenment which encouraged the discarding of all religious practices not supported by reason or the modern social context; on the other hand, the desire of the German Jews to affirm their responsibilities as German citizens by eliminating such conflicting elements in Judaism as the loyalty to Zion and the Hebrew liturgy. Thus a major transformation in religion, comparable to social and cultural emancipation, took place in Central European Judaism.

The Jews of Central Europe, the most completely emancipated in the world, also represented the community of women who were at the forefront of emancipation. Although a high proportion of Jewish women was active in this movement, no specifically Jewish movement existed until the beginning of the twentieth century, with the reappearance of anti-Semitism. This community, the most thoroughly emancipated and acculturated community of Jews, was the first to be attacked by the Nazis.

In 1935 the Nuremberg Laws were enacted in Germany, prompting many European Jews to immigrate to Israel, among them families whose daughters would be among the subjects of our study. Austria fell in a bloodless coup in March 1938; in September the Sudetenland was ceded to Germany; in March 1939, the remainder of Czechoslovakia was invaded. The community of 55,000 Jews in Palestine at the end of World War I grew 10-fold with successive waves of immigration from Europe, reaching 550,000 in 1939 on the eve of World War II. By this time, one-half of the women of our study had reached Israel.

Mass extermination of the Jews of the Greater Reich was carried out in 1943: 18,000 German Jews, 60,000 Austrian Jews, and 243,000 Czech Jews died; in 1944, 100,000 Hungarian Jews died. At the same time, the British Mandate Government Palestine enforced a virtual blockade against Jewish immigration to Palestine, as set out in the White Paper of 1939. Thus from the time of the White Paper, throughout the years of World War II until the establishment of the State of Israel in 1948, Jews reached Israel only by complex escape routes through Europe and illegal immigration ships making secret night landings on the coast of Israel. As we shall show, the shadows of European history interact with the developmental rhythms of the life cycle for the women of Central Europe.

The typical Central European woman in our study, born during the collapse of the German and Austro-Hungarian empires, is representative of the middle-class modern woman of her generation. Most of the Central European women were educated in the countries of their birth, at least to the level of some secondary education, and did not migrate to Israel until young adulthood. Three-fifths of the women in our study escaped Europe before World War II; the remainder came as survivors of the war, often of the concentration camps, shortly afterward.

Adolescence ended for the Central European women, as war spread across Europe. For most, the choice of immigration and thus the nature of survival were in their parents' hands: Those whose parents were unable to leave Europe were often left without family at the end of the war. Thus the task of young adulthood, the establishment of a new family, was for many of the Central European women the creation of a second family after the loss of the first.

The political safety offered by the State of Israel did not represent physical safety and certainly not physical comforts. The early years of the State of Israel were years of economic austerity—a ration of a single egg to a family each week. Under these circumstances the families of the Central European women were small, typically consisting of one or two children born in a relatively brief period of childbearing some time after marriage. Thus, in their 40s and 50s, the Central European women of our study are still likely to have teenage children at home. What is more, they look back with regret on the children they did not bear, though they do not regret at all the loss of fertility which comes with menopause; it is the grown children who might be with them today, not the babies they might bear and have to tend, that they regret not having. As one woman put it, looking back on the economic austerity of the period of early statehood, "The government of Israel cheated me out of my third child." As we shall see, however, although the period of economic austerity coincided with young adulthood for all the women in our study, it was the filter of cultural values and education that translated economic privation into small families—a common response among the modern women; among transitional and traditional women, a very different response was seen.

THE TURKS

Turkey, geographically divided between Europe and Asia, is perhaps symbolic of the transitional Turkish women in our study. Steps toward emancipation and reform, including separation of religious and secular law,

representative government, mass education, and the unveiling of women—
with the attendant connotation of liberation from the confines of the traditional female role—were initiated by Ataturk when he came to power in
1924, at the close of the decade in which the women of our study were born.
Thus, the modernization of women's lives taking place a century ago in
Europe occurred in the lifetimes of the Turkish women in our study. They
may be considered transitional in two ways: both as participants in a transitional period in Turkish history and as immigrants from a modernizing
society into a modern society.

The minority Jewish and Christian communities of Turkey were well
advanced over the Moslem majority in regard to the education of children;
this was a paradoxical consequence of the opposition of the Ottoman government to mass literacy, which over the centuries had produced a disparity
in education between Moslem and non-Moslem still apparent today. The
Jewish communities of Turkey were well organized in the early part of the
century, and the Alliance Universelle Israelite established a broad network
of schools, making education the rule rather than the exception. As a consequence, the Jewish women of Turkey were advantaged over their non-
Jewish peers, in contrast to the Persian women, who met double discrimination, both as women and as Jews. The advantage of the Jewish women of
Turkey can be seen in their relatively high literacy rate: two-thirds of the
Turkish women in our study are literate, although Lerner reported in 1958
that only 14% of the women of Turkey were literate (see Table 1 for a
comparison by ethnic group of selected demographic characteristics).

During the early childhood of the women in our study, significant steps
were taken to advance the status of women in Turkey, which is quite advanced by Middle Eastern standards. In 1926 polygamy was made illegal,
and women gained equal rights in divorce; in 1933 women were granted
political rights. Unveiling was accomplished by persuasion and example
rather than by decree, and the veil in Turkey gradually disappeared. This
successful transition is highlighted by comparison with neighboring countries: Persian and Afghanistan leaders, impressed by the pace of social
change in Turkey under Ataturk, returned home and decreed the unveiling
of women. In both cases, opposing conservative forces reinstated the veil,
which persisted until more basic educational and social reforms created an
atmosphere in which unveiling could be accepted—unstable reforms that
have yielded once more to revolution and reaction under Khomeini.

The near-equal standing of the Jewish community in Turkey ended
abruptly in 1942 with the imposition of the *varlik*, a capital levy on property and profit that was arbitrarily fixed. Although the tax was abolished after
only a year, property and funds were never returned, and the Jewish community suffered heavy losses. No official anti-Jewish actions were taken

TABLE 1

Selected Social Characteristics by Ethnic Group (percentages)[a]

	Ethnic group				
Item	Central Europeans	Turks	Persians	North Africans	Arabs
N =	(287)	(176)	(160)	(239)	(286)
Illiterate	0	29	61	60	96
Married before age 16	0	5	35	37	30
Married at age 21 or older	78	51	15	20	22
Husband selected by family	7	46	75	56	95
Conflict with family over choice of spouse	17	23	42	28	16
Seven or more pregnancies[b]	8	19	64	67	79
One-half or fewer of pregnancies brought to live birth[b]	47	17	6	4	4
Seven or more live births[b]	0	5	53	59	72
No children dead after birth[b]	92	77	52	42	22
Five or more living children	0	14	68	68	76
Five or more children currently living at home	0	3	29	36	53
Children now under age 14	16	30	47	57	56
Total childbearing span less than 7 years	70	35	13	20	10
Satisfied with number of children borne	28	47	39	48	59
Wishing to have borne more children	68	38	35	42	19
Wishing to have borne fewer children	3	16	26	10	22
Grandchildren	32	62	79	76	78
Working outside the home (full or part time, including family business or agriculture)	42	21	29	25	35
Feels "needed" by extended family member	46	60	62	51	17
Husband illiterate	0	25	49	53	66
Husband nonmanual worker	77	36	16	22	12
Currently religiously orthodox	21	30	57	85	98
Currently believe family should choose spouse	1	12	21	19	52

[a]Taken from N. Datan, A. Antonovsky, & B. Maoz (1981). *A Time to Reap: The Middle Age of Women in Five Israeli Subcultures* (p. 18). Baltimore: The Johns Hopkins University Press.

[b]Percentage based on medical sub-samples.

subsequent to the *varlik*, but latent anti-Jewish feelings erupted from time to time. With the establishment of the State of Israel, close to one-half of the Jewish community emigrated from Turkey. The taxes required for permission to emigrate left many without financial resources; prohibitions against Jewish landowning had kept them from learning agricultural skills. Those who came to Israel settled, for the most part, in lower-income neighborhoods of urban communities, like those in which the women of our study live.

Thus the Turkish women of our study were born into a period of cultural transition that would see women slowly emerging from the subordinate status symbolized by polygyny and the veil. In their lifetimes they would experience a second transition: migration from a modernizing culture to a modern culture. The process and the price of these transitions is expressed in the life of the typical Turkish woman in our study, who is transitional in two ways. First, when there is a single response typical of this group, it is intermediate between modernity and tradition. Second, this is a group with greater internal variation than groups at the modern and traditional extremes; thus a measure of central tendency conceals those among the Turkish women who are more modern than most, as well as those who are still fairly traditional. In the description that follows, these qualifications should be borne in mind.

Although literacy is high among the Turkish women, both by comparison to the non-Jewish Turks and the more traditional women in this study, 29% of the Turkish women are illiterate—a striking comparison to the Central European women, a culture in which illiteracy is unknown and probably unthinkable. Born into the period of Ataturk's reforms and a program of social changes that would be particularly important for the lives of women, the Turkish women had the chance but not the guarantee of a new life.

Some changes toward modernization can be seen in the family life cycle of the Turkish women. Most were married in Turkey, rarely before the age of 18 years. Nevertheless, some traditions lingered: Close to one-half the women in our study were married to husbands chosen by their families, and not all accepted the family's choice willingly. For most, migration to Israel came in late adolescence or young adulthood: almost one-quarter reached Palestine before the start of World War II, and another one-quarter managed to immigrate during the years of the war despite the British White Paper restricting Jewish immigration. Within the first years after the establishment of the State of Israel, another two-fifths of the Turkish women reached Israel. Thus, like the Europeans, the Turks are *vatikim*, veterans of long standing in Israel whose transition to adulthood was made in the same years as geographical migration to a new country and culture.

The Turkish women's families are just a little larger than the European families: Most have between two and four children. Childbearing reflects this group's transition toward modernity. For some, the quickening of the family life cycle which is characteristic of modernity and normative among the Europeans can be seen. It was more often the case that the childbearing period lasted a decade or more; thus, in middle age, almost three-quarters of the Turkish women have married children, most of them with grand-children, while a few still have children under the age of six at home. This shift becomes successively more pronounced with increased tradition.

THE PERSIANS

The history of the Jews of Persia began in the sixth century B.C., during the reign of Cyrus. This community, part of the ancient Babylonian Jewish community, was a center of creativity from which the Talmud sprang. However, the early history of the Persian Jews, in which creativity and prosperity were rarely interrupted by persecution, came to an end with the rise of Islam. The Shiite Moslem clergy instigated persecutions that con-tinued from the sixteenth century until the revolution in 1920 and have resumed once more under the rule of Khomeini. For centuries, Persian Jews were forced to choose between conversion to Islam and payment of costly ransoms; both alternatives progressively impoverished the Jewish commu-nities. In 1920, during the decade in which the women of our study were born, the Jews of Persia were granted equality under the law. But this had very little effect on ancient customs and traditions of ostracism; indeed, discrimination against Jews by the Moslem majority increased with the rise of nationalism.

In the first part of the twentieth century, urbanization and indus-trialization—the very forces that had led to a movement for the emancipa-tion of European women—further exacerbated the low economic status of the Persion Jews, crowded out of their marginal niches as peddlers and small tradesmen. At the same time, anti-Semitism increased in the rural villages, causing Jews who had traditionally lived as shepherds to immigrate to the large cities, and adding to the squalor and overcrowding of the ghettos and to the number of beggars who lined the streets.

Within the city ghettos the Jews lived in primitive, insanitary housing, often corwded 10 or 15 to a room. Eye and skin diseases were endemic and malnutrition more common than not. Most of the ghetto inhabitants were sickly and short-lived, earning an inadequate living or none at all. The illiteracy, poverty, and disease which characterized the lives of the Persian poor showed their cumulative effects in the lives of women and children. The rate of illiteracy was higher among women, and their health hazards were multiplied by early marriage and frequent pregnancies, and the endless work both in the home and out of it. Women very often worked outside the home as maids and laundresses, and their husbands were beggars. Yet the status of women was inferior to that of men, and a woman, though she might work to support the family, was under the absolute authority of her husband. The standard of education was low and the educational system disorganized, with the result that girls seldom went to school at all—allowing little hope that they might improve their lives.

The traditional segregation and seclusion of the Persian women was symbolized by the veil. In 1935, during the adolescence of the women of our study, Riza Shah, attracted by Ataturk's program of social reform in neighboring Turkey, decreed the compulsory unveiling of women. However, lacking the necessary support of an underlying client of social change, this decree ended with his abdication in 1941, when conservative opinion reasserted itself and large proportions of women returned without protest to the veil. The practice of veiling and the accompanying social restrictions on women were most often found among the poor. Unlike the Jews of Turkey, the Persian Jews had no strong community organization, and the women suffered from the inferior status of women, compounded by the inferior status of the Jew.

The establishment of the State of Israel opened up a period of mass migration from Persia. An estimated 35,000 of a total of 90,000 Jews migrated to Israel between 1948 and 1955. Lacking both agricultural and white-collar skills, the Persian Jews were only slowly absorbed into the lower and lower-middle classes of the urban Israeli population. In Tel Aviv, as they had been in Persia, the Persians are neighbors of the Turks; but the Persian Jews have failed, both as a nation and as a religious community, to make the strides toward modernization that were achieved by the Turkish Jews.

The price of this failure seems to be greatest for the Persian women. The years of birth of the women in our study cluster around 1919, shortly before Riza Pahlavi came to power. However, there is little evidence that this revolutionary leader's efforts toward modernization had much impact on the lives of these women. Almost three-quarters of the Persian women had less than 4 years of schooling; most are illiterate. Marriage came early; one-fifth of the women in our study were married before age 14 and another two-fifths by age 17. Three-quarters of the Persian women were married to husbands chosen by their families, and of these almost one-half report retrospectively that they did not accept their family's choice willingly. Most of the husbands are older than their wives by 6 years or more. Childbearing started early and continued for many years—a span of 13 years or more for over half of the Persian women. Thus, nearly half the women still have children at home aged 13 or younger—indeed, 10% of these middle-aged women have children aged 5 or younger, and 9% have as many as 7 or more children still living at home. On the other hand, 85% of the Persians have married children, and almost all of these have grandchildren.

Thus, the demographic characteristics of the Persian women are those of traditional women. The Persians, however, are traditional women who immigrated to a modern society quite some time ago. One-quarter of the Persian women came to Palestine before the founding of the State of Israel; one-half came just a few years thereafter. Most immigrated as adults between the ages of 25 and 40.

Like the Turks, the Persian women are in transition, but they have farther to go. The transitional women, born in countries where the transformation from folkways to modernity was taking place fairly rapidly, were then transplanted to a country where modernization was complete and where their relatively traditional lifestyles were outmoded. The undercurrent of discontent running through the responses of the Persian women, whose self-reported psychological well being is the lowest of our five ethnic groups, may reflect the fact that the transition they made was the greatest, bringing with it the stress of meeting the demands of a modern environment with traditional responses. Perhaps the Persians have lost the benefits of traditional folkways while not yet deriving any of the benefits of modernity.

THE NORTH AFRICANS

The Jewish settlements in North Africa data back to antiquity and are believed to have begun with Jews who came to North Africa together with Phoenician colonizers, to be joined later by exiles from Palestine after the destruction of the Second Temple in A.D. 70. The Jews of North Africa were the first to return to settle in *Eretz Yisrael* after the destruction of the Second Temple; since that time, there have been successive small waves of migration from North Africa to Israel, particularly during periods of persecution.

With the Moslem conquest of North Africa, old Jewish communities revived and new communities were born. Jews expelled from Spain during the Spanish Inquisition found refuge in North Africa. During the years in which Moslem culture flourished, Jewish culture and intellectual life flourished too; however, with the decline of Moslem culture, the aristocratic Jewish communities sank into squalor. The Moslem decline was further compounded for the Jews by Moslem persecution. The spiritual climate that had once produced scholars and sages dwindled to insignificance in the centuries of persecution, and most of the Jews of North Africa sank into illiteracy.

Until the beginning of the twentieth century, the North African Jews were subjected to conditions of severe oppression and discrimination, amounting almost to slavery. They were employed at compulsory labor and subjected to humiliating regulations, forced to wear distinctive black clothing and skullcaps, and upon leaving the walled Jewish quarter, made to remove their shoes. The gates of the Jewish quarter were locked at night. Within its walls, overcrowding and unsanitary conditions prevailed.

In 1912, shortly before the first of the women of this study were born, the establishment of the French Protectorate in North Africa introduced a number of changes, making it possible for Jews to leave the walled Jewish quarter and take up trained professions and positions in civil service. However, at the same time that mobility into the professional classes were growing, migration from the small primitive villages of the interior brought a stream of unskilled Jews to the cities, who settled in the Jewish quarter. Thus two strata of North African Jewry were created: an upper, modernizing stratum that came under the influence of the French and lost contact with the Jewish quarter, and a lower stratum that remained within the confines of its walls and its traditions.

When the women of our study were born, education was the prerogative of boys and generally consisted of no more than a few years of religious schooling. The position of women was clearly subordinate to men; bigamy, common in the past, had decreased only recently. Village women had no employment outside the home and indeed were forbidden to leave it; in the cities, women's work was rare, except for a few seamstresses, governesses, and prostitutes. This situation was to improve steadily through the efforts of the international Jewish community. The Alliance Universelle Israelite, which had brought literacy to the Turkish women, established schools in North Africa as well; the Organization for Rehabilitation and Training created trade schools. During the childhood of the women of this study, major strides toward universal education were made, but few of our subjects profited in any way from these changes: 60% of these women are illiterate.

A woman's life was one of ritual and tradition throughout: from the attempts before her birth to ward off the Evil Eye and ensure the birth of a son to the ritual purification of the menstrual cycle and childbirth. This very traditional woman was, during the generation of women in our study, to be replaced by a woman increasingly exposed to education and Western culture. It was not, however, the modern women who immigrated to Israel. A mass exodus of Jews from North Africa followed the establishment of the

State of Israel and the accompanying rise in Arab nationalism. The upper stratum of North African Jewry migrated to France; those with nowhere else to go and little or nothing to bring with them came to Israel. The women of our study settled in two towns abandoned by Arabs in 1948 in the foothills of the Judean Mountains, and isolated in an agrarian setting. The pace of modernization is slower here than in the cosmopolitan cities of Israel, and affluence, for the North Africans, is not next door but rather an intercity bus ride away.

The North African women married young; almost one-fifth were married before the age of 14, and another fifth married by age 16. Most married men chosen by their families and approved the choices; those who chose their husbands had their families' blessings. Education, if any, marriage, and childbearing all preceded immigration to Israel; virtually all the North African women in our study came to Israel after the founding of the state. This, then, is a population of new immigrants whose traditional lifestyles were shaped before their migration to a modern state.

More than half the North African women had a childbearing span of greater than 13 years. Some (17%) have as many as seven or more children now living at home; most (57%) have children 13 or younger, some (9%) aged 5 or younger. Nearly all (84%) have married children; of these, most now have children of their own. Despite a family life cycle much like that of the Persian women, the North African women do not express the deep discontent of the Persians. While more than one-fourth of the Persian women looked back on childbearing and wished they had borne fewer children, the North Africans look upon their large families as blessings and often wish they had even more children. Their tranquility may be in part a product of the more gentle transition from a modernizing country to modernizing towns. But it is also possible to speculate that the rhythm of revolution and reaction in the social history of Persia, more often than not a revolution in women's rights followed by reactionary repression, left its scars upon the Persian women, who face a modernizing world without the resources of modernity or the blessings of the traditional family life cycle. Tradition brings its own contentment to the North Africans, and, as we shall see, to the Moslem Arabs, whose lives were not interrupted by the trauma of migration.

THE MOSLEM ARABS

Raphael Patai has suggested that the Moslem Arab villages represent the survival into the twentieth century of a life not far removed from Biblical tribal life. Most villagers can say that their families lived in the same village (or a neighboring community) for as long as can be remembered; both marital and political alliances are made on the basis of traditional kin groupings. One consequence of the stability of village life is the persistence of the traditional subordinate status of women in the male-oriented village.

Despite continuity with the past, the 50 years since the end of the Ottoman Empire have brought changes to the Arab village. While one may still see horse-drawn wooden plows, it is becoming more common to see the technology of modern farming; the marketing of produce links the villagers to the cities. Like the immigrant Jewish women in our study, the Moslem Arab women's lives have been changed by the political tides of war. The establishment of the State of Israel left the Arabs a minority, isolated by cease-fire lines from the rest of the Arab world. Families were dispersed in the war of 1948, and while there was some reunion after the Six-Day War of 1967 with relatives on the West Bank, the Golan and Gaza, reunion was not complete.

Introduction of public health care by Jewish settlers brought a dramatic drop in maternal and infant mortality; this, together with the persistence of traditional values favoring large families, makes the birth rate among Israeli Arabs one of the highest in the world. The consequent population growth and the growth in economic prosperity have led to increased numbers of nuclear family households, as opposed to the traditional patrilocal extended family households which in previous generations accommodated orphaned children as well as mothers bereaved at or after birth. Nevertheless, male–female relationships have remained more traditional than other aspects of village life: Women have the right to vote, to have accounts at banks; the home is slowly modernizing, and kitchen appliances are becoming more common though not yet universal. Yet the village Moslem Arabs are the most traditional of the various population sectors of Israel, and little change has occurred in the traditional patriarchal climate in the lifetimes of the women in our study.

The subordination of women begins at birth, when a daughter enters the world as a disappointment to her parents; sons are preferred, and a daughter's birth may not even be announced. Girls begin household duties at a very early age; until the establishment of the State of Israel and compulsory schooling for both sexes, only boys had the privilege of education, and the women of our study are almost entirely illiterate (96%), although their daughters reached 100% literacy in a single generation.

The Arab women in our study married somewhat later than the Persians or the North Africans, a consequence of a bride-price higher in Israel than in neighboring Arab countries. The median age at marriage was 17; almost all women married husbands chosen by their families, and very rarely opposed the choice. One third married husbands a decade or more older than themselves; by the time of our study, one fifth had been widowed.

Childbearing has taken up a major part of the Arab women's lives; four-fifths have been pregnant seven times or more, and close to three-fourths have borne seven or more live children. More than one-half the Arab women still have five or more children living at home, and over one-half still have children under the age of 13. Yet as a consequence of the long childbearing span, greater than 13 years for more than two-thirds of the Arab women, four-fifths also have grandchildren.

The Arab women continue to reaffirm traditional values, with a less shift toward modernity than any other group. Half still feel a family should choose the husband, and nearly all characterize themselves as devout keepers of religious tradition. Thus, while the land around them has changed dramatically in their lifetimes, within the villages change is taking place more slowly and without the discontinuity of migration.

THE LESSONS OF HISTORY

Those who do not remember their history, Vico has said, are condemned to repeat it. Ours was a somewhat different experience: We did not intend to learn history at all, but found that we had to go back into time and the specific birthplaces of the women in our study in order to understand the differences among women of a single birth cohort. Among the most dramatic lessons to be learned, we believe, is the near-invisibility of women in the histories of men. Yet women gained the most from Ataturk's reforms and suffered most from Riza Shah's attempts to bring reform to Persia. The gains and losses are easily summed up: With modernization, loss of life at birth can be prevented; large families are no longer needed to ensure survival of a population; increased education soon becomes a need; with increased education, birth rate drops, but the time given to the individual child is greater and so, we may say, life becomes more precious.

If women wrote history, that might be its lesson. But of these five cultures, the most modern are the Central Europeans; their family life cycle reflects the optimistic picture of modernity we have just presented, but their personal histories bear the scars of a war made possible only through the advances of modernity. It has been said that in a shooting war the arts perish first. We would argue that in a shooting war it is women's work that perishes: the labor of childbearing and the years of toil that bring a child into adulthood; the cheapening of lives that seems to go hand in hand with the confinement of women to the home and childbearing, a kind of species wisdom that recognizes that though life may not be held precious it nevertheless must be sustained.

The historical lessons we have suggested are a serendipitous by-product of our research: A survey of women in five such different cultures told us too much about their differences yet too little to explain them, and we were forced to turn to history to understand these women better. This chapter provided an occasion to sum up the five histories side by side with the family life cycles of the women in each of these cultures. This compressed overview has led us to a moral—not the neat methodological moral some might hope for, tying history to the social context and both to the life cycle, but the complex and humbling moral so often learned in the study of history, and so often forgotten. Each of the cultures whose history we have sketched has had its moment of glory, when scholarship was precious, peace prevailed, and, so far as we can see, in those untroubled times the lives of women were lived well. And each moment of glory has been eclipsed by war, nations have sunk into squalor, culture has perished, illiteracy and disease have flourished in the ruins. It has been said that the measure of a civilization is the status of its women: to that we would add the value of children, the care of the old; in short, the nurture of the life cycle. This historical review has shown that such nurture is more uncommon than a life-span developmental psychologist might want to suppose; and the loss of nurture is at the expense of the human condition.

REFERENCES

Datan, N. (1975). Normative life crises: Academic perspectives. In N. Datan & L. H. Ginsberg (Eds.), *Life-span developmental psychology: Normative life crises*. New York: Academic Press.

Datan, N. (1981). After the apple: Post-Newtonian metaphysical theory for jaded psychologists. In N. Datan & H. W. Reese (Eds.), *Life-span developmental psychology: Dialectical perspectives on experimental research*. New York: Academic Press.

Datan, N., Antonovsky, A., & Maoz, B. (1981). *A time to reap: The middle age of women in five Israeli sub-cultures*. Baltimore: The Johns Hopkins University Press.

Godden, R. (1959). *The River*. New York: Viking Press.

Neugarten, B. L., & Datan, N. (1973). Sociological perspectives on the life cycle. In P. B. Baltes & K. W. Schaie (Eds.), *Life-span developmental psychology: personality and socialization*. New York: Academic Press.

Patai, R. (1959). *Sex and family in the Bible and the Middle East*. New York: Doubleday.

Riegel, K. F. (1977). The dialectics of time. In N. Datan & H. W. Reese (Eds.), *Life-span developmental psychology: Dialectical perspectives on experimental research*. New York: Academic Press.

CHAPTER 8

Hardship in Lives:
Depression Influences from the 1930s
to Old Age in Postwar America*

GLEN H. ELDER, JR.
JEFFREY K. LIKER
BERNARD J. JAWORSKI

It is only when you have lived through experiences and digested them that you come to acquire enough sense to know how to deal with them.
BERKELEY WOMAN, 1900 GENERATION

INTRODUCTION

Hard times are frequently bad times in life experience, but they may also be developmental under certain conditions. People suffer and learn from the same events. Both themes appear in observations of the Great Depression. Upon their return to Middletown in the mid-1930s, Robert and Helen Lynd (1937) found that the "great knife of the depression had cut down impartially through the entire population, cleaving open the lives and hopes of rich as well as poor" (p. 295). Some residents were crushed by the

*This study is based on a program of research on social change in the family and life course. Support from the National Institute of Mental Health (Grant MH-34172), Glen H. Elder, Jr., principal investigator is gratefully acknowledged. We are indebted to the Institute of Human Development (University of California, Berkeley) for permission to use archival data from the Berkeley Guidance Study, and to Jonathan Plotkin and Susan Rose for assistance in the statistical analyses.

Copyright © 1984 by Academic Press, Inc.
All rights of reproduction in any form reserved.
ISBN 0-12-482420-X

event, whereas others found ways to manage. What were the enduring legacies of this economic disaster? At present, studies show only a modest relationship between economic events and health (Ferman & Gordus, 1979). The impact seems weaker than one might expect from popular accounts of economic downturns in people's lives. Why is the relationship not stronger?

Explanations have been sought in a more differentiated view of economic conditions, in greater understanding of resilience in coping and adaptation (Thomas, 1981), and in conditions that made resilience possible (Leiberman, 1975). We know that economic hardship involves more than unemployment, the conventional measure. Losses may occur through job changes, demotions, and illness. Exposure to economic cycles or events also takes various forms, from none at all to direct and indirect. But whatever the economic situation, research on coping has brought greater respect for the resilience of the human personality (Kasl, 1979; Kobasa, 1979). Even in the worst of times, some people manage to come through without undue strain or damage.

Observations of this sort are consistent with an impressive degree of personal stability across 20 or more years (Block, 1971; Costa & McCrae, 1980). The stable person presumably includes men and women endowed with qualities that ensure a measure of independence from environmental stressors. The even tempered, for example, are better equipped to cope with the frustrations and tensions of misfortune than the irritable or explosive. Adaptive potential in this and more general accounts refers to the personal and social resources that facilitate coping (Elder, 1974, Chapter 1). These include good health and a nurturant marriage. Healthfulness ranks among the most critical personal resources across the life course, and positive marital interaction represents a key element in life-span networks of social support.

This study of adults from the 1900 generation views their health risk from drastic economic hardship in the Great Depression as contingent on the adaptive potential they brought to hard times. Economic misfortune was more damaging to some members of the generation than to others, but why? We shall look for an answer in three pre-Depression conditions (social class, marital quality, and emotional health) and in gender differences across life situations. Men and their self-image were directly implicated in Depression losses. Change of this sort also made life very difficult for wives, but it did not as forcefully assault their sense of personal worth (Elder, 1974). A detailed rationale for these hypotheses follows a preliminary orientation to the study sample and design.

The men and women of this study started their families during the prosperous 1920s and experienced the bust and boom of the 1930s and

1940s as spouses, parents, and earners. All are members of the well-known Berkeley Guidance Study (Macfarlane, 1938), a longitudinal investigation of normal development in a sample of 211 middle- and working-class children and their parents. The children were systematically selected from a list of Berkeley births in 1928–1929. Data from interviews and observations were collected annually on husbands and wives up to 1945. Approximately 82 of the women and 40 of the husbands were reinterviewed in 1969–1970 (mean age = 70). As might be expected from socioeconomic-status (SES) differences in mortality and social participation, well-educated men and women were more likely than other persons to be contacted in old age (Maas & Kuypers, 1974). However, the survivors closely resemble other men and women in the Berkeley sample on the incidence and severity of economic hardship during the 1930s.

For some time we have recognized that a full understanding of environmental factors in health requires that investigators "be given the opportunity to study the 'natural experiments' that occur so frequently in our society" (Hinkel, Lawrence, & Loring, 1977, p. 302). The Great Depression established something akin to a natural experiment by exposing individuals to relatively nondeprived and deprived experiences with minimal regard for their particular life histories in the middle and working class. Consistent with this focal point, we follow Klerman's (1979, p. 138) proposal on the "strongest possible methodological design" for studies of social change in health states: "Take one or more factors presumed or demonstrated to be associated with higher risk, such as loss, bereavement, or the closing of a factory, and follow such a sample prospectively through time to observe the emergence of the presumed psychopathology." Though limited in size and locale, this longitudinal sample of the 1900 generation represents an extraordinary opportunity to trace the actual Depression experience of adults to evidence of health across 40 years of their life span. The time span literally exceeds by decades the temporal span of other prospective studies of economic decline in the life span and challenges current understanding of the relationship between economic events and life outcomes. Questions far exceed current knowledge.

1. What life pathways enhance the enduring influence of events in personality and social adaptation?
2. Under what conditions are initial effects that fade likely to surface once again, impairing the ability to thrive and even function at minimal levels?
3. How are adaptive skills from early life activated and applied to the requirements of new situations in middle and old age? How do people use the past in constructive ways?

We begin the study by taking up such questions and follow with a sequence that should enable us to clarify outcomes and their life context. The first part of the sequence focuses on the long-term effects of the Depression hardship, as expressed in old age (1970) through variables that have special relevance to income loss, a sense of self-confidence (self-esteem, self-assurance), and the assertion of self—not passive, feels independent, willing to take action. The second part moves back in time to the 1930s for an assessment of economic hardship in emotional stability (e.g., not excitable, tense, sullen), an index in each of three time periods that offers the best available measure of health at this time. The long-term analysis compares men and their wives as survivors of the Great Depression, whereas the larger 1930s sample enables a more complex analysis of adaptive factors (class, initial health, marital quality) in the lives of men and women. The Depression analysis provides some clues to the nature of both enduring and short-term economic influences.

LINKING ECONOMIC EVENTS AND HEALTH

Adult life under the best of circumstances generally includes setbacks, personal losses, and the countless hassles of daily living. An ability to manage trying situations without undue harm to self and others is one sign of health or personal soundness (Lazarus, 1966). But even the sound individual may be shaken by major life events that are unexpected and abrupt, such as the Great Depression. This event meant drastic life change for many Berkeley adults, a discontinuity rather than a transition. Their health from the 1930s to old age depended, in part, on what they brought to the event: their adaptive resources as well as family roles and related obligations and identities. Underlying all of this is the assumed link between health risk and exposure to loss. Some families managed to avoid heavy income losses.

Exposure to Economic Loss

On the eve of the Great Depression the Berkeley sample numbered 211 families of young mothers, fathers, and their children. Most of the families were white, Protestant, and middle class. Two-thirds were positioned in the middle class and three-fourths were headed by native-born parents. Family income in 1929 averaged $2300 and all but a few of the men were fully employed. Some 3 years later, in the bleakest phase of the Depression, family income had declined by 30%, a figure which is comparable to that of

California families in general. Over this time period the number of Berkeley families at the bottom of the economic ladder (below $1500) more than tripled. Despite such change, the economic collapse was clearly not a major event for a substantial number of the Berkeley adults.

Some families managed to avoid economic misfortune altogether, while others were favored by the sharp decline in prices and the general cost of living. This decline reached one-fourth of the 1929 figure by 1933, according to the U.S. Bureau of Labor Statistics. Substantial deprivations of one kind or another seemed to occur as income loss exceeded one-third of the 1929 figure. These changes included both general and severe budgetary restrictions (involving change of residence or family composition), rapidly mounting indebtedness, exhaustion of savings and loans, and the loss of assets, from insurance to furniture, the family car, and home. Reactions to the fearful piling up of debts symbolized the desperate mood of the times. As one woman put it, "I could lose my mind if I let myself think about it."

With these economic changes in mind, along with prior work on the Great Depression (Elder, 1974), we defined an income loss of 34% or greater as evidence of economic deprivation. Smaller losses were classified as evidence of relatively nondeprived status. Compared to 57% of the working-class families, 36% of the middle-class families were deprived by this criterion. This difference in exposure was coupled with an class difference in the duration of economic hardship. Hard times in the form of income loss came earlier in the working class and stayed longer when compared to the economic experience of the middle class. If past experience with financial hardship and job loss had adaptive value for adults in the working class, this value was surely countered by the prevalence and duration of extreme economic pressure.

Class Differentials in the Great Depression

Persuasive documentation of this class differential is presented in Table 1 for a subgroup of Berkeley families that was studied most intensively across the 1930s.[1] Consistent with our knowledge of family adaptations to depressed economic conditions (Moen, Kain, & Elder, 1983), substantial income loss coincides with the unemployment of men, the labor force entry of women, and dependence on public assistance. These associations per-

---

[1]This group (called the Guidance sample) was matched on social and economic factors in 1929 with a less intensively studied sample (the control sample—N = 101). The total sample equals 211 families. The intensively studied sample is the base for our analyses of hardship effects because it has measures of psychological functioning. All long-term effects into old age are based on survivors of the 211 case sample.

TABLE 1

Evidence of Hard Times in the 1930s among Berkeley Men and Women
by Social Class 1929 and Economic Deprivation, in percentages

| | Percentage of Berkeley families | | | |
| | Middle class | | Working class | |
Indicators	Nondeprived (N = 40–44) %	Deprived (N = 21–24) %	Nondeprived (N = 19–20) %	Deprived (N = 20–24) %
Work status and public aid				
1930–1935				
Husband ever unemployed	5	24	15	62
Wife ever employed	14	25	35	50
On public aid, 1 year or				
more	2	17	15	54
1936–1939				
Husband ever unemployed	5	18	11	35
Wife ever employed	19	38	45	58
On public aid	2	8	—	42
Persistent hardship				
Never above $1200 through				
the 1930s	—	—	30	79
Time of recovery				
Recovered 1929 income only in				
1935–1939	—	71	—	50
1940–1945, or later, or never	—	29	—	50

sisted throughout the 1930s, and in all cases they were much stronger in the
working class. Men from the deprived working class were most likely to be
out of work at some point in the 1930s, *and* to have wives who were
gainfully employed. These men typically faced persistent hardship throughout the 1930s, and their chances of recovery were notably less than the
prospects of men and women from the deprived middle class. For both
deprivational groups, the economic collapse meant hard times for years, not
months, the more common standard of the 1980s.

The class setting of economic deprivation tells us much about the Depression experiences of the Berkeley men and women: the severity of loss,
adaptive resources, and modes of response. Self-esteem and feelings of personal control or mastery are related to higher social standing (Elder &
Liker, 1982, Kessler & Cleary, 1980, Rosenberg & Pearlin, 1978) and so
are problem-solving skills. There is good reason to believe that the absence
of such qualities before misfortune limits a person's chances of recovery.
With little sense of personal worth and mastery, a woman is less able "to

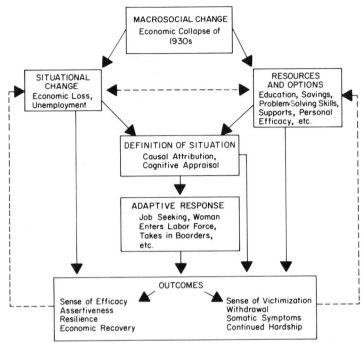

Figure 1. Theoretical model relating macrosocial change to individual adaptations and outcomes.

imagine herself emerging from her privation" (Brown & Harris, 1978, p. 235). In the Oakland study of Depression hardship (Elder, 1974, Chapter 3), loss of status proved to be especially painful to the middle class, but these adults had more resources than members of the lower strata for dealing effectively with family hardship. Their educational, economic, and status advantages were expressed in strong feelings of confidence. By contrast, adults in the working class were especially vulnerable to economic hardships that often seemed unmanageable. For them, hardships undoubtedly reinforced feelings of inadequacy and helplessness.

The individual's class before the Depression thus relates to health outcomes in two general ways: through exposure to economic change and through initial resources and options for coping with life change. Figure 1 traces the effects of large-scale economic change to health outcomes through a sequence of complex interaction processes. Depending on initial resources or adaptive skill, a sharp loss of income may produce outcomes that range from impairment to no effect and even beneficial gains in coping ability. Income loss is typically viewed as a decline in material resources, though it also entails or threatens a loss of social standing, especially in the middle class. The symbolic significance of this loss was vividly expressed by families who invested energy, time, and their reduced income to keep misfortune a private matter. In a study of Oakland families during the 1930s (Elder, 1974, p. 53), a daughter of deprived middle-class parents recalled that her father was extremely stingy in providing her mother with food and clothing money, and yet spent what seemed at the time to be a huge sum of money painting the house because "everybody could see that." The anticipation and experience of status loss may have made a substantial contribution to emotional distress among deprived members of the Oakland middle class.

Gender and the Meaning of Income Loss

Differential exposure to economic change and its experience also refers to differences between the Depression experience of men and women. The gender effect rests on the premise that the meaning of income loss varied between husbands and their wives, with the most adverse effects experienced by husbands. Consistent with self-perception theory (Bem, 1968), income changes due to changes in the wives' status have little direct impact on the self-worth and efficacy of husbands, in fact, much less than the changes in their own status (Augustyniak, Duncan, & Liker, 1984). By and large, substantial income loss directly implicated the status, competence, and identity of men in the 1930s. They were the primary earners. Wives lost their economic support and peace of mind when husbands lost jobs and income declined, but husbands lost a core element of their social significance. Consistent with the individualistic ethos of the times, husbands commonly regarded lost jobs and income as symptomatic of personal inadequacies (Elder, 1974), a diagnosis occasionally shared by wives and children. The more prolonged the deprivation, the deeper the sense of personal blame and helplessness.

Though often troubled to the breaking point by a disintegrating husband and burdened by the domestic tasks of a labor intensive and sometimes crowded household, wives largely escaped the destructive impact of self-recrimination. Indeed, their Depression world often expanded to meet the demand for constructive responses, including gainful employment and the taking in of boarders and lodgers. A study of the Austrian village Marienthal in the 1930s offers a particularly vivid account of women's expanding responsibilities (Jahoda, Lazarsfeld, & Zeisel, 1971). Greater meaning and inner strength could be found through the necessity of meeting such demands. Weller's (1965, p. 242) observation on an Appalachian couple in the depressed 1930s captures well the drama of the divergent impact on husband and wife: "Thus bit by bit, as her husband's role has decreased and as his life has lost meaning, her life has taken on new meaning in the community or at work." At the time, Robert and Helen Lynd (1937) speculated that "it is the world of male roles that has been under most pressure in Middletown in the depression, and that for women the years following 1929 may even in some cases have brought temporary easement of tensions" (p. 179).

Additional insight on gender-role differences in the Depression comes from empirical knowledge of postdisaster adaptations and psychological recovery. Across a number of studies, recovery appears to be most likely among people who become actively engaged in recovery activities, such as the repair of homes and property. In one case, flood victims gained confidence by regaining control of their destiny through self-help activities (Gleser, Green, & Winget, 1981). Such activities were more available to women than to men in the Great Depression. To a substantial degree, Depression women were confronted by a range of action imperatives that concerned family survival and recovery. Management of a doubled up household is one example and gainful employment is another. By comparison, the psychological insult of the Depression losses in men's lives often led to withdrawal and immobilization rather than to recovery (Elder, 1974). Husbands frequently became part of the Depression problem for hard-pressed wives and mothers.

Personal and Social Resources

Basic to the idea of a conditional process is the notion that economic pressures may accentuate dispositions that are brought to the new situation. Extreme economic pressures are likely to accentuate troublesome dispositions, such as irritability, impatience, and anger-out tendencies, that are manageable in less stressful circumstances. The neurotic under extreme pressure becomes more difficult to live with, as statistics on marital instability attest (Costa & McCrae, 1980). Stable people (the "ego resilient," Block & Block, 1980) are more likely to weather misfortune, as suggested by the concept of stamina: "the physical or moral strength to resist or withstand disease, fatigue, or hardship" (Thomas, 1981, p. 41). Lacking this adaptive strength, the economically deprived encountered a higher risk of pathogenic consequences from severe economic pressures. Especially among men, we hypothesize that economic loss had the most adverse effects on emotional stability (1930–1940) in the subgroup that was least stable before hard times. Following the Block's (1980) account of ego resilience, we assume that emotional stability reflects and enables resourceful adaptations.

Moral strength may come from external as well as internal sources. The social and emotional support of an understanding and compassionate spouse can help to mobilize the inner strength for effective coping. *Marital support* refers to emotional resources through bonds of understanding, acceptance, and confidence; the extension of tangible assistance in time, energy, money; the provision of advice and knowledge (Schaeffer, Coyne, & Lazarus, 1981). In largely unknown combinations, these elements of marital support may buffer the stressfulness of deprivational change. Loss is presumably less stressful with marital support available.[2] Accordingly, we hypothesize that the weaker the marriage among couples before hard times in the 1930s, the lower their marital support under deprived circumstances and the higher the health risk from severe economic loss. The buffering effect of marital support should be most prominent among men.

All three dimensions of adaptive potential (class, health, and marital support) apply to the Depression experience of men and women, but they have greater relevance to men who were most directly confronted by the personal tragedy of job and income loss. For men, good health and a loving wife could bolster their sense of worth and control in the face of severe income loss and unemployment. Indeed, these factors are likely to gain significance when neither job nor earnings sustain morale and vitality. The pathogenic influence of economic loss on men should be greatest when both health and marriage were lacking before the Depression.

There is little basis in theory or research for expectations of a positive or developmental outcome from men's economic misfortune, given the character of the change. Specified resources may only lessen the adverse effects of their loss. Abundant resources do not lead to the prediction of beneficial outcomes. Among wives, by comparison, Depression realities could actually enhance their sense of personal worth, mastery, and autonomy. Their entry into the labor market is one plausible route for developing such qualities (see Kessler & McRae, 1982). Positive outcomes of this sort seem most likely if women entered the 1930s with strong marital ties, good health, and the higher-resource level of the middle class.

Definition of the Situation and Causal Attributions

Degree of economic change and initial resources should tell much of the story on why some adults managed the economic crisis of the 1930s better

---

[2]The health function of social support is better documented by assumption than by well-designed empirical research. The hypothesis that social support moderates or buffers the mental and physical health effects of socioeconomic or occupational stress has received some empirical support from rigorous studies (see LaRocco, House, & French, 1980; Payne, 1980). However, other studies fail to support this interaction hypothesis (Lin *et al.*, 1979; Williams, Ware, & Donald, 1981). For an extended discussion of "the stress-buffering role of social support" see essays by Cobb (1976), Dean and Lin (1977).

than others. However, additional knowledge of situational definitions is needed to connect pre-event conditions with subsequent adaptations and health outcomes. Depressive states, maladaptive behavior, and illness are more probable when people bring certain attributional tendencies to negative life changes or events (Peterson & Seligman, 1980; Seligman, Abramson, Semnel, VanBalyer, 1979). Internal attributions (the self is to blame) about negative events tend to lower self-esteem. This type of attribution as well as those that view negative events as global and permanent (vs. partial and unstable) generally foster a state of helplessness and depressed feelings. Depressive attributional styles (internal, global, permanent) increase the risk of subsequent depressive episodes when misfortune strikes again. Especially in the working class of the 1930s, with its prolonged deprivation, family losses may have generated depressive styles that then became a self-fulfilling prophecy, with more adversity and illness.

Cognitive frameworks for interpreting life events provide a suggestive conceptual link between economic hardship and adaptive resources, on the one hand, and the appearance and timing of health outcomes over the 40 years of the Berkeley cohort, on the other. If hardship is linked to unstable or poor health among men because of its situational pressures, a depressive outlook could account for the persistence of this health state into old age, a time span of four decades or more in some cases. But are there sleeper or lagged effects that appear many years after an apparent recovery from the devastation of Depression losses? If women show no reliable sign of adversity from the Depression during the 1930s, can we assume that the Depression did not shape their future life course into old age? These questions are difficult to answer without more knowledge of life-span development or data points that literally extend across the life span (Brenner, 1973, 1979, pp. 68–69). We do not know for sure how long to observe the independent and dependent variables, though important studies (Kasl, 1979) presume the absence of enduring effects of economic hardship from a time span of less than 5 years. Will such effects appear in life experiences when similar situations are encountered?

The last point brings us to a resemblance between the Great Depression and old age, a similarity based on the prevalence of losses, both human and material. Young men and women lost jobs, income, status, homes, and a general feeling of security during the 1930s, and many of these events returned to their lives in the later years. The multiple losses of old age frequently occur simultaneously to magnify a sense of vulnerability. A Berkeley woman of 75 expressed her experience with loss in the following words: "Well, you talk about death every day you lose a friend. The last months I've lost many friends, all good ones, all fine people. Those things make a dent. . . . So it closes in on you. What do you do? You just go along, do the best you can."

The piling up of negative events in old age could activate a long dormant way of construing such events, an attributional style that increases depressed feelings and a sense of helplessness. Such events could also test one's coping ability, an ability possibly strengthened by Depression realities among women who entered the decade with educational skills, good health, and a nurturant family. A spirit of invincibility and selflessness may stem from the mastery experience of surviving the Depression, as well as the more expected attitude of self-pity, bitterness, and martyrdom. In reference to Berkeley women in the 1900 generation, we have suggested that hard times enabled some to master the developmental task of learning to manage or cope with the loss of valued things and significant others.

> The challenge of surmounting the life problems posed by such losses can be viewed as an adaptational orientation for the constraints of infirmity and limited resources during old age. Depression hardship offered a potential form of apprenticeship for women in learning to cope with the invatable losses of old age. [thus] . . . women who experienced the trauma of losing a family home in the 1930s may be better equipped to accept the residential changes of old age. (Elder, 1982, p. 78)

Four concluding observations on the nature and timing of the Great Depression influences set the stage for our empirical analysis. First, the evidence reviewed to this point suggests that men were more likely than women to acquire a depressive outlook that accentuated any health difficulties evident before the Depression. Second, adverse responses seem most likely when men lacked a supportive marital relationship and emotional stability, both primary means for resourceful adaptation. Third, a depressive, helpless outlook in the early 1930s may have had a cumulative, reinforcing effect on health disintegration over the decade. The better established this outlook, the greater the chances of more adversity in the late 1930s and beyond, the more severe and prolonged the health impairment. Fourth, a depressive outlook, the exhaustion of emotional resources in marriage, and persistent economic troubles up to old age represent plausible linkages between economic losses in the 1930s and health in old age.

Some evidence of these temporal connections appears in our analysis as we trace the long-term influence of Depression hardship to old age and then return to a more detailed examination of health trajectories from 1930 to 1944. The long-term framework offers an extraordinary view of the Depression's legacy over 40 years, but it is also a fragile study, owing to sample attrition. Out of 211 original families, 82 women and 38 of their husbands were interviewed at the end of the 1960s. In this part of the study, sample resources enabled us to address two issues: (1) the presence or absence of long-term effects from Depression hardship; and (2) the problem of differential effects by gender role. With the 38 couples who have been married since before the Depression, we can investigate whether and how the same economic conditions have different consequences for the health of husbands and wives in old age.

An empirical test of pre-Depression health and marital relationships as adaptive resources in the 1930s requires the archival assets of the Guidance sample ($N = 110$) of the Berkeley cohort. This sample was more intensively studied across the 1930s than a matched sample of 101 cases that includes some members of the 1969 follow-up. Measured on both health and family conditions before and during the economic collapse, the intensive sample enables us to extend the long-term analysis by addressing three issues of adaptive potential and vulnerability. First, are negative health effects present during the Depression years and do they vary as anticipated by gender, class standing, initial health, and marital support? Second, which of these factors, as resource or disability, was most important in accounting for the Depression's influence on health? And third, can we explain persistent disabilities or impairments in terms of an enduring personal change or in terms of continuing economic hardships throughout the 1930s?

DEPRESSION ADVERSITY IN THE LATER YEARS

No attitude has greater relevance to the Depression experience of the Berkeley men and women and to their adaptations in old age than a sense of personal control. People who come to old age with feelings of helplessness are likely to make choices that narrow options and the range of experience. New situations and opportunities are avoided. Efforts to overcome difficulties are minimized or abandoned. In this context, failure and losses reinforce a helpless state of mind, as in health disabilities and widowhood (Bandura, 1981, 1982). Conversely, an efficacious outlook can sustain coping efforts and health in troubled times. Indeed, even in a nursing home (Rodin, 1980), normal declines on health, mental alertness, and activity level can be slowed or reversed when residents are placed in situations that encourage them to take some control over their lives.

Depression experiences increased men's chances of entering the later years without an intact sense of mastery and confidence, especially when compared to the deprived but family-based setting of married women. To provide the most rigorous test of the gender hypothesis, we begin our analysis with the intact couples. At the time of the follow-up in 1969, the survey located 38 couples who had been married since the 1920s, a period of 40 years or more. By definition, each husband and wife occupied the same class position in 1929 and encountered identical (objective) economic conditions in the family. As such, socioeconomic variations *cannot* account for any observed gender difference in the effect of economic loss. The hypothesized gender difference centers on the differential meaning of family deprivation for men and women.

The class hypothesis combines limited resources and the severity of economic hardship in ways that favor a strong link between deprivation and a lack of personal mastery among women in the working class. However, the differential is not as clear for men. In large part, this is due to the multiple meanings of loss among men, including the profound psychological shock of status loss among men in the middle class. Evidence is presented suggesting that the health impact of such loss in the middle class roughly equalled the effect of objective material loss in the working class.

Our model of personal control in the later years includes two dimensions, self-confidence and assertiveness or self-assertion. Both elements are best viewed in a sequence of action, action outcomes, and consequences. Effective action in demanding situations builds confidence in the self and in personal agency, whereas passivity engenders feelings and consequences that undermine confidence. Smith (1968) referred to these sequences as benign and vicious cycles of life-span development:

> Launched on the right trajectory, the person is likely to accumulate successes that strengthen the effectiveness of his orientation toward the world while at the same time he acquires the knowledge and skills that make his further success more probable. His environmental involvements generally lead to gratification and to increased competence and favorable development. Off to a bad start, on the other hand, he soon encounters failures that make him hesitant to try. What to others are challenges appear to him as threats; he becomes preoccupied with defense of his small claims on life at the expense of energies to invest in constructive coping. And he falls increasingly behind his fellows in acquiring the knowledge and skills that are needed for success on those occasions when he does try. (p. 277)

Husband and Wife Functioning:
A Measurement Model

Assertiveness is measured by three-point ratings: "behaves in an assertive fashion in interpersonal situations," does not "give up and withdraw where possible in the face of frustration," and does not tend to "delay or avoid action." The ratings are part of the 100-item California Q-sort (Maas & Kuypers, 1974). All items were sorted per case interview according to a forced normal distribution on how characteristic or uncharacteristic they were of the person. Case reliabilities for the two judges were .70 or greater.

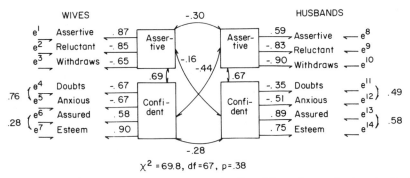

Figure 2. A measurement model of assertiveness and self-confidence for couples (standardized coefficients, N = 38).

Self-confidence includes two 9-point ratings from the Q-sort ("basically anxious" and "overconcerned with own adequacy as a person") and two 7-point interview ratings: self-esteem or feelings of personal worth, and self-assurance as expressed in poise or confidence. To determine whether the two-dimensional model fits the data in this fashion, we constructed a measurement model (Figure 2) using confirmatory factor analysis in LISREL (an analysis of linear structural relations) for husbands and wives. All values are standardized. The factor loadings are statistically significant at the .05 level unless otherwise indicated.

The correlated measurement errors (e.g., .76 linking *doubts* and *anxious* among wives) represent method differences. '*Doubts* adequacy' and *anxious* are Q-ratings based on an ipsative design. High scores on both ratings indicate that they are characteristic of a person. They do not provide information on the standing of the person relative to other people. Despite this difference in measurement, the four indicators are clearly useful measures of self-confidence among men and women during their later years.

The model fits the data at acceptable levels (χ^2 = 69.8, *df* = 67, *p* = .38) and supports the following conclusions. First, the factor loadings on Assertiveness are statistically reliable for both wives and husbands; and the same conclusion applies to the measurement of Self-Confidence. Second, Assertiveness and Self-Confidence are highly related, and their specified indicators are empirically differentiated as expected. There are no ties. That is, measures of Self-Confidence do not show reliable factor loadings on Assertiveness; and the measures of Assertiveness do not also load significantly on Self-Confidence. Third, the only correlated measurement errors reflect a method factor in the measurement of Self-Confidence. For both husbands and their wives, the Q-ratings' errors are significantly correlated (note that the Q-ratings are based on a forced normal distribution which inflates correlations among items). However, both sets of measures function well as indicators of Self-Confidence in the life experience of husbands and wives.

The Berkeley men and women who entered old age with confident feelings about themselves were also typically the men and women who asserted themselves in relationship to life's problems, opportunities, responsibilities, and decisions (correlations of almost .70). This relation and its interpretation presume that Assertiveness and Self-confidence, as measured in Figure 2, have the same empirical meaning for men and women. Can we make this assumption?

At first glance there is reason to reject the assumption. Withdrawal from adversity is more salient in the assertiveness of men, whereas interpersonal assertiveness is more prominent in the self-assertion of women. The factor loadings on Self-Confidence also show modest variation by spouse. A statistically reliable difference between the factor structures of each group would indicate that we are *not* measuring similar concepts in these groups. To test this possibility, the unstandardized factor loadings for each construct were constrained equal across the two groups and the fit of this model was compared to the unconstrained model. The constrained model fits the data well ($\chi^2 = 80$, $df = 72$, $p = .24$). When compared to this baseline, the unconstrained model does not offer a statistically reliable improvement in the goodness of fit ($p = .08$). Hence, we cannot reject the null hypothesis of equal relationships (measure–construct) for men and women.

Our focus on couples in the Berkeley sample brings up an important issue regarding pathways of enduring influence from Depression hardship: the interdependent life experiences and personalities of each marital partner. The well-being of husbands in old age may partially reflect the impact of Depression hardship on wives, whereas husbands may provide a link between the 1930s and the self-confidence and initiative of wives. Even the most resilient spouse might be vulnerable to the life-long emotional demands of a pessimistic, cynical, and resentful mate. From this perspective, the long-term pattern is one of increasing resemblance between husband and wife, an accentuation of similarity over the course of married life. A life style more centered on coping is suggested by a complimentary dynamic in which one spouse maintains a confident, resourceful outlook in the face of a partner's despair and passivity. Complementarity may also arise from need gratification, as when dependency needs are gratified by a dominant mate. Whatever the source, we do find some evidence of complementarity in Figure 2; assertive, self-confident women were not likely to have assertive or self-confident husbands.

This mode of complementarity in Figure 2 is substantial, but the sample is too small to ensure its statistical reliability. For example, a model that assumes that all interspouse correlations are zero produces a goodness of fit that does not differ reliably from the χ^2 value for a model in which only the factor structures of the two groups are constrained to be equal. The χ^2 value increases slightly in the former model, but the increment is not statistically reliable ($p = .15$). One might also argue that the likelihood ratio χ^2 statistic is not valid unless the sample size is large. Recent Monte Carlo simulations (Geweke & Singleton, 1980) suggest that the χ^2 in factor models is valid with subgroups as small as 30 cases. In terms of this analysis, we assume that the primary long-term influence of Depression hardship is expressed through the lives of men for men, and through the lives of women for women.

The Gender Hypothesis on Hardship

Direct support for the gender hypothesis comes from estimates of Depression hardship as a lasting influence on the self-assertion and confidence of husbands and wives. Income loss was the same for each spouse; however, its subjective features had more punishing implications for men who were directly implicated in the loss of job and income. Given that husbands and wives were both exposed to family deprivations, it is noteworthy that husbands in old age show more adverse effects of the Depression experience than their wives. Modest empirical evidence of the "strong woman and defeated man" image of Depression families appears in this aging sample after nearly three decades of post-Depression prosperity.

By far the strongest effect and contrast involves assertiveness. Using the multigroup options of LISREL with income loss as antecedent factor and the three-factor model of assertiveness, we obtained a satisfactory fit with the data for husbands and wives ($\chi^2 = 11.2$, $df = 6$, $p = .08$). The effect of deprivation is negative among the men ($\beta = -.27$, $p < .05$) and positive among their wives ($\beta = .24$, $p < .10$). If we put aside LISREL and its appropriateness for the sample at hand, we find that the very same contrast results from analyses that assume perfect measurement (Assertiveness as measured by an average of the three ratings) and use of ordinary least squares in estimating the effects of deprivation. Both modes of analysis show that men largely experienced the psychological costs of hard times, whereas their wives appear to have gained inner strength from the experience. We have no empirical reason to believe that such differences preceded the Great Depression (Elder, 1982). The self-esteem, self-confidence, and life satisfaction of men and women in 1930 did not reliably predict subsequent income loss.

To test the reliability of this gender difference we compared the goodness of fit of two models, one in which the effects of deprivation for men and women were constrained equal and another one in which the effects were unconstrained. Consistent with our observations, the constrained model does not fit the data as well as the unconstrained type. The latter offers a reliable improvement ($\chi^2 = 5.3$, $df = 2$, $p = .02$) of the fit between model and data.

The gender difference on self-confidence is much less pronounced, owing largely to the absence of any long-term effect of the Depression among women. A LISREL model with economic deprivation and the four-indicator measure of Self-Confidence fit the data reasonably well on husbands and wives ($\chi^2 = 3.4$, $df = 11$, $p = .68$), but Depression hardship only influenced the Self-Confidence of husbands in old age ($\beta = -.21$, $p < 10$). This compares to a beta coefficient of .02 for wives. The two coefficients are not reliably different. We find no difference between the fit of models in which the deprivational effects for men and women are unconstrained versus constrained equal.

Social position before the Great Depression cannot explain or account for the observed difference between husbands and wives in old age relative to their Depression experiences because they shared the same socioeconomic status. But it may contribute to erroneous or misleading estimates in at least two respects. First, economic deprivation is related to lower status. As we have seen, heavy losses were most common in the working class. From this perspective, the influence of deprivation may include the influence of lower status. Second, the couple analysis ignores an earlier finding (Elder, 1982) in which Depression losses posed more of a threat to the health of working class women in old age than to the health of higher-status women. As noted earlier, this class differential seems more clear-cut for women because job, income, and status losses made Depression hardship a damaging experience for men *at all levels* of the class structure.

Social class in 1929 is highly related to economic loss ($r = .53$) among couples; this collinearity means less accurate estimations if both factors are included. We approached the problem by estimating three sets of models: (1) only deprivation as the antecedent variable, (2) only social class in 1929, and (3) both factors. The addition of social class does not substantially change the above set of estimates of deprivation effects among husbands and wives. With social class included in the structural model along with economic deprivation, the effect of deprivation on the assertiveness of men declines only slightly, from $-.34$ to $-.30$; although as expected, collinearity increases the standard error substantially. The change in the *beta* coefficient is even smaller for the Self-Confidence of men. Similar results were obtained on the wives. In all cases, the effect of social class in 1929 is minimal and considerably weaker than deprivation. This conclusion applies to a comparison of single factor models (with Deprivation or class) and to models with both factors. However, the lack of additive effects does not rule out the possibility of statistical interaction between economic deprivation and class.

The Class Difference Hypothesis

This hypothesis cannot be explored among the Berkeley men in old age, owing to the small number of survivors. However, the sample of Berkeley women is large enough to pursue the question of whether the most adverse effects of Depression hardship are concentrated in the lower stratum or working class. Two-fifths of the women entered the 1930s from the working class and this is the group that seems most likely to resemble men on the enduring health costs of the Depression experience. Analyses reported elsewhere (Elder & Liker, 1982) document a class difference in the health risk of Depression hardship that extends beyond the usual expectation of more adverse effects among working class women. With statistical controls on pre-Depression well-being, women from the middle class ranked significantly higher on psychological health in old age if they had experienced Depression losses in the 1930s. Perhaps reflecting their mastery of hard times through employment and enlarged family roles, these women were less inclined to report feelings of self-pity and resentment over losses and setbacks than the privileged nondeprived. In the working class, hard times during the 1930s increased the risk of impaired well-being in old age, and the general pattern of outcomes confirms our expectations. From all angles, the health trajectories of deprived women from the two social strata differ markedly.

If we take these observations into account, there is good reason to expect the largest gender difference on psychological effects in old age among men and women from the middle stratum. Conversely, the Depression's legacy of health impairment is more likely to be shared by aged men and women from the working class. Given the data resources at hand, men could not be divided into high- and low-status groups, leaving us with three groups for analysis. Using the multigroup option of LISREL, we estimated the effect of economic loss on Assertiveness and Self-confidence in old age among three groups: women from the high- and low-status categories and all men. As a baseline for comparison, the "no constraints" model allows the effects of deprivation to be individually estimated; only factor loadings are constrained equal across groups. The structural parameters for a no constraints model are presented in Table 2 along with the goodness of fit values for other models and assumptions.

Figure 3 highlights the effects of percentage of income loss (1929–

TABLE 2

Assertiveness and Self-Confidence in Old Age by Economic Deprivation
in the 1930s: A Comparison of Deprivational Effects among Women and Men

Constructs	Structural parameters for no-constraints model		
	High-status women $(N = 46)$	Low-status women $(N = 33)$	Men $(N = 38)$
Assertiveness			
Metric coefficient	1.55*	−.45	−.95*
Standard error	.49	.51	.47
Beta	.46	−.16	−.34
Self-confidence			
Metric coefficient	.56*	−.43	−.34
Standard error	.26	.43	.30
Beta	.35	−.22	−.21

Selected models and their goodness of fit[a]	Assertiveness[b]			Self-Confidence[b]		
	χ^2	df	Significance (p)	χ^2	df	Significance (p)
Model 1: No constraints	15.7	10	.11	8.9	18	.96
Model 2: Men=low-status women	16.2	11	.13	8.9	19	.97
Model 3: Men=high-status women	28.3	11	.003	13.9	19	.79
Model 4: All groups constrained equal	29.5	12	.003	15.9	20	.72
Model 4 minus Model 2	13.3	2	.005	7.0	1	.009

[a]This part of the table shows the results of fitting four models to the data. In Model 1, we allowed the effects of income loss across the three subgroups to vary. Model 2 adds the condition that the effects of income loss for men and for low-status women are equal (the equal sign should be read as "coefficients constrained to be equal"). Model 3 alters the constraint and Model 4 constrains all three income-loss effects to be equal.

[b]For both outcomes, assertiveness and self-confidence, Model 1 is a significantly better fit than Model 3, which assumes that the deprivation effect for men is the same as the effect for high-status women ($p = .001$). Model 2 also represents a better fit in both cases than does Model 4.

*$p < .05$.

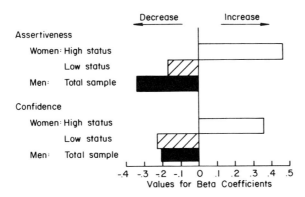

Figure 3. Deprivation effects on assertiveness and self-confidence in old age, 1930s–1970.

1933) on old-age functioning by displaying in bar graph form the degree and direction of the effect. All of the horizontal bars depict beta coefficients (standardized) that are drawn from Table 2. Ideally, we would use unstandardized coefficients for group comparisons, as our analysis in Table 2 does. However, the variable range of these coefficients clearly handicaps their use in this manner. The figure shows that income loss increased the assertiveness and self-confidence of high-status women; and diminished the psychological well-being of low-status women and of the surviving men.

Overall, the long-term costs of economic misfortune during the 1930s appear to be very similar for surviving men and lower-status women in the old age sample of the Berkeley 1900 generation, although the respective processes undoubtedly differ. Even these modest costs of diminished self-adequacy and assertiveness are striking when we take into account the extraordinary span of time and the countless intervening events that could attenuate the Depression's impact. No study up to the present has reported consequences of an historical event over a longer span of the life course.

The structural parameters in Table 2 clearly show the resemblance between men and lower-status women, as well as the contrasting experience of women from the middle class. A model in which the deprivational effect for men is constrained to be equal to the effect for lower-status women fits the data well on both constructs, Assertiveness and Self-Confidence. The fit is much less satisfactory when the path coefficient for men is constrained equal to the coefficient for higher-status women. The most powerful test of our expectations in this area entails a comparison of the goodness of fit for Model 2 (men = lower-status women) and Model 4 in which all path coefficients are constrained to be equal. Particularly on Assertiveness, the fully constrained model (Number 4) amounts to a very poor fit in relation to the data, much poorer than Model 2.

Alternative modes of statistical analysis have produced corresponding results (Elder, 1982). In an analysis of covariance design, we compared the effects of Depression hardship among women from the two status groups, high and low, with socioeconomic resources in 1929 as the covariate. The results consistently show a positive effect in the former group and negative effect in the latter group. The outcome measures included self-reported health, the Q-ratings used in this research, a global index of psychological health, and an index of life satisfaction. According to mean values, women with a background in the deprived middle class generally ranked highest on health in old age, as indexed by the preceding measures, whereas women from the deprived working class typically scored at the bottom. The latter were most likely to feel victimized by life circumstances.

One might argue that the old-age difference between nondeprived and deprived men as well as the women from the low-status group reflects a difference that was prominent before the economic crisis; the deprived were simply recruited from a pool of the least resourceful men and women. Our research to date does not support this view (Elder & Liker, 1982; Liker & Elder, 1983) and neither do the consequences of Depression hardship among high-status women. Selection for misfortune in the 1930s has no application whatsoever to these women. But the selection issue also leads us to initial resources that might condition the effect of income loss. Resourceful men and women should be least vulnerable to the health risk of hard times. The process by which economic misfortune has an effect that endures is undoubtedly linked to prior resources. Such issues focus analysis on the 1930s.

HARD TIMES AND HEALTH IN THE 1930s

Three questions on hardship and health structured our inquiry in the Depression decade. The first puts the gender hypothesis to a test in the 1930s. Is economic loss a more negative factor in the health of men when compared to the health of women? The second question focuses on the conditional properties of this relationship within groups of husbands and wives. Does the health effect of economic loss vary by class, marital support, and initial health? Is it more negative among men from the working class, among discordant marriages, and when health was initially impaired? The third question concerns the issue of enduring versus persistent effects. What happened to the emotional health of men when they recovered their jobs and income? Did they continue to show the imprint of Depression losses?

Wills and Langner (1980, p. 167) argue that demoralization, with its psychological and physical symptomatology, is most likely to stem from "events that have long-term consequences, that are outside the individual's control, and eventually wear people down." This suggests that the most lasting and dramatic effect occurred in families that remained deprived throughout the 1930s. A measure of persistent hardship and recovery in the late 1930s provides an opportunity to put this conclusion to a test. In the lives of women, we have pointed to their response to family hardship as one medium by which the Depression had a lasting effect on their health. Gainful employment represents such a response. Another role was added to the multiple responsibilities of the household. A large number of deprived women entered the labor force. If greater independence and self-confidence resulted from this life change in some cases, other employed women were undoubtedly overwhelmed by the burden and drudgery of their life situation.

The best available measure of psychological health during the 1930s in the Berkeley sample is a 7-point interview scale of emotional stability (archive label is "nervous stability"). Persons with high scores are described as "exceptionally stable," even in the "face of trying circumstances." The lowest-scale category includes men and women who were judged extremely disturbed, or erratic. A tradesman in the latter category was characterized by the interviewer and by informants as very quarrelsome and moody on the job, erratic and irritable at home, and generally a threat to the well-being of his wife and children. The pre-Depression measure (obtained in 1930) for men and women is based on interviews with married couples and on home observations by a field worker. Beyond this baseline interview, only annual interviews with the wife and home observations provided the basic data for ratings of each spouse's emotional stability.

According to in-depth analyses (Liker & Elder, 1983), the change in data source from 1930 to the later 1930s does not bias health measures on the Berkeley men in ways one might expect from wives' reports on husbands. First, the emotional stability of the husband and the wife is not related within or between the time periods, 1930 and 1933–1935. Second, the emotional health of the husband and the wife is equally stable across these time points. To maximize sample size and scale reliability, the yearly ratings were averaged for selected time periods during the early stage of the study. In addition to the base-line of 1930, three periods are represented in the analysis: 1933–1935, 1936–1938, and 1939–1944.

The decision to rely upon the scale of emotional stability for detailed analyses emerged from a confirmatory factor analysis (not shown here) in which we viewed the personal stability of men and their wives in 1930–1931 and 1933–1935 as a construct with three indicators: low Emotional Stability, Irritability (high scorers are "quick to flare up or become fretful"), and Tension/Worrisomeness. Irritable and Tense are based on the data sources used for emotional stability. This model extends across the first half of the depression decade and assumes that the primary influence of each spouse's stability on the other occurs over time—it is not simultaneous. Second, the model assumes that measurement errors by rating are correlated over time because each particular rating may capture a specific aspect of personality other than personal stability. Emotional Stability has the highest factor weights and thus emerges as the most reliable measure of personal stability and functioning in the 1930s.

Three other conclusions deserve notice. First, the general construct of personal stability represents an enduring orientation across the two time periods despite the economic crisis (coefficients range from .81 to .89). We see remarkably little evidence of noteworthy alterations in the behavior of men and women as they experienced hard times, suggesting that individual differences in stability are highly stable (Costa & McCrae, 1980). Another way of putting this observation is to note that the most resilient men and women before economic misfortune were typically the most resilient in adapting to their new circumstances. Second, the personal stability of each spouse had no reliable lagged effect on the psychological functioning of the other mate, as indexed in this study. No evidence suggests that a stable wife enhanced the personal stability of her husband, although she could have more indirect effects by stabilizing the husband's social relationships, including that of marriage itself. Third, severe income loss had substantially different effects for husbands and wives, just as we observed in the later years of life. Controlling for health in 1930, economic deprivation reduced the stability of men during the worst phase of the 1930s and actually enhanced the stability of wives ($\beta = -.25$ and .12), although the latter is not a reliable effect. The picture in old age, some 40 years after the Depression, closely resembles our observations on husband and wife differences in the 1930s.

A number of pathways could lead to an income loss during the 1930s and one might argue that the gender difference is due less to the degree of loss than to unemployment and its more direct effect on men. According to this formulation, job loss has a direct, negative effect on the distress of men in addition to an indirect effect through loss of income. Not surprisingly, unemployment is a major source of income loss among the Berkeley families, but it is only one source. Moreover, job loss does not have a reliable impact on men *apart* from their loss of income.

The analysis up to this point has concentrated on the main effect or influence of relative income loss among men and women. Especially among the Berkeley men, the severity of hardship in the working class, the emotional strain and toll of marital discord, and the handicap of poor health identify conditions that could enhance the risk of impairment under strong economic pressures. Conversely, there is good reason to believe that men with stamina and a strong marriage were best able to weather the economic crisis. At least before the crisis, stable men and women typically had the support of their spouses. Personal and marital health are correlated (rs = .30 to .41). But the unstable who were most in need of support were least likely to receive it. By comparison, socioeconomic standing told little about a person's emotional stability or marriage (rs = .01 to .04) on the eve of the Great Depression.

Adaptive Potential and Vulnerability

The emotional well-being of women and men during the worst years of the Depression (1933–1935) had far more to do with their health before hard times than with their 1930 marital quality, social class in the late 1920s, or their actual loss of income in the 1930s. According to our analysis, these factors account for nearly two-thirds of the variation in men's health during the Depression and for slightly more than two-fifths of the variation among women. In both cases, the major source of emotional stability during the Depression is emotional stability before the crisis, an explained variance of nearly 40%.[3] No other factor is consequential for the well-being of women, not even the initial quality of their marriage. By contrast, a good marriage before economic hardship improved the Depression well-being of men, even apart from the adaptive value of good health.

For this and subsequent analyses on the 1930s, our measure of economic hardship is the percentage difference between family income in 1929 and the lowest annual income figure in the early 1930s (from 1933 to 1934–1935). This continuous measure provides more efficient estimates of economic hardship than our prior contrast between relatively nondeprived and deprived men and women up to old age. Nevertheless, both measures yield comparable results. The continuous measure is available only for the intensively studied Berkeley families which represent the focal sample here; the dichotomy must be used on the full sample, owing to the lack of complete income records.

---

[3]The beta coefficients predicting emotional stability in 1933–1935 for men and women are relative income loss, beta = −.13 and .08 (females); social class in 1929, beta = −.07 and .08; marital quality (a 5-item scale), beta = .20 and .09; and emotional stability, 1930–1931, beta = .65 and .61. The R^2 for men is .63, for women, .45. The five items of the marital quality index include the closeness of each mate to the other, the friendliness of husband and wife to each other, and a general measure of adjustment to each other. All of these ratings are five points and represent the average judgment of the interviewer and a home visitor.

TABLE 3

Men's Emotional Stability in Relation to Economic Deprivation in Three Periods
of the 1930s and Early 1940s: Regression Coefficients

| Factors[a] | Regression coefficients | Emotional stability by time period ($N = 101$) Effects of deprivation and pre-Depression factors, including 1930s health | | |
		1933–1935	1936–1938	1939–1945
Economic change				
Percentage income loss	β	−.13	−.02	−.02
(high loss = high %)	b	(−.006)*	(−.0006)	(−.0008)
Resources, 1930				
Emotional stability	β	.65	−.06	−.10
(5 = high, 1 = low)	b	.62**	−.05	−.07
Marital quality	β	−.20	−.25	−.08
(5 = high, 1 = low)	b	−.24**	−.25**	−.07
1930s Emotional stability				
1933–1935	β	—	.51	.28
	b		.43**	.20**
1936–1938	β	—	—	.54
	b			.45**
Constant		7.04	3.35	1.57
R^2		.63	.51	.55
Number of cases		100	97	94

[a]SES was statistically controlled.
*$p < .05.$ **$p < .01.$

As shown in Table 3, the emotional stability of men in the Depression
had much less to do with the economic pressures they faced than with their
initial health and marital support. The effects of income loss for the total
sample are remarkably weak. Note also the lack of any direct effect of
deprivation and pre-Depression resources on health in the late 1930s and
early 1940s. Across both periods, 1936–1938 and 1939–1945, the influence of initial resources if fully mediated through the health trajectory of
individuals. We find little evidence of lagged or sleeper effects except in the
case of marital quality before hard times. This factor remains predictive of
good health among men in the last half of the Depression decade, and then
diminishes to insignificance by the Second World War. Both individual
change and continuity are well represented in these temporal patterns.

Three orienting conclusions emerge from this preliminary picture of
economic crisis and health across the Depression decade. First, economic
deprivation is relatively inconsequential as a main effect on the emotional

stability of men and women in the total sample, with adverse effects restricted to men. Second, only two potential resources mattered for men's health (initial health and a quality marriage), and only initial health turns out to be predictive of women's stability across the 1930s. Social class prior to the economic crisis is not predictive of health in this period when other factors are statistically controlled. Third, the long-term effects of economic loss and the pre-depression resources are largely mediated by intervening health states. Thus an accentuation of initial instability through deprivation and limited resources might well persist beyond the immediacy of Depression hard times.

With most of the Depression's impact expressed in the lives of men, we give particular attention to this subgroup in our analysis of deprivational influences by social class (a 1929 Hollingshead index based on education and occupation), marital support, and initial health. Across the decade, the effect of deprivation on men's stability does not follow a consistently different pattern by social class (table not shown). Middle class is defined by Strata I, II, and III. Strata IV and V include working-class families. Initial class position is generally irrelevant to the well-being of men in the Depression. All of the regression coefficients for deprivation effects in 1933–1935 and 1936–1938 show a negative outcome on health, but they average less than $-.10$. Class standing is more relevant to the health status of women, particularly after 1935. Deprived women from the middle class show a relative gain in emotional stability for 1936–1938 ($\beta = .18$), whereas their counterparts in the working class became less stable than more fortunate women in this stratum ($\beta = -.21$). The difference between these contrasting effects is not reliable, although the general pattern is similar to that observed some 30 years later in old age (see Table 2). The main exception is that the two groups of women actually become less alike on health outcomes across this time period. The lifelong process may entail the cumulative nature of class advantage and disadvantage and of mastery and setback. Initial class differences should expand as this dynamic evolves from early adulthood to old age. The advantaged became more advantaged, and the deprived more deprived.

Marital support before the Depression crisis represents a more direct and precise measure of adaptive resources than class position (class is linked to a variety of personal and social resources), and it has substantial implications for health under conditions of material hardship (Burke & Weir, 1977). These implications take at least two forms that are summarized by the terms *buffer* and *bolster*. In the *buffer* condition, economic deprivation is most likely to have adverse effects on adult health when marital relationships are strained, discordant, or weak. Strong, nurturant marriages protect spouses from the pathogenic effects of role loss or life change by eliciting definitions of the situation and emotional responses that improve effective coping (Lin, Simone, Ensel, & Kuo, 1979). The ability to maintain a sense of perspective is one benefit of feedback in marriage. Assurance of personal worth is another.

The *bolster* condition stresses the joint effect of economic hardship and a strong marriage. Marital support protects couples from the health risk of economic stressors, but it also facilitates individual and family adaptations that can enhance or improve physical and psychological well-being. For example, heavy income losses may require labor intensive activities that lead to stronger family ties. Marital support could also enable women to step out of their domestic worlds so as to provide additional family income. New responsibilities of this sort have the potential to increase personal confidence and assertiveness.

The buffer account explains how marital support reduces the illness risk of economic stress whereas the bolster mechanism specifies how stress actually encourages developmental growth. With the adverse effects of income loss most prominent among men, the buffer function of marital support has greatest relevance. The bolster effect suggests at least one way some Berkeley women were strengthened by the experience of the Depression's hardships.

Both of these observations are supported by outcomes from a series of regressions. With adjustments for initial stability, social class, and marital quality, we find that economic loss only diminished the emotional stability of men who entered the 1930s with relatively weak marriages (Figure 4). Marital quality in 1930–1931 is measured by an average of five scale scores: closeness of each spouse to the other, friendliness of each spouse to the other, and a general scale of mutual adjustment. Weak and strong marriages were defined by scores below and above the median. For both 1933–1935 and 1936–1938, deprived men who lacked a strong marriage experienced a significantly higher risk of emotional instability than the nondeprived ($\beta = -.19$, $p < .10$). For strong marriages, the effect shifts to the positive side, especially during the late 1930s ($\beta = .20$). The interaction effect of deprivation and discord on men's stability is statistically reliable only for 1936–1938 ($p < .10$). By the end of the 1930s, then, we find that the quality of men's marriages before hard times made a notable difference in their health career. Weak marriages accentuated the negative effects of income loss, whereas strong marriages enhanced the possibility of good health even in hard times.

Unlike the men, the Berkeley women who encountered Depression losses with a conflicted marriage *were not* more likely to suffer greater instability than the nondeprived. However, the support of a strong marriage did markedly increase chances that some benefits would be derived from

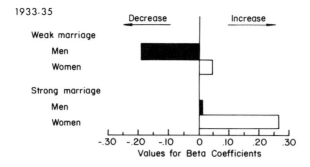

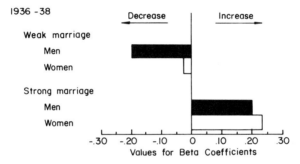

Figure 4. Deprivation effects on emotional stability of men and women, 1933–1935/1936–1938 by strength of marital bond, 1930–1931.

economic misfortune. This effect appears in both the first and second half of the 1930s (average $\beta = .25$ vs. coefficients of .04 or $-.02$ for the weak marriage group). The interaction effect is not statistically reliable, but the overall pattern for women offers greater empirical support for the benefits of strong ties (the bolster effect) than for the health costs of weak ties under economic pressure. Overall, weak ties seemed to matter for men, but not for their wives. In terms of emotional stability, the rewards of strong marital ties in hard times were experienced more by wives than by husbands.

Over the long course of Depression, health and marital support are interdependent. Parallel studies (Liker & Elder, 1983) of the Berkeley couples and their families indicate that Depression losses generally weakened marital ties by producing adverse change in the husband's health and personality. Men who were unstable before the Depression frequently became more irritable and explosive following a heavy loss of income, and these changes increased marital tension and conflicts, sometimes leading to incidents of domestic violence. We find no conclusive evidence of a causal process in which economic loss increased men's explosiveness by undermining their marriage and spouse's regard. However, the developmental benefits of hard times among initially stable wives did tend to minimize the detrimental influence of deprivation on marital relations.

When we focus on coping resources before hard times in the 1930s, marital support is far overshadowed by the protective power of emotional stability, though it is important to appreciate the interdependence of good marriages and good health, previously discussed. With much overlap between the two resources, we cannot be entirely successful in appraising their relative influence. But emotional stability before the Depression clearly still represents the best single predictor of how men and women fared under the economic pressures of the Great Depression.

Initial Health and Depression Influences

Husbands and wives were likely to remain in good health across the 1930s if they entered the decade in good health. Approximately one-third of the health variation among these men and women during the Depression era reflects their health before the economic collapse. Such continuity assumes different meaning for the sexes. In the case of men, health assessments before economic troubles tell us something about their vulnerability to the negative effects of income loss. Among women, the assessment identifies women who were most likely to acquire inner strength under the pressures of hard times. Vulnerability and adaptive potential are two sides of the Depression's impact.

The basic design for this analysis includes two groups that were distinguished in 1930 by scores below and above average on intial stability. Even without complex statistical analyses, it is clear that initial health played a most critical role in the health experience of hard-pressed men. For example, the adverse effects of deprivation among men were entirely confined to those who were judged unstable before their economic misfortune. Less than 10% of the deprived stable men were judged unstable in 1933–1935 (scores of 5–7). This compares among unstable men with 40% of the nondeprived and nearly 90% of the deprived. The analysis tells us much less about the emotional well-being of women in the 1930s, except that the initially healthy were most likely to meet the challenge of Depression pressures in their lives.

A more precise account of these differences was obtained for each health group by estimating with ordinary least squares the effects of income loss, marital quality or support in 1930, emotional stability in 1930, and social class as of 1929. Figure 5 presents a clear picture of the contrasting

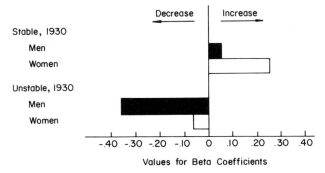

Figure 5. Deprivation effects on emotional stability of men and women, 1933–1935, by initial stability, 1930–1931.

effects for husbands and wives. Heavy income loss entailed very substantial health costs for initially unstable men, but not for unstable women. By comparison, such losses brought moderate gains in health for initially healthy women, though not for equally healthy men. Without any doubt, the men who were most vulnerable to economic stress were those whose health suffered most from misfortune during the Depression.

Men were especially vulnerable to the substantial health risks of Depression hardships and marital discord (Table 4). A broken or conflicted marriage accentuated the instability of unstable and stable men. Women who were unstable before hard times were likely to remain so throughout the Depression, but they were not particularly vulnerable to the strain of economic losses. Instead, the Depression relevance of initial health for women takes the form of adaptive potential. The interaction of hard times and initial health is statistically reliable ($p < .05$). Women endowed with good health before the 1930s frequently acquired even greater stability and resilience amidst the adaptive requirements of economic misfortune. In a sense, the extraordinary demands experienced by these women brought out their coping potential.

Both good health and a strong marriage enabled large numbers of men and women to survive conditions of heavy income loss with a sense of well-being. This joint influence is clearly shown by a comparison of four conditions: above and below average scores on initial stability and marital quality. In deprived circumstances, 92% of the men who entered the 1930s with poor health and a weak marriage were judged unstable in 1933–1935 (scores of 5–7 = unstable). This figure compares with 75% of the men who had strong marriages and poor health, and with 30% of the men who possessed initial good health and a weak marriage. It is noteworthy that not a single case from the good health–marriage category became unstable (as

TABLE 4

Emotional Stability of Men and Women by Economic Deprivation and Initial Resources in Groups Defined by Pre-Depression Stability: Regression Coefficients by Time Period

Stability by sex, time period, and initial health: Regression coefficient

	Men				Women			
	1933–1935 Initial health		1936–1938 Initial health		1933–1935 Initial health		1936–1938 Initial health	
Antecedent factors[a]	Stable 1930–1931	Unstable 1930–1931	Stable 1930–1931	Unstable 1930–1931	Stable 1930–1931	Unstable 1930–1931	Stable 1930–1931	Unstable 1930–1931
Income Loss, %								
beta	.04	−.36***	.09	−.27**	.25**	−.06	.23*	.09
(metric)	(−.001)	(−.012)	(.003)	(−.010)	(.008)	(−.002)	(.007)	(.001)
Marital quality, 1930–1931								
beta	.19	.22***	.34**	.27**	.02	.17	.01	.25
(metric)	(.19)	(.22)	(.33)	(.27)	(.02)	(.18)	(.009)	(.28)
Emotional stability,[b] 1930–1931								
beta	.32**	.54***	.12	.43***	.52***	.30**	.11	.20
(metric)	(.51)	(.60)	(.19)	(.49)	(.62)	(.47)	(.12)	(.32)
R²	18%	69%	19%	58%	36%	25%	12%	14%
N	49	51	50	51	54	50	52	53

[a] SES in 1929 is included in each equation as a control.

[b] Statistical interaction of income loss and emotional stability yielded a t-ratio of 2.18 for men in 1933–1935; and 2.56 for men in 1936–1938. Among women, the only reliable interaction occurred in 1933–1935, $t = 1.99$.

*$p < .10$. **$p < .05$. ***$p < .01$.

defined here) by 1933–1935 or 1936–1938. By contrast, poor health and a weak marriage before hard times were still a health risk 10 years later. Either condition or both increase the probability of ill health to about .33.

As noted earlier, marital quality adds little to the health status of women. Less than 12% of the women who entered the 1930s with good health were judged emotionally unstable, and marital support made no reliable difference in this state. However, women in poor health before the 1930s were more likely to avoid ill health in the Depression if they had the emotional support of their husbands; 38% were judged in ill health during 1933–1935, compared to 60% of the women in poor health *and* weak marriages. This joint condition is the only state that is linked to a reasonable chance for poor health by the 1940s (27%).

In the case of women, both marital support and good health before hard times functioned as modes of adaptive potential that fostered effective coping and even some growth under difficult circumstances. These factors and perhaps the qualities associated with higher status enabled women to make the best of their situation. We have noted adaptations that could account for the developmental gains of stable women, from the managerial demands of running a large household with pooled resources to gainful employment. For purposes of exploring this positive influence, we chose to focus on labor force entry as a growth-producing transition among resourceful women in particular. Following this inquiry, we conclude by examining the effect of "continuing economic troubles" on the emotional instability of men during the late 1930s.

Women's Health and Employment

As Depression crises hit one household after another, a good many Berkeley women entered the labor force to bolster family income, particularly late in the 1930s when their children were older. A fifth of the women obtained jobs by 1935. By the end of the decade, new entrants totaled 34% of the sample. We assumed that economic pressures increased the health of initially stable women through Depression employment. Employment could bring a new sense of personal work and confidence, as well as skills to cope effectively on one's own. To test this proposition we estimated the effects of labor-force entry in the 1930s on emotional stability during the late 1930s (1936–1938). Entry represents a life change in the sense that all women who were classified as entrants were not employed during 1929. Measures of economic deprivation, emotional stability, marital quality, and social class were included in the ordinary least squares equations (Table 5).

Stable women who acquired employment at some point in the 1930s were likely to show even better health than nonworkers by the end of the

TABLE 5

Economic Influences on Women's Emotional Stability:
Regression Coefficients in Two Time-Periods[a]

Factor	Regression coefficients	Effects on period measure of emotional stability[b]	
		1936–1938	1939–1945
% Income loss from 1929 to	beta	.35	.26
mid-1930s	(metric)	(.008)**	(.008)*
Entered labor force in 1930–	beta	.35	.16
1939 (0 = no; 1 = yes)	(metric)	(.64)**	(.28)
Number of cases		52	52

[a]N = Women above median on emotional stability, 1930–1931.
[b]All equations include measures of SES in 1929, emotional stability (1930–1931), and marital quality (1930–1931) as controls.
$*p < .10$; $**p < .05$.

decade. By enhancing the well-being of stable women in the 1930s, Depression employment increased prospects for good health during World War II as well. The process suggests a causal chain in which women's employment links deprivation and health. However, labor force entry did not account for or explain the effect of Depression hardship, at least not according to the evidence at hand. Economic deprivation and work entry were largely independent influences on women's health in this sample.

More details are needed on both sets of influences. As Kohn's (1977) research shows, the substantive complexity, routinization, and autonomy of work bear upon the development of intellectual flexibility, a sense of personal control, problem-solving skills, and morale. Most of the work options available to women in the 1930s were not of the challenging variety that enhance development. Unsatisfying jobs were perhaps a damaging influence to women who had little in reserve emotionally in 1930. Indeed we find that labor force entry among unstable women was a negative factor in their health by the end of the 1930s ($\beta = -.14$). The constrast between the influence of work entry on stable and on unstable women is statistically reliable ($p < .05$). Neither length of time in the Depression labor force nor the status level of the job yielded additional insights on women's health.

Continuing Economic Troubles in Men's Lives

A model of enduring impairment in the lives of Depression men should include the persistence of hard times up to World War II. At least in part,

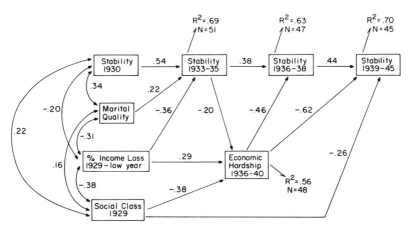

Figure 6. Emotional stability of men, 1930–1945, by economic deprivation in early 1930s and continued hardship (standardized regression coefficients. Sample includes men below average on stability in 1930–1931).

the form and duration of ill health may reflect a continuation of hard times. We know that a good many low-status families that suffered heavy losses in the Depression were still hardpressed at the beginning of World War II. The Depression's long arm could be expressed through chronic conditions of this sort, as well as through initial change in the health trajectories of deprived men that persisted over time.

To sort out these alternative pathways in men's lives, we constructed a causal model for emotional stability among men (up to 1945) who entered the Depression lacking emotional stability (below the median), the only group affected by hard times. We begin with three types of pre-Depression resources (a nurturant marriage, good health, and the asset of a middle class position) and economic loss as givens or variables not to be explained. Beyond this point, the model includes emotional stability at three time points and an index of persistent economic hardship after 1935. Men received one point on this index for each of the following conditions: (1) never recovered 1929 income or remained chronically deprived throughout the 1930s, (2) received public assistance after 1935, and (3) lost a job in the late 1930s. Index scores range from 0 to 3. Figure 6 presents only the causal paths that are statistically reliable ($p < .05$), except for the path between stability, 1933–1935, and hardship which is included for its suggestive value on reciprocal influence.

From the earliest stage of the Great Depression to the middle of World War II, economic adversity made initially unstable men even more unstable, particularly when economic troubles continued. Income loss at the Depression's outset lessened the emotional stability of men in 1933–1935 and also increased the probability of persistent economic hardship later in the 1930s. An even more influential predictor of persistent hardship is social standing as of 1929. The men who were still down economically by the late 1930s include a disproportionate number of the unskilled. Continuing hardship, in turn, generated more unstable behavior among men at the end of the 1930s and even during World War II. All long-term effects of income loss before 1935 were mediated through the powerful destabilizing effect of this loss and through its expression in persistent hardship.

What we see in Figure 6 is the substantial influence of environmental stresses on men who were least equipped to cope with such hardship in the first place. Environmental variations and deprivations have powerful effects on behavior when people are most dependent on external support, social accommodation, and continuity. Under dependency circumstances, decremental change profoundly alters life routines and psychological functioning. Unstable tendencies are least apt to be managed in the midst of family pressures and genuine hard times and may lead to behavior that makes bad conditions even worse.

The Depression experience is very different for men and women with stamina or emotional stability before hardship. Economic loss during the early 1930s had little adverse effect on the Depression health of these men and women, and we find no reliable evidence that continuing economic troubles diminished their well-being over time. To the best of our knowledge, stable men did not become more resilient under Depression stresses, though stable women show modest signs of such gains. A process of *accentuation* accurately depicts the relationship between economic stress and health. Dispositions were accentuated for the most part; they were not transformed.

OVERVIEW

Economic change raises profound questions about the life chances and health of individuals and cohorts. Downturns in the economy restrict options, overburden the support of family and friends, and undermine the self-attitudes and perspectives that nurture good health. An upswing in the economy may bring new opportunities as well as stronger pressures through rising aspirations and expectations. Most lifetimes are punctuated by ups and downs, even by cycles of ups and downs. Thus children of the 1920s were socialized in Depression hardship, entered adult roles and family responsibilities in the affluent 1940s and 1950s, and now face old age in a period of economic retrenchment. In this study we have traced the economic misfortune and welfare of men and women who were born around the turn of the century. Their lives span the prosperous 1920s, the depressed 1930s and booming postwar era, and the fiscal constraints of old age in the 1970s and 1980s.

The study is organized around the thesis that drastic economic hardship in the Great Depression influenced the health of men and women differentially according to their adaptive potential before the economic decline. Building upon the literature, we hypothesized that relative income loss (1929–1933) entailed more adverse consequences for the psychological health of men than women. Such effects were also proposed for adults in the working class, when compared to the middle class, and for those with marital discord and poor health at the outset. The subjects are members of the Berkeley Guidance Study and its longitudinal sample. The study was launched in the late 1920s with parents of infants. Slightly more than 200 parents were studied with varying degrees of coverage across the 1930s up to 1945, and a large number participated in a follow-up nearly 25 years later, 1969–1970. The original sample is predominantly middle class, white, and native-born.

The analysis begins with the Berkeley men and women in old age some 30 years after the Depression and then moves back to the Depression experience for a detailed assessment of the relationship between hard times and health. As a first step, the analysis of old age examined the long-term effects of Depression hardship on self-confidence and assertiveness for men and women. The results of this work support a gender-role hypothesis. With or without adjustments for the initial social class, Depression losses sharply diminished the self-confidence and assertiveness of men, and generally bolstered these states among women. Further analysis identified a class difference in the long-term effects of deprivation among women. Economic loss generated feelings of confidence and independence among women from the middle class, as of 1929, whereas the effects among lower-status women were consistently negative. Working class women most closely resemble men on the detrimental health effects of the hardships caused by the Depression.

The general pattern of results in old age corresponds with results from a more complex investigation of economic pressures and health during the 1930s. We measured emotional health at four points with a single rating (an average of annual ratings) called emotional stability: 1930, 1933–1935, 1936–1938, and 1939–1945. In total effect, economic deprivation increased the health risk for men and produced no reliable impact on the lives of women. The effect of economic loss for men and women did not vary by social class before the Depression, though substantial differences were observed in relationship to initial health and marital support. The most adverse effects of income loss on the emotional well-being of men were restricted to men who were judged relatively unstable at the outset and lacked the support of a nurturant marriage. Just as continuing economic hardship during the late 1930s substantially increased chances for enduring impairment up to the mid-1940s, economic recovery generally increased the chances for health recovery among men.

Instead of bringing a greater risk of impaired health to women, family deprivation enhanced their resilience and competence when conditions were supportive. This effect appears among women with the marital support of their husbands and especially among those who entered the 1930s in reasonably good health. Initially stable women in hard times were most apt to become stronger, more resilient persons when they had a good marriage and gainful employment during the 1930s. Class differences in the effects of hardship on health during the 1930s were much weaker than those observed in old age, some 30 years later.

From beginning to end, this study provides empirical support for the notion that situational influences on behavior are contingent on what people bring to the new situation. The health consequences of hardship in the Great Depression varied principally by gender, marital support, and initial health. Gender structured the personal meaning of family deprivation in ways that made the event especially damaging to the well-being of men. The buffering and bolstering role of a nurturant marriage in the health of men and women underscores the developmental and protective significance of social support and integration during times of crisis. And good health prior to misfortune or setbacks offered the inner resources to survive and even grow amidst hardship.

Historical studies and the investigation of hardship influences across many years are typically faced with conditions that leave much to be desired. Available data and sample limitations are relevant examples in this study. A contemporary study would undoubtedly favor established and multiple measures of health instead of the single rating on which much of our analysis rests. This rating of emotional stability was merely the best measure available to us, as indicated by parallel analyses with codes of behavioral impairment and confirmatory factor analyses. Whatever the measurement limitations, it is clear that our results generally mesh with the standard literature on life change. Small size and attrition over time are two important sample limitations, but they do not challenge the results we have reported. Questions about measure reliability, validity, and normality arise when sample size is small, and we have taken the precaution of analyzing the data with techniques that made different assumptions, especially in regard to the long-run effects of Depression hardship. The same pattern of effects emerged from our use of adjusted means, analysis of covariance, and an analysis of linear structural relations (LISREL).

The results of this study support five conclusions regarding historical change in the life course. First, such change differentiates the life experience of people within a birth cohort as well as between cohorts. A good many Berkeley men and women lost heavily on material status and goods, whereas others passed through the decade largely untouched. Second, the life-course effects of historical change varied according to the prechange state of the individuals, their life stage, and their resources. According to project research to date, children, adolescents, young adults, and middle-aged adults were subjected to different encounters with hard times; a difference that reflects age-related social roles and options. Third, individual and family adaptations to new conditions in historical change are influenced by pre-event resources. An example is the women who worked in the 1920s and then reentered the labor force under economic pressure in the 1930s. Fourth, the nature of these adaptations or responses may well provide some clues to the long-term effects of a changing environment.

A major challenge for life-span analysts is to understand the process by which early setbacks or losses continue to influence human functioning many years and even decades later. This knowledge bears directly on coping variations in old age. As Leiberman (1975, p. 136) observes, "We can always point to some individuals who seem to grow as a result of the crisis, other individuals who appear to handle the situation without showing any marked effects, and still others who wither—who cannot cope, who experience severe psychological distress or become somatically impaired." Such life variations may correspond with prior experience regarding adaptations to personal loss. The Depression experience of some Berkeley men and women enables us to make sense of their diverse ways of aging.

REFERENCES

Augustyniak, S., Duncan, G. J., & Liker, J. K. (1985). Income dynamics and self-conceptions: Linking theory and method in models of change. In G. H. Elder, Jr. (Ed.), *Life course dynamics: Trajectories and Transitions, 1968–1980.* Ithaca, New York: Cornell University Press.

Bandura, A. (1981). The self and mechanisms of agency. In J. Suls (Ed.), *Social Psychological Perspectives on the Self.* Hillsdale, NJ: Erlbaum.

Bandura, A. (1982). Self-efficacy mechanism in human agency. *American Psychologist, 37,* 122–147.

Bem, D. J. (1968). Self-perception theory. In L. Berkowitz (Ed.), *Cognitive theories in social psychology.* New York: Academic Press.

Block, J. (1971). *Lives through times.* Berkeley: Bancroft.

Block, J. H. & Block, J. (1980). The role of ego-control and ego-resiliency in the organization of behavior. In W. A. Collins (Eds.), *Minnesota Symposium on Child Psychology,* Vol. 13, Hillsdale, New Jersey: Erlbaum.

Brenner, M. H. (1973). *Mental health and the economy.* Cambridge: Harvard University Press.

Brenner, M. H. (1979). Influence of the social environment on psychopathology: The historic perspective. In J. E. Barrett (Ed.), *Stress and mental disorder.* New York: Raven.

Brown, G. W., & Harris, T. (1978). *Social origins of depression: A study of psychiatric disorder in women.* New York: Free Press.

Burke, R. J., & Weir, T. (1977). Marital helping relationships: The moderators between stress and well-being. *The Journal of Psychology, 95,* 121–130.

Cobb, S. (1976). Social support as a moderator of life stress. *Psychosomatic Medicine, 38,* 300–314.

Costa, Jr., P. T., & McCrae, R. R. (1980). Still stable all these years: Personality as a key to some issues in adulthood and old age. In P. B. Baltes & O. G. Brim, Jr. (Eds.), *Life-span development and behavior.* New York: Academic Press.

Dean, A., & Lin, N. (1977). The stress-buffering role of social support. *The Journal of Nervous and Mental Disease, 165,* 403–417.

Elder, Jr., G. H. (1974). *Children of the Great Depression.* Chicago: University of Chicago Press.

Elder, Jr., G. H. (1982). Historical experiences in the later years. In T. Hareven (Ed.), *Aging and life course transitions.* New York: Guilford.

Elder, Jr., G. H., & Liker, J. K. (1982). Hard times in women's lives: Historical influences across 40 years. *American Journal of Sociology, 88,* 241–269.

Ferman, L. G., & Gordus, J. P. (Eds.), (1979). *Mental health and the economy.* Kalamazoo, MI: Upjohn Institute.

Geweke, John F., & Singleton, Kenneth J. (1980). Interpreting the likelihood ratio statistic in factor models when the sample size is small. *Journal of the American Statistical Association, 75,* 133–37.

Gleser, G. C., Green, B. L., & Winget, C. (1981). *Prolonged psychological effects of disaster: A study of Buffalo Creek.* New York: Academic Press.

Hinkle, J., Lawrence E., & Loring, William C. (Eds.). (1977). *Effect of the man-made environment on health and behavior.* Atlanta, Georgia: Center for Disease Control.

Jahoda, M., Lazarsfeld, P. F., & Zeisel, H. (1971). *Marienthal: The sociography of an unemployed community.* New York: Aldine.

Kasl, S. V. (1979). Changes in mental health status associated with job loss and retirement. In J. E. Barrett (Ed.), *Stress and mental disorder.* New York: Raven Press.

Kessler, R., & Cleary, P. (1980). Social class and psychological distress. *American Sociological Review, 45,* 463–478.

Kessler, R. C., & McRae, Jr., J. A. (1982). The effect of wives' employment on the mental health of married men and women. *American Sociological Review, 47,* 216–227.

Klerman, G. S. (1979). Discussion, Part II. In J. E. Barrett (Ed.), *Stress and mental disorder.* New York: Raven.

Kobasa, S. C. (1979). Stressful life events, personality, and health: An inquiry into hardiness. *Journal of Personality and Social Psychology, 37,* 1–11.

Kohn, M. L. (1977). *Class and conformity.* Chicago: University of Chicago Press.

LaRocco, J. M., House, J. S., & French, Jr., J. R. P. (1980). Social support, occupational stress, and health. *Journal of Health and Social Behavior, 21,* 202–218.

Lazarus, R. S. (1966). *Psychological stress and the coping process.* New York: McGraw-Hill.

Leiberman, M. A. (1975). Adaptive processes in later life. In N. Data & J. H. Ginsburg (Eds.), *Life-span developmental psychology: Normative life crisis.* New York: Academic Press.

Liker, J. K., & Elder, Jr., G. H. (1983). Economic hardship and marital relations in the 1930s. *American Sociological Review, 48,* 343–359.

Lin, N. R., Simione, R. S., Ensel, W. M., & Kuo, W. (1979). Social support, stressful life events and illness: A model and empirical test. *Journal of Health and Social Behavior, 20,* 108–119.

Lynd, R. S., & Lynd, H. M. (1937). *Middletown in transition: A study in cultural conflicts.* New York: Harcourt.

Maas, H. S., & Kuypers, J. A. (1974). *From thirty to seventy: A forty-year longitudinal study of adult life styles and personality.* San Francisco: Jossey-Bass.

Macfarlane, J. W. (1938). Studies in child guidance. I. Methodology of data collection and organization. *Monographs of the Society for Research in Child Development, 3,* 1–254.

Moen, P., Kain, E., & Elder, Jr., G. H. (1983). Economic conditions and family life: Contemporary and historical perspectives. Prepared for Conference on Economics and Families, the National Academy of Sciences, January. In R. R. Nelson & F. Skidmore (Eds.), *American Families and the Economy: The High Cost of Living.* Washington, DC: National Academy Press.

Payne, R. (1980). Organizational stress and social support. In C. L. Cooper & R. Payne (Eds.), *Current concerns in occupational stress.* New York: Wiley.

Peterson, C., & Seligman, M. E. P. (1980). *Helplessness and attributional style in depression.* Paper presented at the Heidelberg Symposium on the Development of Metacognition, the Formation of Attributional Styles, and the Formation of Self-Instruction, Heidelberg University.

Rodin, J. (1980). Managing the stress of aging: The role of control and coping. In S. Levine & H. Ursin (Eds.), *Coping and health.* New York: Plenum.

Rosenberg, M., & Pearlin, L. I. (1978). Social class and self-esteem among children and adults. *American Journal of Sociology, 84,* 53–77.

Schaefer, C., Coyne, J. C., & Lazarus, R. S. (1981). The health-related functions of social support. *Journal of Behavioral Medicine, 4,* 381–406.

Seligman, M. E. P., Abramson, L. V., Semnel, A., & VanBalyer, C. V. (1979). Depressive attributional style. *Journal of Abnormal Psychology, 88,* 242–247.

Smith, M. B. (1968). Competence and socialization. In J. A. Clausen (Ed.), *Socialization and society.* Boston: Lilly, Brown.

Thomas, C. B. (1981). Stamina: The thread of life. *Journal of Chronic Disease, 34,* 41–44.

Weller, J. (1965). *Yesterday's people.* Lexington: University of Kentucky Press.

Williams, A. W., Ware, Jr., J. E., & Donald, C. A. (1981). A model of mental health, life events, and social supports applicable to general populations. *Journal of Health and Social Behavior, 22,* 324–336.

Wills, T. A., & Langner, T. S. (1980). Socioeconomic status and stress. In I. L. Kutash, L. B. Schlesinger, and Associates (Eds.), *Handbook on stress and anxiety.* San Francisco: Jossey-Bass.

CHAPTER 9

Fatherhood: Historical and Contemporary Perspectives*

ROSS D. PARKE
BARBARA R. TINSLEY

INTRODUCTION

Changes both in the structure of American families, as well as in the roles and functions of individual family members are a continuing focus of theoretical and empirical investigation. Many of the most significant of these changes are reflected in the role of the father in the contemporary family. In this chapter, the qualitative and quantitative shifts reflecting changes in social conditions that have taken place in fathering activities since the 1950s are assessed. Our focus is on historical change in fathering, but to appreciate shifts in the paternal role, complementary changes in the behaviors of other members of the family are also noted. A second aim is to illustrate the value of examining historical change in families for increasing our understanding of family functioning. A final purpose is to cast the study of fathers and families in a life-span framework in order to explore the utility of this approach for future theory building and research in this area.

THEORETICAL ASSUMPTIONS

We begin by presenting assumptions concerning the study of families. First, to fully understand the changing nature of the father's role in the

* Preparation of this chapter was supported by NICHD Grant HEW PH5 05951, NICHD Training Grant HDO 7205-01, and the National Foundation March of Dimes. We are grateful to Elaine Fleming for research assistance and to Sue Chapman and Sally Parsons for their assistance in the preparation of this manuscript.

203
Copyright © 1984 by Academic Press, Inc.
All rights of reproduction in any form reserved.
ISBN 0-12-482420-X

family, it is necessary to recognize the interdependence among the roles and functions of all family members (Parke & Tinsley, 1981). It is being increasingly recognized that families are best viewed as social systems. Consequently, to understand the behavior of one member of a family, the complementary behaviors of other members also need to be recognized and assessed. For example, as men's roles in families shift, changes in women's roles in families must also be monitored.

Second, fathers indirectly influence other family members, in addition to their direct influence through interaction. Examples of fathers' indirect impact include various ways in which fathers modify and mediate mother–child relationships. In turn, women affect their children indirectly through their husbands by modifying both the quantity and quality of father–child interaction (Lewis & Fiering, 1981; Parke, 1979, 1981; Parke, Power, & Gottman, 1979). In addition, recognition is being given to the embeddedness of families within a variety of other social systems, including both formal and informal support systems as well as the cultures in which they exist (Bronfenbrenner, 1979; Cochran & Brassard, 1979; Parke & Tinsley, 1982).

A further assumption that guides our essay is the importance of distinguishing among individual time, family time and historical time. *Individual time* is each family member's life course. *Family time* is defined as the timing of transitional life events for the family as a unit (e.g., residential relocation). *Historical time* provides the social conditions for individual and family transitions; an example is the 1960s—Vietnam War era. These distinctions are important because individual, family, and historical time do not always harmonize (Elder & Rockwell, 1979; Hareven, 1977). For example, a family event, such as the birth of a child—the transition to parenthood—may have very profound effects on a man who has just begun a career in contrast to one who has advanced to a stable occupational position. Moreover, individual and family time are both embedded within the social conditions and values of the historical time in which they exist (Hareven, 1977). The role of father, as is the case with any social role, is responsive to such fluctuations.

Finally, in this chapter two types of explanations typically offered for change over the course of time in behavior—*period* and *cohort* explanations are examined. According to Cherlin (1981)

> Period explanations refer to the consequences of events that occur during the period studied. The view that patterns of marriage and childbearing changed as a result of a contemporaneous, society-wide shift in values can be considered a period explanation. . . . Cohort explanations refer to the consequences in later years of the early experiences or shared characteristics of particular birth cohorts. The view that the psychological impact of growing up in the depression—

or the size of one's cohort—influenced one's later family life can be considered a
cohort explanation. (1981, pp. 42–43)

However, these explanations are not mutually exclusive, as Cherlin further
argues:

> Since each cohort lives in a different period and therefore is subject to a different
> set of period-based influences, it is difficult to determine whether social change
> from generation to generation is produced by the differing characteristics of the
> cohorts involved or by society-wide changes during the time period studied.
> Period-based and cohort-based effects, in other words, are often confounded.
> (Cherlin, 1981, p. 43)

As far as possible, attention is addressed to the relative plausibility of these
two types of explanations for accounting for changes in fathering.

In Search of a Baseline

One of the major tasks in an analysis of historical changes in fathering
is to define the sometimes elusive historical baseline against which to com-
pare subsequent changes. A number of problems need to be recognized. It is
incorrect to assume stability in fathering behavior over historical time. Instead, both the quality and quantity of father involvement has fluctuated
widely even over the past century (Bloom-Feshbach, 1981; Lummis, 1982).
Second, change is not always linear at the quantitative or qualitative levels.
Nor is it assumed that increased participation has been, is, or will be the
dominant trend. Moreover, at the qualitative level, change occurs at varying
rates in different spheres of fathering. Third, due to the shifts in methodology, it is, at best, difficult to make comparisons in fathering between
two points in historical time. It is against this backdrop of difficulties that
we approach this topic. Instead of asserting that there is a true (and in any
case, an arbitrarily selected) baseline, we first briefly sketch some of the
main findings concerning fathers of the past decade, largely obtained using
intact nuclear families. Secondly, shifts that are taking place in the society
are documented and where data permit, comparisons are made between
these traditional families and families who were selected specifically because
they differ from the traditional familial arrangement along one or more
dimensions. By careful selection of comparison groups, a tentative picture of
the interplay between historical or secular changes in society and fathering
activities can be drawn. Our analysis takes advantage of the fact that in
complex Western industrialized societies, change occurs at different rates in

various subgroups of the population, thus permitting comparisons among groups who differentially vary from a traditional family pattern. A final aim is to evaluate the impact of these shifts on children's social and cognitive development.

A Portrait of Traditional Families

In studies of relatively traditional families, it has been consistently found that from birth on mothers feed and caretake more than fathers with both infants and older children (see Lamb, 1981; Parke, 1979; Parke & Tinsley, 1981, for reviews). Even when adjustment are made for the amount of time available for caregiving activities of mothers and fathers, the same pattern of greater mother participation is evident. This pattern is present not only in U.S. samples (Kotelchuck, 1976; Rendina & Dickerscheid, 1976), but in other countries, such as Great Britain (Richards, Dunn, & Antonis, 1977), Australia (Russell, 1978), and France and Belgium (Szalai, 1972) as well. There are, however, both wide individual differences across families in the level of father participation and in a later section, some of the factors that modify the father's contribution to caregiving is considered.

Two qualifications merit brief mention. A distinction between *competence* and *performance* is useful in studies of father involvement in caregiving. According to Parke and Sawin (1976), fathers are capable of executing caregiving tasks (e.g., feeding) and exhibit as much sensitivity to infant cues during feeding as mothers. Moreover, using the amount of milk consumed as an index of competence, fathers and mothers were found to be equally skillful in this task. Fathers do have the capability to execute caregiving activities competently even though they generally contribute less time to this type of activity than mothers.

Second, although research on the father's influence in infancy has centered primarily on the direct impact of the father's behavior (e.g., as a feeding or stimulatory agent), his influence may be indirectly mediated through the mother or other members of the family as well (see Lewis & Fiering, 1981; Parke et al., 1979; for detailed discussion of this issue). For example, even when they are not directly participating in feeding, fathers can indirectly affect this activity by modifying the behavior of the feeding agent. The father's indirect role in feeding is well illustrated by Pedersen's (1975) investigation of the influence of the husband–wife relationship on mother–infant interaction in a feeding context. Feeding, however, is not the only important interactional context and next we turn to another significant context—play.

Play: The Distinctive Roles of Mother and Father

Although mothers contribute to caregiving more than fathers, fathers are not necessarily uninvolved with their infants. Both mothers and fathers are active playmates for their infants and children; however, fathers devote a higher proportion of their time with their children to play than do mothers. For example, in one recent study of middle-socioeconomic-status (SES) families, Kotelchuck (1976) found that fathers devote nearly 40% of their time with their infants to play, whereas mothers spend about 25% of their time in play. Further evidence comes from Lamb (1977) who observed interactions among mother, father, and infant in their homes at 7 to 8 months and again at 12 to 13 months. Lamb found marked differences in the reasons that fathers and mothers pick up their infants: Fathers were more likely to hold the babies to play with them, whereas mothers were more likely to hold them for caretaking purposes.

Fathers and mothers differ not only in quantity of play, but in the style of play as well. Fathers' play is more likely to be physical and arousing, whereas mothers' play is more verbal, didactic, and toy-mediated (see Parke, 1979; Parke and Tinsley, 1981; Power & Parke, 1982). Mothers and fathers provide distinctly different types of stimulation and learning opportunities (Power & Parke, 1982). Only by considering *both* mother and father as separate but interdependent members of the family system can we understand early infant development.

UNPLANNED AND PLANNED CHANGE: EFFECTS ON FATHERING

Although this traditional portrait of father as playmate and mother as caregiver is still valid for many families, a variety of changes in the secular sphere suggests that this pattern is undergoing revision. In this section, some of the changes that have modified this traditional view of fathers and mothers are outlined. Two types of changes merit distinction: *unplanned* and *planned* change. Many of these types of changes are unplanned and/or may not have been specifically implemented to alter fathering roles. These changes could be viewed as naturally occurring experiments in social change, but as we demonstrate, many of these changes had unanticipated effects on fathers and family organization. In contrast, planned change is restricted to deliberate intervention strategies that are directly producing alterations in the relative distribution of gender role-related behaviors of men and women. In the following section, we focus on unplanned change, and in a later section, on planned change.

UNPLANNED CHANGES IN FATHERING

Over time, unplanned modifications in fathering behavior result, to a large extent, from changing social conditions in our society. We examine such influences on paternal behavior as the impact of shifts in the medical sphere on fathering, including changes in childbirth procedures, advances in care of preterm infants, and hospital visitation practices. In the economic sphere, the effects of the sharp rise in maternal employment are explored. Recent shifts in the timing of first parenthood are examined for their effects on fathering. What is the impact of the increases in divorce and remarriage on fathering behavior? The extent to which the level and quality of maternal and paternal caregiving and play is modified in response to these differing sets of changes is answered by these analyses. In addition, this exercise begins to define the limits of the plasticity of maternal and paternal roles and to provide some preliminary clues concerning the relative impact of differing types of social change on parenting behavior as well as some insights concerning the aspects of parenting most susceptible to secular change.

The Impact of Changes in the Medical Sphere on Fathers' Role in the Family

A variety of changes in medical practices and hospital operation have taken place since the 1950s. In this section, a number of these changes, including the rise in the number of cesarean-section deliveries, the increase in the survival rates of low-birth-weight preterm infants, and the shortened lying-in period following childbirth are examined. In addition the impact of liberalized hospital visitation practices for fathers as well as greater paternal participation in labor and delivery on fathering are explored.

For a variety of reasons, there has been a dramatic increase in the percentage of cesarean-section deliveries since the early 1970s. In 1970, only 5.5% of infants were delivered by cesarean section; in 1980 this figure was 18% (Bottoms, Rosen, & Sokol, 1980). Recent research suggests that cesarean childbirth can alter fathers' level of participation in routine care-taking activities. In a recent study, Pedersen, Cain, Zaslow, and Anderson (1980) found that fathers of cesarean-delivered infants engaged in significantly more caregiving at 5 months than fathers in a comparison group whose infants were vaginally delivered. Although the fathers of the cesarean-delivered infants were more likely to share caregiving responsibilities in several different areas on an equal basis with the mother, fathers in the comparison sample tended to only "help out", with the mothers still meeting the major proportion of caregiving needs. Other investigators have found similar patterns. In an interview study of 85 couples and nine additional women through pregnancy, birth, and their child's infancy, Grossman, Eichler and Winickoff, (1980) found that in families in which the infant was cesarean-delivered, fathers seemed more involved with their infants than fathers of vaginally delivered infants when the infants were 2-months-old. Vietze, MacTurk, McCarthy, Klein, and Yarrow (1980) also report that cesarean delivery results in more active paternal caretaking. Seventy-five families with a first child were observed through the first year of life. Fathers of cesarean-delivered infants demonstrated more soothing behavior toward their infants than fathers of vaginally delivered infants at 6 months, although this was not maintained by the infants' first birthday. The most probable explanation of these findings suggests that mothers, as a result of the surgery, are unable to assume a fully active role in caregiving during the early postpartum weeks. Fathers, as a result of their increased involvement in early care, continue this caregiving activity even after the time that the mothers are able to resume a more active role, although it appears that fathers of vaginally delivered infants catch-up by 12 months.

The Pedersen *et al.* (1980) study, as well as other studies of the effects of cesarean birth on paternal involvement, underlines the importance of the early postpartum period for establishing role definitions. However, this should not imply that these early established patterns are not modifiable. As noted here previously, Vietze *et al.* (1980) found that by the end of the first year these differences in father participation between the two types of deliveries have disappeared. Although these differential patterns of increased father involvement in caregiving appear to be short-lived, the long-term impact of this heightened involvement early in the father's career as a parent either on the father himself, the mother, or the child remains to be determined. For example, it might be argued that fathers who experienced early involvement may be more responsive to future demands for participation at later time points during such temporary events as maternal illness or more permanent alterations such as maternal employment. Moreover, this research again reminds us of the importance of considering indirect effects in the family system, in this case, that the mother's behavior and needs—as a result of the cesarean birth—may modify father–infant interaction (Pedersen *et al.*, 1980).

Another situation that may increase the father's role in early caregiving is the premature birth of a baby. Approximately 14% of the infants in the United States are born prematurely, and due to dramatic advances in the care and treatment of premature infants, the mortality rate for this high-risk population has shown impressive decreases. Whereas the mortality rates for preterm infants in the United States weighing between 1000 and 2500 grams was approximately 20% in 1950 (Eastman, 1950; cited by Leiderman, 1983) mortality rates for this population have now dropped to approximately 5% (Leiderman, 1983). To cite a typical example, the Los Angeles County University of Southern California Medical Center had the following change in perinatal mortality: $\frac{55}{1000}$ total births in 1969 to less than $\frac{20}{1000}$ in 1978. These changes have been particularly striking with low-birth-weight infants (Hodgman, 1982).

A number of factors associated with the birth of a preterm infant may increase father involvement. First, the context of care for preterms may elicit greater father involvement. Part of the reason for the lower rates of mortality for preterm infants is the change toward centralized hospital units that specialize in the care of high-risk infants. Because one facility usually covers a large geographic region, infants are often transported from the delivery hospital to a central high-risk nursery. The mother usually is not transported, which means that it is the father who has the major amount of contact with the infant. There is some evidence (Leiderman & Seashore, 1975) that suggests that this situation may be stressful and may be a contributor to family disharmony due to the fact that mothers are being supplanted by fathers as the primary parent. Alternatively, the opportunity for the father to have contact and to be involved early in the infant's care may, in part, account for the finding that fathers continue to show a high level of interest in the infant even after the mother is able to participate more fully, as indexed by rates of hospital visitation by fathers to see their preterm infants. Moreover, fathers contribute in this situation, not only by their direct participation, but indirectly as well. Research by Minde, Trehub, Corter, Boukydis, Celhoffer, and Marton (1978) has shown that mothers who have supportive husbands tend to visit their premature babies in the hospital more often and that mothers who visit more often have fewer parenting problems later than mothers who visit less frequently. Again, we see that fathers can influence their infants indirectly by affecting the mother–infant relationship.

Paternal support in families with preterm infants continues beyond the hospital period. Investigators in both England and the United States have recently found that fathers of premature infants are more active in feeding, diapering, and bathing their infants than fathers of term babies, not only in the hospital but later at home as well (Hawthorne, Richards, & Callon, 1978; Yogman, 1983). These fathers' more active participation in caregiving is particularly helpful because premature infants usually need to be fed more often than term infants and experience more feeding disturbances. Premature infants also can be less satisfying to feed and to interact with because they are often less responsive to parental stimulation than term infants (Goldberg, 1979). Thus, prematurity may elicit greater father involvement in caretaking at least partially because of the father's desire to relieve the mother of full responsibility for the extra time and skill required for caring for these infants. In turn, the father may indirectly influence the premature infant by positively affecting the mother–infant relationship. Finally, fathers probably play an important role in providing emotional as well as instrumental support to mothers which is especially important in view of the stress associated with the premature birth of an infant (Parke & Tinsley, 1982; Tinsley & Parke, 1984a).

Play patterns, as well as levels of involvement in caregiving may be different for fathers of preterm infants than fathers of term infants. In a comparative observational investigation of the interaction patterns of fathers with preterm and term infants in the high-risk nursery and at home shortly after the infants' discharge, styles of father–infant play with the preterm and term infants differed (Tinsley, Johnson, Szczypka, Parke, 1982). Fathers exhibited their characteristic higher rate of physical play— but only when the infant was born at term. When the infant was born prematurely, there was no mother–father difference in play style. The differences were particularly marked by 3 weeks; during the hospital period, there were no differences between mothers and fathers in their treatment of either term or preterm infants. Possibly fathers assume that the premature infant is fragile and unable to withstand robust physical stimulation which in turn leads to an inhibition of fathers' usual play style. Follow-up observations are currently underway to determine the stability of this pattern over later developmental points in the first year of infancy. In sum, play, as well as caregiving, can be altered by the medical status of infant, but it is clear that to understand fathers' role shifts in response to premature birth requires that fathers be viewed in the context of the family system.

Another change in fathering is increased paternal participation in labor and delivery. Even as late as 1972, fathers were permitted in the delivery room in only 27% of American hospitals and not until 1974 did the American College of Obstetricians and Gynecologists endorse the father's presence during labor. By 1980, fathers were admitted to delivery rooms in approximately 80% of American hospitals.

The effects of the fathers' presence are not yet well understood. Some evidence indicates that women whose husbands participated in both labor and delivery reported less pain, received less medication, and felt more positive about the birth experience than women whose husbands were present only during the first stage of labor (Henneborn & Cogan, 1975). Fathers may be indirectly affected themselves by the reduction in maternal medication, in light of earlier research (Parke, O'Leary, & West, 1972) that found that fathers interact less with heavily medicated infants and more with active, alert infants. Other evidence indicates that the presence of a supportive companion—although not necessarily a father—results in a significantly lower incidence of problems of labor and birth (cesarean birth, meconium staining, fetal distress) (Sosa, Kennell, Klaus, Robertson, & Urrutia, 1980)

Moreover, fathers' presence during the second stage of labor and delivery increased the mothers' emotional experience at the birth; mothers reported the birth as a "peak" experience more often if fathers were present. Similarly fathers' emotional reactions to birth were heightened by being present at the delivery (Entwisle & Doering, 1981). In another study based on paternal observations and interviews, Petersen, Mehl and Leiderman (1979) found that a more positive birth experience for the father was associated with enhanced attachment to the infant. These investigators also found that longer labors at home, in contrast to hospital delivery, were associated with greater paternal attachment. Finally, they note that birth-related events were stronger predictors of attachment than were data from the pregnancy period, thus arguing that self-selection factors were not as important as the birth experience itself on subsequent involvement with the baby. Together the evidence tentatively suggests that the presence of the father has positive benefits for both mothers and fathers. Finally, in light of the data demonstrating that maternal medication during labor and delivery can have depressive and disorganizing effects on infants (Conway & Brackbill, 1970; Murray, Dolby, Nation, & Thomas, 1981), paternal presence may indirectly benefit the infant as well.

A related issue concerns the impact of extended father–infant contact during the newborn period on the subsequent father–infant relationship. Recently Keller, Hildebrandt, and Richards (1981) compared fathers who received extended contact alone with their infants (approximately 4 hours) with fathers who followed a traditional schedule of contact of only visiting their wives and babies together during the postpartum period. Behavioral assessments at 6 weeks postpartum indicated that extended-contact fathers engaged in significantly greater en face behavior and more vocalizing during feeding than traditional-contact fathers. Moreover, the extended-contact fathers had a more positive attitude toward baby care, were responsible for a greater percentage of baby care, viewed their infants as more attractive, and reported playing with their babies longer each day than traditional-contact fathers. Although these findings are interesting and are consistent with earlier work with mothers (See Klaus & Kennell, 1982), in light of reports of failure to replicate earlier findings on extended maternal contact

(Svejda, Campos, & Emde, 1980) as well as recent critiques (Goldberg, 1983; Lamb & Hwang, 1982) of prior research in this area, considerable caution in interpreting the results of this study is necessary.

Finally, because there has been a gradual reduction in the average length of hospitalization following childbirth over the past three decades, it may be that opportunities for father–infant contact in the hospital are becoming less critical. At the same time, a reduced lying-in period may increase the importance of father participation in the period immediately after the baby goes home. The impact of length of postpartum hospitalization on levels of father involvement in caregiving merits exploration, as would the impact of these variations on the subsequent father–infant relationship.

A number of other changes in hospital practices, including more liberal visitation rules as well as the trend toward family pediatric units, which permit a parent to stay with an older hospitalized child, may be altering the father–child relationship. Finally, the increasing availability of paternity leaves may provide fathers with greater opportunity to participate in the early care of the infant.

A life-span perspective on these shifts in medical practices requires consideration of both the cohort as well as the time of testing. It is not possible from the available data to assess whether the shifts in delivery practices, such as the increase in cesarean sections, affect fathers of different cohorts in similar ways. Examination of samples to assess this issue would be worthwhile because it is not clear whether these changes would have produced similar shifts in father involvement in another time period. For example, in a more traditional era, characterized by more rigid gender roles for mother and fathers, a cesarean-section delivery may not necessarily have led to increased paternal involvement. Female members of the family's social network such as friends or relatives (parents or in-laws) may have been called upon to assist the new mother. However, in light of decreased geographical proximity between families and extended kin, family support systems are often less available which, in turn, increases the likelihood of father involvement. Given that the use of social networks for child care related activity is negatively correlated with the father's involvement in child care, (Bloom-Feshbach 1979), it is suggested that if the grandparents and other members of the social network are helping with child care in a situation such as a cesarean-section birth, there is less impetus and opportunity for the father to be involved in this type of support. Thus, several societal trends converge to create a situation in which fathers are naturally encouraged to increase their participation in caregiving. In summary, these data clearly underscore the role played by changes in the medical sphere on shifts in both quantity and quality of fathering.

It is not only the medical context of childbirth that is promoting change, but the timing of the onset of childbearing is important as well. In the next section, we examine this issue.

The Impact of Timing of Parenting on the Father's Role

Patterns of the timing of the onset of parenting are changing, although those changes are not evident from an examination of the median age of parents at the time of the birth of their first child. In the first half of the 1950s the median age of a woman at the birth of her first child was 22.2 years, whereas in the 1975–1979 period it was approximately the same— 22.3 years. This apparent pattern of stability, however, masks the impressive expansion of the range of the timing of first births during the 1970s. During this period, women were having babies earlier *and* later than in previous decades. Two particular patterns can be identified. First, there was a dramatic increase in the number of adolescent pregnancies, and second, there was an increase in the number of women who were postponing childbearing until their 30s. Between 1970 and 1980, there was an increase in the rate of childbirths to adolescent mothers. Similarly, between 1970 and 1979, the number of first babies born to women between 30 and 34 years old doubled. What are the consequences of this divergent pattern of childbearing?

A number of factors need to be considered in order to understand the impact on fathering of childbearing at different ages. First, the *life-course context,* which is broadly defined as the point at which the individual has arrived in his social, educational, and occupational timetable, is an important determinant. Second, the *historical context,* namely the societal and economic conditions that prevail at the time of the onset of parenting, interacts with the first factor in determining the effects of variations in timing. Let us consider early and delayed childbirth in light of these issues.

EARLY-TIMED CHILDBEARING

The most significant aspect of early entry into parenthood is that it is a nonnormative event. Achieving parenthood during adolescence can be viewed as an accelerated role transition (Russell, 1980). As McCluskey, Killarney, and Papini (1983) note, "School age parenting may produce heightened stress when it is out of synchrony with a normative life course. Adolescents may be entering parenting at an age when they are not financially, educationally, and emotionally ready to deal with it effectively" (p. 49). In addition, adolescent childbearers are at higher medical risk, due to poorer diets, malnutrition, and less intensive and consistent prenatal care. In the educational sphere, early childbearing is negatively associated with educational attainment—especially for females (Card & Wise, 1978). Similarly, early onset of parenthood is linked with diminished income and assets as well as poverty, relative to individuals who delay childbearing (Card & Wise, 1978, Presser, 1980); again the effect is particularly severe for women. In turn, this has long-term occupational consequences with early child-bearers overrepresented in blue-collar jobs and underrepresented in the professions. Another issue is that early childbearing is more likely to be unplanned; according to one estimate (Presser, 1974), for 15–19-year-old women, 80% of the births were unplanned, whereas for a 24–29-year-old group only 30% were unplanned. Similarly, although only 9% of the 24–29-year-old women gave birth out-of-wedlock, 60% of the teenagers were unmarried. Other estimates differ but still suggest a higher-than-average probability that adolescents are unmarried at the time of conception and/or at the time of delivery. One estimate (Alan Guttmacher Institute, 1976) suggests that of the U.S. teenagers who gave birth, one-third are conceived within wedlock, one-third marry during pregnancy, and one-third give birth out-of-wedlock. However, marriage often occurs in the first 2 years after the delivery; again estimates vary but approximately one-quarter of the unmarried women tend to marry within 2 years (Furstenberg, 1976; Presser, 1980). Teenage marriages tend to be highly unstable; separation and/or divorce is two to three times as likely among adolescents than women who are 20 years or older (Baldwin & Cain, 1980).

In part, this pattern is due to the fact that the fathers also are often adolescents, and as in the case of teenage mothers, are often unprepared financially and emotionally to undertake the responsibilities of parenthood (Parke, Power, & Fisher, 1980). In view of the low rates of marriage and high rates of separation and divorce for adolescents, adolescent fathers, in contrast to "on-schedule" fathers, have less contact with their offspring. However, contact is not absent; in fact, several studies of unmarried adolescent fathers maintain a surprising amount of paternal involvement for extended periods following the birth. For example, in a study of 138 unmarried adolescent mothers in Minnesota, Nettleton and Cline (1975) found that 50% of the 45 mothers who did not relinquish custody of their infants dated the father during the infant's first year of life. Moreover, 20% of these 45 eventually married the fathers of their children. Similarly, 46% of the 180 unwed mothers Lorenzi and his colleagues (Lorenzi, Klerman, & Jekel, 1977) interviewed in New Haven either married the child's father or were seeing him on a regular basis 26 months after the birth. Although the number of women who have regular contact with the men who fathered their children declined over the child's first 2 years (56% at 3 months, 40% at 15 months, and 23% at 26 months), a small but constant proportion of the mothers at each time point (18%) reported that they saw the father only occasionally. In addition, most of the fathers who visited the mothers also visited the child. Finally, Furstenberg (1976) noted similar rates of visitation as late as 5 years after the birth. Twenty-one percent of the fathers were living with their children, another 20% visited their offspring on a regular basis, whereas 21% visited occasionally. An interesting and consistent pattern in these studies is that a significant number of fathers establish a stable live-in relationship with their child after 1 or 2 years (Furstenberg, 1976; Lorenzi et al., 1977)—a period that is often necessary to complete formal education and/or secure regular employment. As will be discussed later, a delay in regular father–child contact does not necessarily preclude the development of a satisfactory father–child relationship or diminish the father's impact on his child's later development. Evidence indicates that adolescent-father involvement has a positive impact on the child's social and cognitive development (Furstenberg, 1976).

How have increases in the rate of adolescent childbirth altered the father's role? Or to pose the question differently, how was being an adolescent father different in a historical period when adolescent childbearing was relatively rare than in a period when the rate is significantly higher? First, as rates of adolescent childbearing rise and the event becomes less nonnormative or deviant, the social stigma associated with the event may decrease. In combination with increased recognition that adolescent fathers have a legitimate and potentially beneficial role to play, adolescent fathers' opportunities for participation have probably expanded. Second, the increased availability of social support systems such as day care may make it easier for adolescent fathers (and mothers) to simultaneously balance educational and occupational demands with parenting demands. Clearly, longitudinal studies of the long-term impact of achieving fatherhood during adolescence are necessary, as well as more investigation of the impact of adolescent fatherhood during different historical periods.

POSTPONED CHILDBEARING

A variety of contrasts exist between becoming a parent in adolescence and initiating parenthood 15 to 20 years later. In contrast to adolescent childbearing, when childbearing is delayed, considerable progress in occupational and educational spheres has potentially already taken place. Education is generally completed and career development is well underway for both males and females.

The aim of a recent study by Daniels and Weingarten (1982) was to determine whether the patterns of parental involvement vary as a function of early- versus later-timed parenthood. These investigators interviewed 72 couples. Half of the couples, who formed the early-timed group, had their first child when the wife was on the average 21.5 years old, whereas the remaining couples who formed the late-timed group began their parenthood when the wife was on the average 30.5 years old. In addition, three generations were represented a decade apart. One-third of the sample (12 early- and 12 late-timed parents) were in their early 20s in 1980, one-third were in their early 40s, and one-third were in their early 50s.

The oldest cohort, born in the late 1920s and early 1930s had their children between 1945–1955 and early-timed parenthood was the usual pattern. Childbearing began at 21 years of age, approximately 14 months after marriage. Late-timed parenthood was nonnormative. The middle-age cohort was born in the late 1930s and began their parental careers in the 1955–1970 period. This was a transition sample, which contained parents who were following the older pattern of early parenting as well as parents who were delaying the onset of parenting. The youngest cohort was born in the 1950s, and their children were born in the 1970s. Late timing was more common and a longer spread between marriage and childbirth was evident. In this cohort, the average age of marriage was 27 years, but the onset of parenthood was delayed approximately 4 years. Semistructured open-ended clinical interviews were conducted with both spouses. Although some quantitative results were generated by this method, the main results were qualitative and are of value mainly as hypotheses for future systematic evaluation.

Although our focus is on fathers, the impact of the timing of the onset of parenthood can best be appreciated by examining the effects on both mothers and fathers—consistent with our view that fathers are best understood as part of the family system.

The timing of parenthood has a major impact on career patterns of women. Daniels and Weingarten (1982) distinguish two patterns of work outside the home and parenting: A simultaneous pattern in which work outside the home and parenting coexist in the parents' lives and a sequential pattern in which work outside the home and parenthood follow one another. One of their main findings was that the early-timed mothers were 8 times more likely to follow a sequential than a simultaneous pattern, whereas the late-timed mothers were more evenly divided into simultaneous (16 mothers) and sequential (20 mothers) patterns. Suggestive cohort effects are evident among the late-timed mothers. There is a clear trend across the three cohorts, who had children in either the 1950s, 1960s or 1970s, for mothers to move from a sequential pattern in the 1950s to a simultaneous pattern by the 1970s. In the oldest cohort, twice as many late-timed mothers followed a sequential pattern (8 mothers) rather than a simultaneous pattern (4 mothers); in the middle cohort, 7 mothers followed the sequential pattern and 5 mothers adopted the simultaneous pattern; and in the youngest cohort the reverse was true, where 7 followed the simultaneous pattern and 5 followed a sequential pattern. Although these data require replication with larger samples before confidence can be placed in this trend, the findings underscore the importance of considering how various cohorts manage early- and late-timing decisions. For women in the oldest group, in which delayed childbearing was nonnormative, the compromise involved acceptance of a sequential strategy in which career was temporarily interrupted. In contrast, for women in the youngest cohort, the climate of the 1970s with the more liberal attitudes toward maternal employment led to more of these women pursuing both parenthood and careers simultaneously.

Each of these patterns has distinct advantages and disadvantages. When childbearing begins early, career development is typically delayed and less time is available for negotiating both marital and personal identity issues. When both parenthood and career begin simultaneously, both may be potentially compromised by the necessity of dividing time and energy across two domains. On the other hand, both career and parenthood are underway by a relatively young age. Delaying the onset of parenting, of course, means that a career is already established, that marital stability may be achieved, and that the issue of personal identity may be more settled. If a sequential pattern is followed, the opportunity to devote onself to parenting more fully is available, but this approach disrupts career advancement and leads to loss of income. If a simultaneous pattern is followed, there is not the obvious career interruption. There may be work–family conflicts, however, but these are probably fewer than in the case of the early simultaneous pattern due to greater career security.

Mothers who delay childbearing may also qualitatively interact differently with their infants. Ragozin and her colleagues (Ragozin, Bashman, Crnic, Greenberg, & Robinson, 1982) found that both maternal attitudes and behavior were affected by maternal age. In a comparison of mothers between 18- and 38-years of age, they found with maternal age there were positive linear increases in the amount of caretaking responsibility, and satisfaction with parenting and a negative linear relationship for social time away from their infant. Moreover, observed interaction between mothers and their 4-month old infants indicated that maternal affect increased with maternal age. Similarly, older mothers were more successful in eliciting vocal and imitative responses from their infants—an index of their social and cognitive teaching skills. However, these mother–infant interaction effects were evident only for primiparous mothers, and as parity increased, the relationships between maternal age and parity became negative. As Ragozin *et al.* note: "It appears that having previously experienced parenthood, a mother becomes more interested in extra-familial roles as she grows older—more ready to 'get on with her life'. Thus, older multiparous women exhibit less positive affect and less optimal behavior toward infants. In contrast, the older primiparous woman having more experience in non-parenting roles, is more committed to the parenting experience" (Ragozin *et al.*, 1982, p. 633). In summary, not only career patterns are affected by timing of parenthood, but as this study clearly illustrates, maternal roles and behavior are affected as well. Unfortunately, Ragozin *et al.* provide no information concerning the extra-familial work patterns of these women.

What are the consequences of these patterns for father involvement? Again, as for mothers, both early and late timing have advantages and drawbacks for fathers. Men who have their children early have more energy for certain types of activities that are central to the father role, such as physical play (Parke & Tinsley, 1981). Similarly, the economic strain that occurs early is offset by avoiding financial problems in retirement due to the fact that children are grown up and independent earlier. In turn, early fathering generally means beginning grandfathering at a younger age, which in turn, permits the early-timed father to be a more active grandparent (for a discussion of these issues, see Tinsley & Parke, 1984b). In spite of these advantages, when men become fathers early, there are two main disadvantages: financial strain and time strain, due to the competing demands imposed by trying simultaneously to establish a career as well as a family. In contrast, the late-timed father avoids these problems. The late-timed father's career is more settled permitting more flexibility and freedom in balancing the demands of work and family. Second, patterns of preparental collaboration between the parents may already be established and persist into the parenthood period. In their study, Daniels and Weingarten found early-timed fathers are less involved in the daily care of a preschool child. According to Daniels and Weingarten (1982), three times as many late-timed fathers, in contrast to their early-timed counterparts, had regular responsibility for some part of the daily care of a preschool child. Possibly, the increase in paternal responsibility assumed by fathers in late-timed families may account for the more optimal mother–infant interaction patterns observed by Ragozin *et al.* (1982). Observational analyses of father–offspring interaction patterns in early- and late-timed families would be helpful.

Other evidence is consistent with the finding of greater father involvement when childbearing is delayed. Bloom-Feshbach (1979) reported that the older a father is at the time of his first child's birth, the more he is practically involved with the caretaking of his infant. However, age of father was not associated with expressive–nurturant aspects of the father–child relationship; possibly infant–father attachment, for example, may not be altered by age of the father. Other research suggests one possible mediator of greater father involvement among older fathers. In a recent short-term longitudinal study, Feldman, Nash, and Aschenbrenner (1983) found that one of the predictors of paternal involvement in infant caregiving was low job salience. Although it is possible that older fathers can afford to invest less in their career and therefore, low job salience may be tapping a similar dimension, it is possible that time in career and job salience are independent. Assessment of job salience and its relationship to paternal caregiving in early- and late-timed fathers would help clarify this issue.

As the findings in this section demonstrate, the timing of the onset of parenthood is a powerful organizer of both maternal and paternal roles. In the future, investigators need to examine not only both maternal and paternal interaction patterns with each other and their children, but within the context of careers as well. More detailed attention to cohort issues is warranted as indicated by the suggestive findings of Daniels and Weingarten (1982). Presumably the decision to delay the onset of parenthood was easier in the 1970s than in earlier decades due to increased acceptance of maternal employment, less rigid role definitions for men and women, and the greater availability of support services such as day care which would permit a simultaneous family–career option.

The Impact of Women's and Men's Employment Patterns on the Father's Role in the Family

The relationships between employment patterns of both women and men and their family roles is increasingly being recognized (Bronfenbrenner and Crouter, 1982; Hoffman, 1984). In this section, a variety of issues concerning the links between the worlds of work and family are considered in order to illustrate the impact of recent shifts in work patterns on men's family roles. The impact of changes in the rate of maternal employment on both quantitative and qualitative aspects of father participation are examined, as well as the influence of variations in family work schedules. Finally, historical changes in the nature of mens work are briefly examined.

WOMEN'S EMPLOYMENT

Since the mid-1950s, there has been a dramatic shift in the participation rate of women in the labor force. The rise has been particularly dramatic for married women with children. Between 1950 and 1978, the employment rate more than tripled for married mothers of preschoolers, doubled for those with school-age children only, and increased by one-half for those with no young children (U.S. Bureau of the Census, 1979). How have these shifts affected the quantity and quality of the father's contribution to family tasks such as housework and childcare?

Quantitative Effects

Problems arise in interpreting the main data source—time-use studies—because these studies often fail to control for the family size and the age of children. As Hoffman (1984) notes, "Since employed-mother families include fewer children, in general and fewer preschoolers and infants, in particular, there are fewer childcare tasks to perform" (p. 439). Therefore, the differences between families with employed and nonemployed mothers may, in fact, be underestimated. A second problem is that, as noted earlier, the differentiation of tasks performed by fathers is often very crude, and in some studies, it is impossible to determine what specific aspects of the father's family work, such as primary child care, non-care-related child contact, or housework are affected. In spite of these limitations, some trends are clear.

In general, fathers increase the proportion of time that they devote to the total family workload when mothers are employed outside the home. However, this increase often emerges as a result of wives reducing the amount of time they devote to housework and childcare rather than due to increases in the absolute amount of time men devote to these tasks. Consistent with the classic analysis of Blood and Wolfe (1960), in a more recent time-diary study of housework and childcare in Syracuse, New York, Walker and Woods (1976) found that husbands' proportion of all family work (i.e., combining that performed by both husband and wife) rose from 16% (1.6 of 9.7 hours) to 25% (1.6 of 6.4 hours) when wives were employed. Other studies (see Pleck, 1983), confirm the general finding that fathers' proportional share increases not because they are contributing more absolute time, but because mothers are spending less time on home tasks. However, these findings are not without significance because the impact of the mother and the father on children is likely to be different in families in which the father and the mother are more equal in their household participation.

Moreover, there is some recent evidence for absolute increases in fathers' contributions to family work when wives are employed, especially in father–child contact. Robinson (1977), in a diary study of a national sample, found a modest increase of 19 minutes a day in men's total child-contact time, an increase of 16.5%, when women were employed outside the home. Similarly, Pleck (1981) in an analysis of a survey using respondents' summary estimates found that fathers with employed wives performed about a half-hour per day more family work that includes housework, childcare, and parent–child contact. Although the proportion of time fathers in the Pleck study spent in child-centered activity and housework was not determined, other evidence indicates that child contact is more likely to increase than housework (Hoffman, 1984). If this hypothesis is supported, these modest absolute increases assume greater importance because they directly affect the nature of the father–child relationship.

Other evidence is consistent with this hypothesis that fathers' involvement with children will be especially likely to increase when mothers are employed. Child variables such as age, appear to determine whether or not fathers' family-work shifts with maternal employment. Walker and Woods (1976) found an increase in fathers' family-work with maternal employment when the youngest child was 1 year of age or younger or the couple had five or more children. Similarly, Russell (1982) in a recent study of the impact of maternal employment on Australian fathers found that maternal employment altered fathers' involvement in family work only when there were children under 3 years of age. Fathers in this case were slightly more involved when mothers were employed (4.4 hours vs. 3.15 hours for employed vs. nonemployed, respectively). Moreover, Russell found that when mothers are employed, the quality of responsibility that fathers assume shifts: Fathers with employed wives spent time taking sole responsibility for their children, compared to fathers with nonemployed wives (4.7 hours vs. 1.0 hours).

It is clear that there is an increase in father participation when mothers work outside the home, but the data fit well Rappaport's concept of a *psychosocial lag* (Rappaport, Rappaport, & Strelitz, 1977). According to this concept, men's roles in the family are changing at a slower rate than shifts in women's roles in paid employment. Part of the explanation for the relatively modest size of the shift in men's family work when women enter the job market may be due to the fact that there has been a "value shift in our culture toward greater family involvement by husbands . . . which has effects even on those husbands whose wives are not employed" (Pleck, 1983, p. 47). A similar trend is found in the reduction in time devoted to household tasks by nonemployed women as well as employed women (Hoffman, 1984; Robinson, 1977).

These shifts in father participation can potentially have a positive effect on the father–child relationship as a result of increased direct interaction between the father and child, but paternal participation can have an indirect effect on the child by modifying the mother–child relationship (Lamb, 1982).

Unfortunately, a number of problems limits the value of these findings to our understanding of historical trends in fathering. First, most of the available data comes from cross-sectional comparisons of families in which wives are either employed outside the home or not. Although it is assumed that these concurrent data can be extrapolated backwards to provide a picture of how men's participation in family activities have shifted across time as a result of the historically documented increases in women's presence in the workforce, longitudinal studies of the same families as well as repeated cross-sectional comparisons across time are necessary to place this issue on a firmer empirical basis.

In current literature, cohort, time of testing and age of children are often confounded. For example, in the studies that show that the fathers' participation is higher when infants and young children are involved, it is not clear whether this is due to only the age of the children or to the difference in the cohorts whose children are younger at the time of evaluation. Value shifts may elicit greater involvement in the current cohort of new parents, that may not have affected more seasoned parents. Moreover, once a pattern of father participation has been established, possibly these families will continue to participate more equally in childbearing. If this analysis is correct, future surveys may indicate that father participation extends into later childhood age periods. Alternatively, fathers who are involved early may feel that they have contributed and do less at later ages. The importance of considering the timing of the mother's employment as a determinant of the degree of father involvement is clear. Age of the child is not the only variable however; other factors such as employment onset in relationship to the family's developmental cycle as well as the reason for employment need to be considered. Both the age of the parents and their point in the occupation cycle will affect paternal involvement and may interact with maternal employment.

Qualitative Changes in the Father–Child Relationship accompanying Maternal Employment

Examination of the quantitative shifts in father behavior as a consequence of maternal employment is only one aspect of the problem; it is also necessary to examine the impact of this shift on the quality of the parent–child relationship. Some evidence from interviews of a sample of fathers of 7- to 14-month-old infants suggests that maternal employment is related mainly to the level of fathers' instrumental involvement in child-care and not to fathers' nurturant expressive behavior (Bloom-Feshbach, 1979). According to these data, further involvement in practical aspects of child care may be more influenced by shifts in maternal employment than more nurturant expressive aspects of the father–child relationship.

However, this conclusion may be premature, as evidenced by two recent observational studies of shifts in style of parent–infant interaction as a function of maternal employment. In one recent study, Pedersen *et al.* (1980) assessed the impact of dual wage-earner families on mother–infant and father–infant interaction patterns. These investigators observed single and dual wage-earner families for a 1-hour period in the evening with their 5-month-old infants. Fathers in single wage-earner families tended to play with their infants more than mothers did. However, in the two wage-earner families, the mothers' rate of social play was higher than the fathers' rate of play. In fact, the fathers in these dual wage-earner families played at a lower rate than even the mothers in the single wage-earner families. Because the observations took place in the evenings after both parents returned from their jobs, Pedersen *et al.* suggested that the mother used increased play as a way of reestablishing contact with her infant after being away from home for the day. "It is possible that the working mother's special need to interact with the infant inhibited or crowded out the father in his specialty" (Pedersen *et al.* 1980, p. 10). This behavior of the mother is consistent with the studies of maternal employment and infant attachment that found no relationship between employment status and the quality of infant–mother attachment (Chase-Lansdale, 1981; Hock, 1980), but found evidence of insecure infant–father attachment in dual career families, though only for sons and not daughters (Chase-Lansdale, 1981; cited by Hoffman, 1984).

A number of questions about the Pedersen *et al.* (1980) findings remain. It is still unclear whether these patterns of increased mother play continue after the mother–infant relationship is more firmly established than it is at 5 months. Is this pattern of increased play evident in dual wage-earner families in which the mother begins work when the infant is older? Comparison of families in which the age of the infant differs when the mother returns to work would help to clarify these issues.

The style of interaction that the mothers in these working-mother families exhibited was similar to the predominant style of mother play characterized by verbal behavior. Mothers in these families increased the amount of their play with their infants but remained within their stylistic mode. There was no evidence of a shift to a more typically "masculine" style of physical play.

In an even more stringent test of the modifiability of play styles as a function of family organization, Field (1978) compared fathers who act as primary caregivers with fathers who are secondary caregivers, in contrast to the Pedersen *et al.* (1980) families in which both parents were employed outside the home. Mothers and fathers reversed roles in Field's families. Field found that primary-caregiver fathers retained the physical component in their interaction styles just as secondary fathers did. However, in other subtle ways the play styles of primary-caregiving fathers were similar to the play styles of mothers. Primary caretakers—both mothers and fathers— exhibited less laughing and more smiling, imitative grimaces, and high-pitched vocalizations than secondary-caretaker fathers did. However, both primary-caregiving and secondary-caregiving fathers engaged in less holding of the infants' limbs and in more game playing and poking than mothers. Together with the Pedersen *et al.* (1980) study, these data suggest that both mothers and fathers may exhibit distinctive play styles, even when family role arrangements modify the quantity of their interaction. Further research is necessary to assess more completely the modifiability of these interactive styles as a result of differing family arrangements. A complete comparative study of families in which there is a full reversal of primary- and secondary-caregiving roles with traditional families in which the father is the secondary caregiver would clarify the extent to which interactional behavior is dependent on the differential distribution of caregiving tasks. Just as investigators are examining the impact of self-defined concepts of masculinity, femininity, and androgyny on caregiving patterns, it would clearly be worthwhile to evaluate the relationship between gender-role attitudes and parental play styles. Perhaps androgynous individuals would exhibit less stereotypically masculine or feminine play styles.

VARIATIONS IN WORK SCHEDULES

A variety of shifts have taken place in recent years that have resulted in either reduced work time or more flexible arrangement of work schedules. One change is the shift from a 6- to a five-day work week, but some have argued that the shorter work week in the United States may have diminished the working hours only for white collar occupations such as clerical or low-level administration (Kanter, 1977; Willmott, 1971). Other groups such as higher-level professionals work long hours on the job, whereas blue-collar workers are more likely to have more than one job (Hoffman, 1984; Riesman, 1958; Wilensky, 1961).

Work schedules can vary considerably across households over time, and examination of these schedules may reveal a clearer picture than an undifferentiated focus on employment per se. Men who worked four 10-hour days a week compared with men who worked the five 8-hour days spent a significantly greater amount of time in child care (Maklan, 1976). The men who worked 4 days a week devoted nearly 4 more hours a week to child care, but there was no difference in the amount of time devoted to housework. These changes toward father assumption of a larger share of child-care tasks may not only improve his relationship with his children but may also alter the mother–child relationship by relieving mother of some of the routine child care.

Flexible hours may also give men more time for fathering. Flexible hours, for example, may permit fathers to stay home later in the morning and get their children ready for school or, alternatively, to be at home to greet the children after school. Relationships between children and fathers might vary if fathers shared in these daily child-care routines. Recent evidence of the effects of flextime is inconclusive. In one recent study of 700 people in two U.S. government agencies, of which one agency was on flex-time and the other on a regular schedule, Bohen and Viveros-Long (1981) found that neither mothers nor fathers who were on flextime reported spending more time with their children than did workers on regular sched-ules. However, people on flextime generally reported less conflict between their home and work responsibilities than those on regular schedules. Per-haps the quality of the relationship between parent and child may im-prove—even if the amount of time does not shift. However, more research is necessary to explore the value of flextime for families, avoiding such problems as self-selection, before any firm conclusions about the effects of flexible scheduling can be drawn.

OTHER HISTORICAL SHIFTS IN MEN'S WORK

Another issue which shows historical shifts and may alter the father role are changes in the types of occupations in which men engage. As Bronfenbrenner and Crouter (1982) have documented, there have been marked alterations in the nature of mens' jobs over the past century. Jobs have shifted in terms of "absorptiveness"—to use Kanter's (1977) phrase, not necessarily in terms of worker involvement, but in the extent to which there are prescribed responsibilities for other family members such as wives and children. The occupational changes have largely been away from those that involve roles for children, such as small businesses and farming. For example, the proportion of families who own and operate farms has shown a steady decrease since the turn of the century, whereas employment in large organizations has increased. These shifts have altered the interdependence of family life and work life, and reduced children's access and participation in parents' work. In turn, the amount of time, quality of interaction, and the contexts of contact between fathers and children are radically altered by these changes.

Another significant change is the increased rate of geographic mobility, which is often occupationally related. Although the impact of mobility on families is still poorly understood, current evidence does indicate that stress is heightened (Nieva & Rieck, 1980), wives are depressed (Weissman & Paykel, 1972), and children's adjustment is affected (Pulkkinen, 1982) by residential relocation. It is clear that dislocation from existing social support networks may have adverse effects on families' ability to cope with stressful change, which in turn, may affect the father–child relationship. However, evidence suggests that the impact of residence change is often short-lived.

Finally, historical trends in unemployment and the accompanying im-pact on fathers and families merit examination. With the exception of El-der's (1974) work on the effects of job loss during the Great Depression, little attention has been devoted to this topic. As Hoffman (1984) notes, however, there have been a number of significant changes, such as increased availability of federal support, as well as increased gender-role equality and greater acceptance of maternal employment, which could significantly modify the impact of employment in the 1980s, in comparison to the early 1930s. Unemployment has been shown to have a disruptive impact on families; not only is family tension increased (Cobb & Kasl, 1977; Farran & Margolis, 1983), but there is substantial evidence of a link between paternal job loss and intrafamilial violence, including both wife and child abuse. Steinberg, Catalano, and Dooley (1981) found over a 30-month period that increases in child abuse are preceded by periods of high-job loss. As Parke and Collmer (1975) note, there are a variety of reasons for this association, including increased availability of the father, that could heighten the probability of conflict as well as the status loss for the father. More attention to the ways in which job loss alters father and family functioning and how the impact of unemployment has changed since the classic studies of the depression are needed.

The Impact of Divorce on Father's Role

At the same time that many changes are leading to modest increases in father participation in families, another significant change—the dramatic increase in the rates of separation and divorce—is significantly altering and in many cases, decreasing the opportunities for father involvement in family life. The divorce rate has increased dramatically over the last two decades. Divorce rates in the United States remained relatively constant from 1951 to 1965, but have more than doubled since then. The divorce rate fluctuated from 15 to 17 divorces per 1000 married women 14–44-years old between 1951 and 1965 and then increased steadily to 37 per 1000 during 1975–1977 (Kitagawa, 1981). Moreover, estimates of the proportion of "ever married" persons whose first and second marriage may end in divorce show clear historical shifts. According to Kitagawa (1981) the percentage of first marriages that will eventually end in divorce increased from 13% for the cohort of women born during 1900–1904 to 38% for the cohort of women born during 1945–1949. The proportion of second marriages ending in divorce increased from 5% for the 1900–1904 cohort to 44% for the 1945–1949 cohort (Kitagawa, 1981). The absolute increase is due to the increase of population in the United States, particularly to the married population; but the proportional increase is due, in part, to changes in the composition of the population in favor of subgroups with high divorce rates such as married persons in their teens and early 20s. In addition there have been changes in social, psychological, and attitudinal variables that makes divorce a more acceptable solution to marital problems (Cherlin, 1981).

Moreover, children are often involved, and the number of divorced men and women maintaining families doubled between 1970 and 1979. Despite a declining birth rate and a decrease in the number of children under 18 years between 1970 and 1980, there was a 40% increase in the number of children living with one parent. Over 90% of these live with their mothers, and more than half of these children live with a mother who is either divorced or separated (Census Reports, 1980). According to the recent estimate, 1.2 million children each year experience the divorce or separation of parents.

These statistics emphasize the necessity of viewing divorce as a normative event in the 1980s (Hetherington & Camara, 1984). At the very least, the current increase in the rate of divorce may mean that divorce should be viewed as a historical nonnormative event that has affected a high percentage of individuals over the last decade. Although attitudes and laws about child custody are changing, mothers still gain custody in 90% of divorce cases. In 1979, only 10% of children of divorced parents in the United States and 7% in Great Britain lived with their fathers—these proportions have tripled since 1960. Moreover, custody decisions vary with the age of the child with the father being more likely to get custody of school-age children than of infants and young children.

Two issues are addressed in this section. First, what role does the father play when mother has custody. Second, what are the effects of paternal custody? (A full discussion of the impact of divorce is beyond the scope of this chapter. For reviews, see Hetherington, Cox, & Cox, 1979, 1982; Hetherington & Camara, 1984).

MATERNAL CUSTODY AND FATHERS' ROLE

Again, as in our previous discussions, in this situation, fathers can influence their children directly and indirectly. Although our traditional models of socialization emphasize direct effects whereby agent and child mutually influence each other through direct face-to-face interaction, there is some evidence that the father may play an important indirect role when the mother has custody. Face-to-face contact, of course, remains important for fathers and children after divorce, but a number of studies indicate a pattern of gradual decline in father–child contact following divorce. Hetherington *et al.* (1982) found that 2 years after divorce, fathers had much less contact with their children than they had immediately after the divorce. Of the 48 fathers in the study, 19 fathers saw their children once a week, 21 fathers saw them every 2 or 3 weeks, and 8, once a month or less.

Similarly, Fulton (1979) found that in only one-fifth of the families was there a steady pattern of visitation in the 2 years after divorce by the noncustodial parent—usually the father. In 50%, there was a decline in visitation, and in 28% of the families, the noncustodial parents never visited.

In light of these figures, it is important to examine fathers' indirect influence on their children, principally by the support they provide their former wife in her parenting role. Hetherington *et al.* (1979) found that the mothers' effectiveness in dealing with the child was related to support from her ex-husband in childrearing and agreement with her ex-husband in disciplining the child. When divorced couples agreed and supported each other, the disruption in family functioning appeared to be less extreme and the restabilizing of family functioning occurred earlier. However, the most ideal situation for children of divorce is one in which close relationships with *both* parents are maintained. Hess and Camara (1979) compared three groups of children of divorce: children who had positive relationships with one parent and a negative relationship with the other, children who had positive relationships with both parents, and children who had negative relationships with both parents. These three patterns of relationships had strikingly different impacts on children. Those who maintained positive relationships with both parents had the lowest scores on measures of stress and aggression and were rated more highly on work effectiveness and social interaction with peers. When both relationships were unsatisfactory, the negative effects of divorce were most severe. The children who had a positive relationship with one parent were nearly identical to children who had good relationships with both parents on measures of aggression and stress and were between the groups of children who had either positive or negative relationships with both parents in their work effectiveness and their ability to get along with their peers. This coincides with data from Main and Weston (1981) demonstrating that for infants a good relationship with one parent can compensate, at least in part, for a poor relationship with the other parent. Clearly, relationships with both parents need to be considered. Unfortunately, Hess and Camara (1979) did not investigate whether the mother–child or father–child relationship is more important or, more critically, whether it is better for the child to have a positive relationship with the parent who has custody. A situation in which a child lives with one parent but wishes to be with the other obviously is not ideal.

PATERNAL CUSTODY

Although we tend to take maternal custody in divorce cases for granted, it is a twentieth century phenomenon. Before this century, under

English law, children were viewed as property of the husband, and fathers were nearly always granted custody of their children. A father had to be grossly unfit before and exception was made. In 1817, for example, the poet Shelley was denied custody of his children on the grounds of his "vicious and immoral" atheistic beliefs. In our century, by contrast, until very recently, fathers were typically awarded custody only if the mother was viewed as exceptionally incompetent.

The view that mothers are uniquely suited both biologically and psychologically to raise children has prevailed. And this attitude is generally held by the courts who "have long paid up service to a 'best interest' doctrine when child custody is at issue, but in practice, courts have been guided by the generalization that the mothers should be awarded custody except in extreme circumstances" (Santrock & Warshak, 1979, p. 133) Consider this legal opinion from a judge of the New York Family Court:

> The simple fact of being a mother does not by itself indicate a capacity or willingness to render a quality of care different from that which the father can provide. The traditional and romantic view, at least since the turn of the century, has been that nothing can be an adequate substitute for mother love. . . . Later decisions have recognized that this view is inconsistent with informed application of the best interests of the child doctrine and out of touch with contemporary thought about child development and male and female stereotypes. (Cited by Levine, 1976, p. 47)

At the same time that our conceptions of gender roles for mothers and for fathers are changing and the father's competence as a parent and caretaking is being documented and recognized, more fathers are seeking custody of their children. Similarly, as more women join the work force, some women are questioning their allegiance to the mothering role with the result that a small minority of women are not seeking custody of their children (Gersick, 1979). Currently over 10% of the divorced fathers in the United States have custody of their children. Probably this represents a slight increase over earlier decades but no reliable national figures were available until recently.

What are the implications of father custody? Santrock and Warshak (1979) recently investigated the impact of maternal versus paternal custody. Their conclusion is based on a careful evaluation of how fathers and mothers with custody relate to their 6-to-11-year-old children in a problem-solving task in the laboratory. The families were videotaped while parent and child planned an activity together and discussed the main problems of the family. Based on these videotaped observations, Santrock and Warshak found a variety of differences in the children—depending on the custody arrangement. For boys, parental custody appeared to be beneficial: The boys who lived with their fathers were more mature and more sociable and displayed higher levels of self-esteem than boys who were in their mother's custody. For girls, the opposite was the case: They were less demanding, more independent, and more mature when in the custody of their mothers.

A similar picture emerges from ratings that were made when the children were interviewed. Girls who lived with their father were seen as less cooperative and less honest than girls in their mother's custody. Similarly, the boys in paternal custody were more honest and more cooperative than the boys in maternal custody. These findings suggest that paternal custody may be a better arrangement for boys but not for girls when a divorce does occur. Santrock and Warshak note the implication of their findings:

> There appears to be something drastically important about the ongoing, continuous relationship of a child with the same-sex parent. For example, when fathers are given the major role in rearing both boys and girls, they may sense what the psychologically healthy needs of boys are more so than girls. Similarly, when mothers are given virtually sole responsibility for rearing their children, as in a mother custody divorce arrangement, they too may bring to the situation a better sense of girls' needs more so than boys. (1979, p. 116–117)

However, we need to be careful in interpreting Santrock and Warshak's findings or in generalizing from their sample of fathers to all divorced fathers. Men who do receive custody may be unusual in some ways because the awarding of custody to fathers is still uncommon. These fathers may have been unusually talented and devoted parents and that may have been one reason for awarding them custody in the first place.

Children in paternal and in maternal custody have different kinds of lives and experiences. Fathers tend to use additional caretakers such as the mother, babysitters, relatives, day care centers, and friends more than do the mothers. More specifically, children in paternal custody see their mothers more often than children in maternal custody see their fathers. Children whose fathers have custody also are enrolled in day care for more hours a week (24 hours versus 11 hours.)

Whether fathers seek those social supports more often or whether friends, relatives, and neighbors just feel that fathers need more help than mothers in rearing their children has not been determined. Because men are typically perceived as less capable caregivers than women—research evidence aside—it would not be surprising if fathers who raise children by themselves received more unsolicited help. These social support systems appear to be important: Regardless of the type of custody, the total amount of contact with additional adult caretakers is directly linked to the child's warmth, sociability, and social conformity, at least as they show up in the laboratory. It is less clear why these social supports are beneficial. Perhaps they enable children to receive more- and higher-quality adult involvement both from the additional caretakers and from the parent they live with, whose resources are less depleted. Possibly, children in general benefit from contact with a richer and expanded social network of people who can offer additional support as well as alternative role models. Fathers, mothers, and children are best understood when their ties to people and institutions outside the family are considered.

Regardless of the custody arrangements, fathers themselves may learn from the experience of caring for their children that may result following a divorce. Rosenthal and Keshet (1980), who recently studied 129 separated or divorced men, suggest that "men who have separated from or divorced their wives and have taken on some major responsibility for their children's care, find that the demands of that responsibility can become an important focus for their own growth" (p. 71). Moreover, they conclude that children not only need their fathers, but "men need their children. . . . In learning to take care of his children's needs, a man learns to take care of his own" (p. 69).

Many questions remain that require different research strategies to answer. First, more data is necessary concerning the changes in the number of men who seek custody of their children as well as the number who are successful in achieving custody. It may be that men's motivation for custody may be outstripping the rate of change in the legal system. Second, trends in alternative arrangements, such as joint or shared custody, need to be documented, as well as the impact of these newer arrangements on children. Third, investigation of the long-term effects of different types of custody arrangements on children as well as adults are badly needed. Fourth, the ways in which father involvement (e.g., visitation rate) has shifted over time when mother has custody merits documentation. Fifth, has the impact of divorce shifted across historical periods? For example, is divorce experienced by children similarly in the 1960s and in the 1980s? Does the fact that larger proportions of families share similar transitions in the 1980s than in earlier decades modify reactions to the divorce process? Or does the availability of increased support services (see Hetherington & Camara, 1984, for a review) for families of divorce ease the adjustment in the 1980s? These are the kinds of questions that are raised by this type of historical analysis.

REMARRIAGE AND STEPPARENTING

As divorce rates increase, remarriage rates show a corresponding rise. Approximately four out of every five people who divorce eventually remarry, with the rate of remarriage being higher for men than women and higher for younger than older women. As Furstenberg (1982) notes, "In the early part of this century, the interval between divorce and remarriage was nearly 10 years longer on the average than today" (1982, p. 118). Moreover, children are often involved in these family changes resulting in a sizeable proportion of children who live with one parent and one stepparent. The percentage of children under 18 years of age who live in this type of family arrangement has shown a modest but steady increase. In 1960, the figure was 8.6%, which rose to 9.4% in 1970 and to 10.2% in 1978 (Glick, 1979). One recent estimate indicates that over 6 million children in the United States live in stepparent homes (Santrock, Warshak, Lindbergh, & Meadows, 1982). Since maternal custody is the usual arrangement, remarriage means that children experience a stepfather more often than a stepmother.

What are the effects on stepfathers on children? Little is known to date about the impact of this arrangement on children. A beginning step has been undertaken by Santrock *et al.* (1982) who compared intact, divorced mother-headed families and divorced and remarried families (stepfather families). Based on laboratory-based observations of the parents and children, these authors found that the social behavior of children is not necessarily less competent in stepfather families than in intact or in divorced families. In fact, their findings indicate that boys in stepfather families showed more competent social behavior than boys in intact families; this finding corresponded with more competent parenting behavior in those stepfather families. By contrast, girls in stepfather families were observed to be more anxious than girls in intact families. However, the nature of the observational context clearly limits any general conclusions; studies involving a wider range of contexts over time are necessary before any clear conclusions about the impact of stepfathering can be drawn.

PLANNED CHANGE

Many of the shifts noted previously resulted from unplanned and unexpected changes in family organization. However, in recent years, a small minority of families have explicitly explored alternative family arrangements such as rolesharing and reversing family roles. In spite of their rarity, these alternative family arrangements can inform us about the possible ways in which families can reorganize themselves to provide flexibility for mothers, fathers, and children.

In one study, Russell (1982) examined 50 Australian families in which fathers took major or equal responsibility for child care. In these families, fathers and mothers shared about equally (12 hours a week for mothers, 9 hours for fathers) the full range of child-care tasks such as feeding, diapering, bathing, and dressing. In traditional families, by comparison, fathers performed these tasks only about 2 hours a week or 12% of the time. A similar pattern emerges for play and for other significant interactions, such as the parent helping with homework, child helping parent prepare a meal, and so forth. Fathers and mothers were again approximately equal in their division of playful interactions (18 hours for fathers and 16 hours for mothers), whereas in traditional families fathers spend an average of 10 hours and mothers 23 hours a week. However, the two types of families were comparable for the absolute amount of time spent by both parents combined. (53 hours a week in shared-caregiving families and 56 hours a week in traditional families). Types of play activity vary across these two kinds of families. Although Russell found the usual pattern in his traditional families of mothers being more involved in indoor, conventional, cognitive, and toy-oriented activities than fathers and of fathers being more involved in outdoor and physical play than mothers, there were no differences in the types of play activities between mother and fathers in the shared-caregiving families.

These nontraditional role-sharing families have different attitudes toward gender roles than do conventional families. Not surprisingly, fewer of the role-sharing fathers feel that a mother's place is in the home. And the parents in nontraditional families have greater faith in the father's ability to care for children. More than 80% of the fathers and 90% of the mothers in nontraditional families believed that fathers could be capable caregivers—although some felt that fathers were still not as good as mothers. In contrast, only 49% of the fathers and 65% of the mothers in the traditional families felt that fathers were capable of taking care of children.

There are distinct consequences for mothers, fathers, and children from sharing roles. Most commonly, mothers experience difficulties associated with the physical and time demands of a dual role; in Russell's sample, 60% of the mothers reported this strain. On the positive side, mothers reported increased stimulation as a result of outside employment, greater independence, and increased self-esteem. Fathers have mixed reactions as well, with 48% of the fathers reporting difficulties associated with the demands—the constancy and boredom—associated with their full-time caregiving role. On the positive side, 70% of the fathers reported that their relationship with their children improved. Other advantages include: greater understanding of children, greater awareness of mother–housewife roles, and freedom from career pressures.

Other evidence (Radin, 1982) of the effects of these types of alternative family arrangements on children in the United States suggests that children in these families show higher levels of internality—a belief in their own ability to control events—than children in traditional families. In addition, children in the role-sharing families scored higher on verbal ability, and their fathers set higher educational standards and career expectations for their children than fathers in traditional families. Similar findings have been reported recently by Sagi (1982) in a study of the impact of level of paternal involvement on Israeli children. Over half of the fathers were either equally or more involved in child care than mothers. In addition to finding that children of fathers with intermediate and high involvement exhibited more internal locus of control than children of fathers with low involvement, the intermediate- and high-involvement fathers had higher expectations for independence and achievement and offered more encouragement than low-involvement fathers. Empathy varied positively with involvement as well, with the children of the high-involved fathers showing the highest empathy scores.

However, caution is necessary because parents who reverse roles are a very recent phenomenon, and evidence suggesting that children from these families fare better is not conclusive. Such parents may be different in other ways from parents who maintain traditional roles and might have influenced their children differently than traditional parents, no matter which parent stayed home with the children. Moreover, the effect of shared caregiving is usually confounded by the effects of related family characteristics such as maternal employment outside the home. However, it is likely that parents who reverse roles are significantly affected by their choice and that, therefore, the nontraditional environment in which their children develop is at least partially responsible for differences between children from traditional and nontraditional families. As new family role arrangements become more common and more intensively studied, the effects of role reversal and other innovations will be better understood.

In spite of this evidence, other data suggests that mother–father roles may be less amendable to social change than these studies indicate. Lamb and his colleagues (Lamb, Frodi, Hwang, & Frodi, 1982) have taken excellent advantage of a unique national family policy adopted by the Swedish government. The Swedish government has offered the equivalent of paid sick leave (up to 90% of the individual's regular salary) for 9 months for any parent who wished to stay home to care for a new infant. Although between 1974 and 1979 fewer than 15% of new fathers in Sweden took advantage of this opportunity, Lamb and co-workers have studied the growing minority of men who took parental leave for more than month, during which time they had primary responsibility for their infant's care. These nontraditional families were compared with traditional families in which mothers served as primary caregiver. Based on home observations at 3, 8, and 16 months, some surprising findings emerged. Mothers and fa-

thers—regardless of relative involvement in caregiving—differed in characteristic ways: in general, mothers exhibited more of the observed behaviors
(e.g., smiling, touching, vocalizing) than fathers, with only a few exceptions.
This pattern is, of course, similar to prior observations of parents in traditional families. In sum, regardless of their family type, mothers and fathers
behaved in characteristically different ways:

> Differences between maternal and paternal behavior are remarkably robust,
> remaining stable inter- and intra-culturally despite variations in the relative in-
> volvement of mothers and fathers in childcare. This suggests either that behav-
> ioral differences are biologically-based or that they are deeply internalized during
> years of socialization. We will not be able to evaluate these alternative explana-
> tions until we are able to study parents who are themselves reared in a nonsex-
> typed fashion and allocate family responsibilities in a nontraditional fashion.
> (Frodi, Lamb, Hwang, & Frodi, 1982, p. 6)

One source of the discrepancy between the Russell (1982) and Lamb *et
al.* (1982) findings, in addition to methodological, cultural, and age of
children issues, concerns the relative degree of societal support available for
this role shift. Social psychologists (Kelley, 1972) have shown that attitude
change is more likely to occur when effort has to be expended, whereas if
less effort is necessary, less shift in attitude will follow. In Russell's case, role
sharing was a nonnormative activity, whereas in the case of the Swedish
experiment, the participants had extensive societal support for their role
shifts.

Moreover, as Russell (1982) found in a sobering follow-up of his role-
sharing families, only about one-fourth of his families were continuing with
the arrangement 2 years after his first study. A number of factors may
account for the small number of families that choose these alternatives and
persist in them. For example, in general, men are still paid more than
women, so that most families may find that it makes better economic sense
for the father to be the breadwinner. Men may be reluctant even to request
leaves of absence that may jeopardize their job security—particularly in
times of scarce jobs and inflation. In some cases, such as when the mother is
breastfeeding a child, these role reversals may be difficult to implement. The
basic problem, however, may still be one of attitude; as Levine (1976)
points out: "There is still the widespread belief that a man does not belong
at home taking care of children." (p. 153) Until there is some change in this
traditional view about the roles that men and women can or should play in
rearing their children, few families will either try alternative patterns or
persist in them for extended periods of time.

In the final section we address this issue, namely, the ways in which
society can provide support for fathers and families.

CULTURAL SUPPORT SYSTEMS FOR FATHERS
AND FAMILIES

In light of the social and economic changes that are promoting in-creased father involvement in the caregiving of infants and older children, it is important to provide cultural supports for fathering activities. First, there needs to be an increase in opportunities for learning fathering skills. These supports can assume a variety of forms such as the provision of both pre- and postpartum training classes for fathers to both learn and to practice caretaking skills, and to learn about normal infant development (Biller & Meredith, 1974). Parenthood training, however, need not wait until preg-nancy or childbirth. As many have advocated, both early (PTA, 1925, cited by Schlossman, 1976) and more recently (Hawkins, 1971; Sawin & Parke, 1976), parenthood training, including information about infant develop-ment and infant and child care, as well as the economic realities of child rearing, should be provided in high school or even at an earlier age in light of the increasing number of teenage pregnancies. As noted elsewhere (Parke, 1982; Parke & Collmer, 1975), such training may also aid in the prevention of child abuse.

Second, there needs to be increased opportunities to practice and imple-ment fathering skills. To provide the opportunity to share in the early caretaking of the infant, paternity leaves should be given wider support. During the pregnancy period, it would be helpful to institutionalize time to permit the father to attend birth and childcare classes and to share in obste-trician visits with the mother. Other shifts in societal arrangements such as shorter work weeks, flexible working hours, and split jobs, whereby a male and female share the same position, are all changes that will increase the potential participation of males in fathering.

Another positive change involves modification of maternity ward visit-ing arrangements to permit fathers to have more extended contact with their newborn infants. To date, father–infant interaction in the newborn period is largely under institutional control, and as a result, it is frequently hospital policy rather than father interest that determines the degree of father–newborn involvement. Although some countries are still highly restrictive of father–infant visitation, other countries such as Denmark and Sweden and, increasingly, the United States encourage father involvement in labor and delivery, and support frequent visitation during the immediate postpartum period (Klaus & Kennell, 1982).

However, providing the opportunity for contact is only a first step. In addition, supportive intervention that may aid fathers in learning caretaking and social interactive skills can be provided during this early postpartum period as well. Recent evidence of the impact of hospital-centered intervention for fathers comes from a recent investigation by Parke and his colleagues (Parke, Hymel, Power & Tinsley, 1980; Tinsley, Hymel, Power & Parke, 1979).

Fathers viewed a videotape that portrayed other males engaged in play, feeding, and diapering. In contrast to a control group who saw no videotape, the fathers exposed to this 15-minute presentation were more knowledgeable about infant perceptual capacities, were more responsive to their infants during feeding and play, and fed and diapered their babies more often at 3 months in the home. However, the effect held only for fathers of boys; fathers of girls were unaffected by the intervention. The same gender effect is similar to other reports of greater father involvement with sons than daughters (see Parke, 1979, for a review of this research).

However, efforts to modify father involvement need not be restricted to the newborn period. In a recent study, Dickie and Carnahan (1979) provided training to mothers and fathers of 4- to 12-month-old infants in order to increase their competence. Utilizing Goldberg's (1979) notion of competence as parental ability to assess, predict, elicit, and provide contingent response experiences for their infants, these investigators provided eight 2-hour weekly sessions. Training emphasized individual infant variation, knowledge of the infant's temperament and cues, provision of contingent experiences, and awareness of the infant's effect on the parents. Fathers who had participated in the training sessions, in contrast to fathers who had not participated, increased their interactions with their infants; specifically they talked, touched, held, attended the infant more, and gave more contingent responses to infant smiles and vocalizations. The infants of the trained fathers sought interaction more than infants of fathers in the control group. However, mothers in the trained group decreased their interactions; in view of the fact that training did increase the judgments of the spouses' competence, it is possible that the wives of the trained fathers encouraged their competent husbands to assume a greater share of the infant care and interactional responsibilities. Interestingly, this finding underlines the reciprocal nature of the mother–father relationship and provides further support for viewing the family as a social system in which the activities of one member has an impact on the behavior of other family members. Finally, these data are consistent with nonhuman primate findings that father–infant involvement varies inversely with the degree of maternal restrictiveness (see Redican & Taub, 1981; Parke & Suomi, 1981, for reviews).

Other studies (e.g., Zelazo, Kotelchuck, Barber, & David, 1977) suggest that father relationships with older infants (12-month olds) can be modified as well. Intervention need not be restricted to infancy or to any other specific time period. The capacity of both parents and infants for continual adaptation to shifting social circumstances probably overrides the paramount importance of any single time period for the formation of social relationships (Brim & Kagan, 1980; Cairns, 1977). These demonstrations provide further evidence of the plasticity and modifiability of paternal behavior and suggest that fathers can learn to adopt new roles as family systems evolve in new ways. At the same time, these studies suggest that more attention needs to be given to social support systems for fathers—as well as mothers—in order to facilitate their execution of parenting activities. Finally, these studies underline the value of a multilevel analytic approach to understanding father's role in the family that recognizes the embeddedness of fathers and families within a wider network of social network of social systems, including institutions and communities (Brim, 1975; Bronfenbrenner, 1979; Parke & Lewis, 1981).

EFFECTS OF CHANGES IN FATHERING ON CHILDREN AND PARENTS

The impact of these shifts in fathering for children and parents themselves is an important, but still poorly understood issue. Let us briefly examine each of these effects in turn.

The Impact on Children

Although many of fathers' contributions to the child's development overlap with those of other agents in the child's world (Lamb, 1981; Parke, 1981), there is evidence that variations in father involvement do substantially affect childrens' social and cognitive development (Lamb, 1981; Parke, 1981; Radin, 1982). However, the extent to which changing social conditions and consequent modifications of the father's role alter the child's development remains unanswered. Due to the recency of many of the changes explored in this chapter, only short-term evaluation of resulting developmental modification for the current generation of children is feasible. Although it is attractive to assume that evidence of the impact of existing variations in fathering on children's development can form the basis for understanding future variations, it is misleading to assume that continuing increases in father participation will produce orderly linear modifications in children's development. First, there may be a threshold for father effects beyond which no greater effect of involvement will be found, which would suggest that increases in father participation may not significantly alter children's development. Second, it is probably misguided to focus on quantity of involvement in light of the extensive literature that shows that the quality of parental behavior rather than quantity is a better predictor of child outcome. Third, it is unlikely that all areas of development would be equally affected by changes in father (and mother) family roles. Rather than searching for global outcomes in either the social and cognitive domain for evidence of the impact of historical shifts in fathering, specific aspects of children's development should be addressed which are most likely to yield effects.

For example, earlier studies of the effects of maternal employment provide an instructive guide by demonstrating that certain specific areas such as gender-role stereotypes and career aspirations were more likely affected than general measures of social and cognitive development. Similar specificity of effects is likely to be found as a result of shifts in fathering as well. Moreover, the specific impact on children will vary with the type of secular change; it is unlikely that shifts in medical practices, timing of parenting, or divorce will all have uniform effects on children's development. Fourth, both short- and long-term outcomes need to be studied. Many of the variations in family reorganization may have relevance for children only at later points in the life cycle, such as the advent of their own parenting careers. This suggests that the stage of the child's development needs to be taken into account because the impact will vary with the developmental level of the child.

The Impact on Father and Mother

These changes may have at least as much and possibly a greater impact on fathers themselves. A number of areas may be affected including the father–child relationship, the father's self-perception of his own gender role, as well as his attitude toward women's roles. In addition, the marital relationship may be affected, as well as the father's attitude toward and involvement in his outside occupation.

Some evidence (e.g., Russell, 1982) indicates that fathers' relationships with their children improve as a result of increased involvement. Self-perception of their gender roles may shift toward greater androgyny (Russell, 1982). As a result of increased involvement with their own children, fathers may increase in empathy and in their sensitivity to a wider range of social cues. This hypothesis awaits empirical evaluation. In the work sphere, fathers may become less involved as a result of their increased family involvement. Alternatively, men who try to maintain a high work commitment at the same time as an increased family involvement may experience heightened role strain and possibly increased marital conflict. As in the case of children, the effects on fathers will depend on a variety of factors including the age of the father, career position, as well as the age of the child at the time of evaluation. The reason for the increase in father participation merits consideration because forced versus voluntary increases may yield different effects on fathers.

Another result of these changes are shifting expectations that all fathers engage in increased caregiving. In turn, fathers who participate may come to be considered the norm, and relatively uninvolved fathers may be viewed as more nonnormative. The role of shifting expectations in promoting further change in fathering merits investigation.

Finally, it is important to recognize that the assumption of a causal link between shifts in fathering and changes in fathers themselves needs to be validated, in order to eliminate the alternative possibility that fathers who become more involved already differ on these dimensions.

Since changes in the paternal role potentially modify maternal behavior as well, it is important to evaluate the impact on mothers as well. Again, changes in a variety of spheres merit examination, including changes in the mother's relationship with her children and her spouse, as well as changes in her occupational sphere. Although it is assumed that some positive effects may flow from shifts toward more egalitarian family roles, such as reduced strain between family and work roles, the possibility that some women may resent the intrusion of fathers into the child-rearing domain merits investigation. In the final analysis the value system of individual families merit consideration (Parke *et al.*, 1980). Although cultural and social norms concerning father participation may be changing, families endorse these norms at different rates. In families who embrace more traditional role divisions for mothers and fathers, increased father involvement may produce negative rather than positive effects.

CONCLUSIONS AND FUTURE TRENDS

Many issues remain. A better category system is required for organizing events that may alter family life. Although our distinction between the effects of planned and unplanned change represents a beginning in this direction, a more sophisticated taxonomy is required not only for purposes of organizational convenience, but to permit better prediction as well. Such a system should begin to illuminate the variables that compose the event (timing, duration, intensity), as well as the short- and long-term impact of the event on families.

Second, more explicit guidelines are required to illuminate which aspects of family processes are most likely to be altered by historical events and which processes are less amendable to change. For example, are fathers biologically prepared to interact in a physical manner with their children while mothers are biologically programmed to interact in less physical and more verbal modes? If this assumption about differences in parental play style is, in fact, true, rates of interactions would be more likely to change than style. Alternatively, the restraints may be more solely environmental, and as opportunities for adult male and female participation in child care and child rearing become more equal, some of the stylistic differences may diminish.

Third, the historical events discussed in this chapter were treated relatively separate only for the convenience of exposition. In fact, it should be stressed that these events often co-occur rather than in any singular fashion. Moreover, the impact of any historical change may be different as a result of occurring in the same period as another change or changes. For example, divorce rates and women's increased presence in the workplace covary and probably each event has different meaning without the other's change. This implies the need for multivariate designs that would capture the simultaneous impact of multiple events on fathering activities.

Longitudinal investigations are needed in order to disentangle cohort- and period-based explanations for these trends. Moreover, an intergenerational perspective (Tinsley & Parke, 1984b) would be useful for understanding the varying influences of cohort, period, and other environmental factors on fathers and families. Do the grandfathers (and grandmothers) of 1980 behave differently than their counterparts of two decades ago? Not only would examination of how their relationships with their adult children change be worthwhile, but documentation of changes in the grandparent–grandchild relationship would be interesting as well.

In spite of the array of issues that remain unresolved, this essay has illustrated the value of a life-span historical approach for raising new questions about fathers and families that are not readily evident from other theoretical perspectives. These are concerns that must be addressed in the evolution of a sophisticated systems model that captures the dynamics of family functioning.

References

Alan Guttmacher Institute. (1976). *11 million teenagers: What can be done about the epidemic of adolescent pregnancies in the U.S.* New York: Planned Parenthood Federation of America.

Baldwin, W., & Cain, V. (1980). The children of teenage parents. *Family Planning Perspectives, 12,* 34–43.

Biller, H., & Meredith, D. (1974). *Father power.* New York: Doubleday.

Blood, R., & Wolfe, D. (1960). *Husbands & wives.* New York: Free Press.

Bloom-Feshbach, J. (1979). *The beginnings of fatherhood.* Unpublished doctoral dissertation, Yale University.

Bloom-Feshbach, J. (1981). Historical perspectives on the father's role. In M. E. Lamb (Ed.), *The role of the father in child development* (2nd ed). New York: Wiley.

Bohen, H., & Viveros-Long, A. (1981). *Balancing jobs and family life: Do flexible work schedules help.* Philadelphia: Temple University Press.

Bottoms, S. F., Rosen, M. G., & Sokol, R. J. (1980). The increase is the Cesarean birth rate. *New England Journal of Medicine, 302,* 559–563.

Brim, O. G. (1975). Macro-structural influences on child development and the need for social indicators. *American Journal of Orthopsychiatry, 45,* 516–524.

Brim, O. G., & Kagan, J. (1980). *Constancy and change in human development.* Cambridge: Harvard University Press.

Bronfenbrenner, U. (1979). *The ecology of human development: Experiments by nature and design.* Cambridge, MA: Harvard University Press.

Bronfenbrenner, U., & Crouter, A. (1982). Work and family through time and space. In S. B. Kamerman & C. D. Hayes (Eds.), *Families that work: Children in a changing world.* Washington: National Academy Press.

Cairns, R. B. (1977). Beyond social attachment: The dynamics of interactional development. In T. A. Alloway, P. Pliner, & L. Krames (Eds.), *Attachment behavior.* New York: Plenum.

Card, J., & Wise, L. (1978). Teenage mothers and teenage fathers: The impact of early childbearing on the parent's personal and professional lives. *Family Planning Perspectives, 10,* 199–205.

Chase-Lansdale, P. L. (1981). *Effects of maternal employment on mother–infant and father–infant attachment.* Unpublished doctoral dissertation, University of Michigan.

Cherlin, A. J. (1981). *Marriage, divorce, remarriage.* Cambridge, MA: Harvard University Press.

Cobb, S., & Kasl, S. (1977). *Termination: The consequences of job loss* (Publication No. 77–224). Washington, DC: DHEW (NIOSH).

Cochran, M. M., & Brassard, J. A. (1979). Child development and personal social networks. *Child Development, 50,* 601–616.

Conway, E., & Brackbill, Y. (1970). Delivery medication and infant outcome: An empirical study. *Monographs of the Society for Research in Child Development, 35,* 24–34.

Daniels, P., & Weingarten, K. (1982). *Sooner or Later: The timing of parenthood in adult lives.* New York: Norton.

Dickie, J., & Carnahan, S. (1979). *Training in social competence: The effect on mothers, fathers and infants.* Paper presented at the Biennial Meeting of the Society for Research in Child Development, San Francisco.

Eastman, J. J. (1950). *Williams obstetrics* (10th ed.). New York: Appleton-Century-Crofts.

Elder, G. H. (1974). *Children of the great depression.* Chicago: University of Chicago Press.

Elder, G. H., & Rockwell, R. (1979). The life course and human development: An ecological perspective. *International Journal of Behavioral Development, 2,* 1–21.

Entwisle, D. R., & Doering, S. G. (1981). *The first birth.* Baltimore: Johns Hopkins University Press.

Farran, D. C., & Margolis, L. H. (1983, April). *The impact of paternal job loss on the family.* Paper presented at the Biennial Meeting of the Society for Research in Child Development, Detroit, Michigan.

Feldman, S. S., Nash, S. C., & Aschenbrenner, B. G. (1983). Antecedents of fathering. *Child Development, 54,* 1628–1636.

Field, T. (1978). Interaction behaviors of primary versus secondary caretaker fathers. *Developmental Psychology, 14,* 183–185.

Frodi, A. M., Lamb, M. E., Hwang, C. P. and Frodi, M. (1982, March). The Swedish experiment: Paternal involvement in infant care. Paper presented at the International Conference on Infant Studies. Austin Texas March

Fulton, J. A. (1979). Parental reports of children's post-divorce adjustment. *Journal of Social Issues, 35,* 126–139.

Furstenberg, F. F. (1976). *Unplanned parenthood.* New York: Free Press.

Furstenberg, F. F. (1982). Remarriage and intergenerational relations. In R. Fogel, E. Hatfield, S. Kiesler, & J. March (Eds.), *Aging: Stability and change in the family.* New York: Academic Press.

Gersick, K. E. (1979). Fathers by choice: Divorced men who receive custody of their children. In G. Levinger & O. C. Moles (Eds.), *Divorce and separation.* New York: Basic Books.

Glick, P. C. (1979). The future of the American family. *Current Population Reports* Series P-23, No. 78.

Goldberg, S. (1979). Premature birth: Consequences for the parent-infant relationship. *American Scientist, 67,* 214–220.

Goldberg, S. (1983). Parent-infant bonding: Another look. *Child Development, 54,* 1355–1382.

Grossman, F. K., Eichler, L. S., & Winickoff, S. A. (1980). *Pregnancy, birth and parenthood.* San Francisco: Jossey-Bass.

Hareven, T. K. (1977). Family time and historical time. *Daedalus, 106,* 57–70.

Hawkins, R. P. (1971). Universal parenthood training: A proposal for preventative mental health. *Educational Technology, 11,* 28–35.

Hawthorne, J. T., Richards, M. P. M., & Callon, M. (1978). A study of parental visiting of babies in a special care unit. In F. S. W. Brimble-Combe, M. P. M. Richards, & N. R. C. Roberton (Eds.), *Early separation and special care nurseries.* London: Simp/Heinemann Medical Books.

Hennenborn, W. J., & Cogan, R. (1975). The effects of husband participation on reported pain and the probability of medication during labor and birth. *Journal of Psychosomatic Research, 19,* 215–222.

Hess, R. D., & Camara, K. A. (1979). Post-divorce relationships as mediating factors in the consequences of divorce for children. *Journal of Social Issues, 35,* 79–96.

Hetherington, E. M., & Camara, K. A. (1984). Families in transition: The processes of dissolution and reconstitution. In R. D. Parke, R. Emde, H. McAdoo, & G. P. Sackett (Eds.), *Review of Child Development Research* (Vol. 7). Chicago: University of Chicago Press.

Hetherington, E. M., Cox, M., & Cox, R. (1979). Family interaction and the social, emotional and cognitive development of children following divorce. In V. Vaughan & T. B. Brazelton (Eds.), *The family: Setting priorities.* New York: Science and Medicine Publishing.

Hetherington, E. M., Cox, M., & Cox, R. (1982). Effects of divorce on parents and children. In M. E. Lamb (Ed.), *Nontraditional families.* Hillsdale, NJ: Erlbaum.

Hock, E. (1980). Working and nonworking mothers and their infants: A comparative study of maternal caregiving characteristics and infant social behavior. *Merrill Palmer Quarterly, 26,* 79–101.

Hodgman, J. E. (1982). Pregnancy outcome, neonatal mortality. In P. W. Berman & E. R. Ramey (Eds.), *Women: A developmental perspective.* Washington: U.S. Government Printing Office.

Hoffman, L. W. (1984). Work, family and the socialization of the child. In R. D. Parke, R. Emde, H. McAdoo, & G. P. Sackett (Eds.), *Review of child development research* (Vol. 7). Chicago: University of Chicago Press.

Kanter, R. M. (1977). *Work and family in the United States: A critical review of research and policy.* New York: Sage.

Keller, W. D., Hildebrandt, K. A., & Richards, M. E. (1981, April) *Effects of extended father–*

infant contact during the newborn period. Paper presented at the meeting of the Society for Research in Child Development, Boston.

Kelley, H. H. (1972). *Attribution in social interaction.* In E. E. Jones, D. E. Kanouse, H. H. Kelley, R. E. Nisbett, S. Valins, & B. Weiner (Eds.), *Attribution: Perceiving the causes of behavior.* Morristown, NJ: General Learning Press.

Kitagawa, E. M. (1981). New life styles: Marriage patterns, living arrangements and fertility outside of marriage. *Annals of the American Academy of Political and Social Science, 453,* 1–27.

Klaus, M. H., & Kennell, J. H. (1982). *Parent-infant bonding* (2nd ed.). St. Louis: Mosby.

Kotelchuck, M. (1976). The infant's relationship to the father: Experimental evidence. In M. E. Lamb (Ed.), *The role of the father in child development* (pp. 329–344). New York: Wiley.

Lamb, M. E. (1977). Father-infant and mother-infant interaction in the first year of life. *Child Development, 48,* 167–181.

Lamb, M. E. (Ed.). (1981). *The role of the father in child development* (2nd ed). New York: Wiley.

Lamb, M. E. (1982). Maternal employment and child development: A review. In M. E. Lamb (Ed.), *Nontraditional families.* Hillsdale, NJ: Erlbaum.

Lamb, M. E., Frodi, A. M., Hwang, C. P., & Frodi, M. (1982). Varying degrees of paternal involvement in infant care: Attitudinal and behavioral correlates. In M. E. Lamb (Ed.), *Nontraditional families* Hillsdale, NJ: Erlbaum.

Lamb, M. E., & Hwang, C. (1982). Maternal attachment and mother-infant bonding: A critical review. In M. E. Lamb & A. L. Brown (Eds.), *Advances in Developmental Psychology* (Vol. 2). Hillsdale, NJ: Erlbaum.

Leiderman, P. H. (1983). Social ecology and childbirth: The newborn nursery as environmental stressor. In N. Garmezy & M. Rutter (Eds.), *Stress, coping and adaptation: A developmental perspective.* New York: McGraw-Hill.

Leiderman, P. H., & Seashore, M. J. (1975). Mother-infant separation: Some delayed consequences. In H. Hofer (Ed.), *Parent-infant interaction.* New York: Elsevier.

Levine, J. A. (1976). *Who will raise the children: New options for fathers (and mothers).* New York: Lippincott.

Lewis, M., & Fiering, C. (1981). Direct and indirect interactions in social relationships. In L. P. Lipsitt (Ed.), *Advances in infancy research* (Vol. 1). New York: Ablex.

Lorenzi, M., Klerman, L., & Jekel, J. (1977). School age parents: How permanent a relationship? *Adolescence, 12,* 13–22.

Lummis, T. (1982). The historical dimension of fatherhood: A case study 1989–1914. In L. McKee & M. O'Brien (Eds.), *The father figure.* London: Tavistock.

McCluskey, K. A., Killarney, J., & Papini, D. R. (1983). Adolescent pregnancy and parenthood: Implications for development. In E. C. Callahan & K. A. McCluskey (Eds.), *Lifespan developmental psychology: Non-normative life events.* New York: Academic Press.

Main, M., & Weston, D. R. (1981). The quality of the toddler's relationship to mother and father: Related to conflict behavior and the readiness to establish new relationships. *Child Development, 52,* 932–940.

Maklan, D. (1976). *The four day workweek: Blue collar adjustment to a nonconventional arrangement of work and leisure time.* Unpublished doctoral dissertation, University of Michigan.

Margolis, L., & Farran, D. (1982). Unemployment: The health consequences for children. *North Carolina Medical Journal,*

Minde, K., Trehub, S., Corter, C., Boukydis, C., Celhoffer, L., & Marton, P. (1978). Mother–child relationships in the premature nursery: An observational study. *Pediatrics, 61,* 373–379.

Murray, A. D., Dolby, R. M., Nation, R. L., & Thomas, D. B. (1981). Effects of epidural anesthesia on newborns and their mothers. *Child Development, 52,* 71–82.

Nettleton, C. A., & Cline, D. W. (1975). Dating patterns, sexual relationships and use of contraceptives of 700 unwed mothers during a two-year period following delivery. *Adolescence, 37,* 45–57.

Nieva, V. F., & Rieck, A. (1980, September). *Job related moves: Effects on whole-family conflicts, stresses and satisfactions.* Paper presented at the Annual Meeting of the American Psychological Association, Montreal.

Parke, R. D. (1979). Perspectives on father-infant interaction. In J. Osofsky (Ed.), *The handbook of infant development.* New York: Wiley.

Parke, R. D. (1981). *Fathers.* Cambridge: Harvard University Press.

Parke, R. D. (1982). Theoretical models of child abuse: Their implications for prediction, prevention and modification. In R. H. Starr (Ed.), *Child abuse prediction.* Cambridge: Ballinger.

Parke, R. D., & Collmer, C. W. (1975). Child abuse: An interdisciplinary perspective. In E. M. Hetherington (Ed.), *Review of child development research* (Vol. 5). Chicago: University of Chicago. 1975.

Parke, R. D., Hymel, S., Power, T. G., & Tinsley, B. R. (1980). Fathers and risk: A hospital based model of intervention. In D. B. Sawin, R. C. Hawkins, L. O. Walker, & J. H. Penticuff (Eds.), *Psychosocial risks in infant–environment transactions.* New York: Bruner/Mazel.

Parke, R. D., & Lewis, N. G. (1981). The family in context: A multi-level interactional analysis of child abuse. In R. W. Henderson (Ed.), *Parent-child interaction: Theory, research and prospect.* New York: Academic Press.

Parke, R. D., O'Leary, S. E., & West, S. (1972). *Mother-father-newborn interaction: effects of maternal medication, labor and sex of infant.* Proceedings of the American Psychological Association, pp. 85–86.

Parke, R. D., Power, T. G., & Fisher, T. (1980). The adolescent father's impact on the mother and child. *Journal of Social Issues, 36,* 88–106.

Parke, R. D., Power, T. G., & Gottman, J. (1979). Conceptualizing and quantifying influence patterns in the family triad. In M. E. Lamb, S. J. Suomi, & G. R. Stephenson (Eds.), *Social interaction analysis: Methodological issues.* Madison: University of Wisconsin Press.

Parke, R. D., & Sawin, D. B. (1976). The father's role in infancy: A re-evaluation. *The Family Coordinator, 25,* 365–371.

Parke, R. D., & Suomi, S. J. (1981). Adult male-infant relationships: Human and nonhuman primate evidence. In K. Immelmann, G. Barlow, M. Main, & L. Petrinovitch (Eds.), *Behavioral development: The Bielefeld Interdisciplinary Project.* New York: Cambridge University Press.

Parke, R. D., & Tinsley, B. R. (1981). The father's role in infancy: Determinants of involvement in caregiving & play. In M. E. Lamb (Ed.), *The role of the father in child development* (2nd ed.). New York: Wiley.

Parke, R. D., & Tinsley, B. R. (1982). The early environment of the at-risk infant: Expanding the social context. In D. Bricker (Ed.), *Intervention with at-risk and handicapped infants: From research to application.* Baltimore: University Park Press.

Pedersen, F. A. (1975, September). *Mother, father and infant as an interactive system.* Paper presented at the Annual Convention of the American Psychological Association, Chicago.

Pedersen, F. A., Cain, R., Zaslow, M., & Anderson, B. (1980, April) *Variation in infant experience with alternative family organization.* Paper presented at the International Conference on Infant Studies, New Haven, CT.

Peterson, G. H., Mehl, L. E., & Leiderman, P. H. (1979). The role of some birth-related variables in father attachment. *American Journal of Orthopsychiatry, 49,* 330–338.

Pleck, J. H. (1981). *Wives' employment, role demands and adjustment* (Final report). Wellesley College Center for Research on Women. Unpublished manuscript.

Pleck, J. H. (1983). Husbands' paid work and family roles: Current research issues. In H. Z. Lopata & J. H. Pleck (Eds.), *Research on the interweave of social roles* (Vol. 3): *Families & jobs*. Greenwich CT: JAI Press.

Power, T. G., & Parke, R. D. (1982). Play as a context for early learning: Lab and home analyses. In I. E. Sigel & L. M. Laosa (Eds.), *The family as a learning environment*. New York: Plenum.

Presser, H. (1974). Early motherhood: Ignorance or bliss? *Family Planning Perspectives, 6,* 756–764.

Presser, H. (1980). Sally's Corner: Coping with unmarried motherhood. *Journal of Social Issues, 36,* 107–129.

Pulkkinen, L. (1982). Self-control and continuity in childhood-delayed adolescence. In P. Baltes & O. G. Brim (Eds.), *Life Span Development and Behavior*. Vol. IV, New York: Academic Press.

Radin, N. (1982). Primary caregiving and rolesharing fathers. In M. E. Lamb (Ed.), *Nontraditional families*. Hillsdale, NJ: Erlbaum.

Ragozin, A. S., Bashman, R. B., Crnic, K. A., Greenberg, M. T., & Robinson, N. M. (1982). Effects of maternal age on parenting role. *Developmental Psychology, 18,* 627–634.

Rappaport, R., Rappaport, R. N., & Strelitz, Z. (1977). *Fathers, mothers & society*. New York: Basic Books.

Redican, W. K., & Taub, D. M. (1981). Male paternal care in monkeys and apes. In M. E. Lamb (Ed.), *The role of the father in child development* (2nd ed.). New York: Wiley.

Rendina, I., & Dickerscheid, J. D. (1976). Father involvement with first-born infants. *Family Coordinator, 25,* 273–379.

Richards, M. P. M., Dunn, J. F., & Antonis, B. (1977). Caretaking in the first year of life: The role of fathers' and mothers' social isolation. *Child: Care, Health and Development, 3,* 23–26.

Riesman, D. (1958). Work and leisure in post-industrial society. In E. Larrabee & R. Myersohn (Eds.), *Mass leisure*. Glencoe, IL: Fress Press.

Robinson, J. P. (1977). *How Americans use time*. New York: Praeger.

Rosenthal, K. M., & Keshet, H. F. (1980). *Fathers without partners*. Totowa, NJ: Rowman & Littlefield.

Russell, C. (1980). Unscheduled parenthood: Transition to "parent" for the teenager. *Journal of Social Issues, 36,* 45–63.

Russell, G. (1978). The father role and its relation to masculinity, femininity and androgyny. *Child Development, 49,* 1174–1181.

Russell, G. (1982). Shared-caregiving families: An Australian study. In M. E. Lamb (Ed.), *Nontraditional families*. Hillsdale, NJ: Erlbaum.

Sagi, A. (1982). Antecedents and consequences of various degrees of paternal involvement in child rearing: The Israeli project. In M. E. Lamb (Ed.), *Nontraditional families*. Hillsdale, NJ: Erlbaum.

Santrock, J. W., & Warshak, R. (1979). Father custody and social development in boys and girls. *Journal of Social Issues, 35,* 112–125.

Santrock, J. W., Warshak, R., Lindbergh, C., & Meadows, L. (1982). Children's and parents' observed social behavior in stepfather families. *Child Development, 53,* 472–480.

Sawin, D. B., & Parke, R. D. (1976). Adolescent fathers: Some implications from recent research on parental roles. *Educational Horizons, 55,* 38–43.

Schlossman, S. L. (1976). Before home start: Notes toward a history of parent education in America, 1897–1929. *Harvard Educational Review, 46,* 436–467.

Sosa, R., Kennell, J. H., Klaus, M. H., Robertson, S., & Urrutia, J. (1980). The effect of a supportive companion on perinatal problems, length of labor and mother–infant interaction. *New England Journal of Medicine, 303,* 597–600.

Steinberg, L. D., Catalano, R., & Dooley, P. (1981). Economic antecedents of child abuse and neglect. *Child Development, 52,* 975–985.

Svejda, M. J., Campos, J. J., & Emde, R. N. (1980). Mother-infant "bonding": Failure to generalize. *Child Development, 51,* 775–779.

Szalai, A. (Ed.). (1972). *The use of time: Daily activities of urban and suburban populations in twelve countries.* The Hague: Mouton.

Tinsley, B. R., Hymel, S., Power, T. G., & Parke, R. D. (1979). *An experimental modification of father–infant interaction.* Paper presented at the American Psychological Association, New York.

Tinsley, B. R., Johnson, P., Szczypka, D., & Parke, R. D. (1982, March). *Reconceptualizing the social environment of the high-risk infant: Fathers and settings.* Paper presented at the International Conference on Infant Studies, Austin.

Tinsley, B. R., & Parke, R. D. (1984a). The person–environment relationship: Lessons from families with preterm infants. In D. Magnusson & V. Allen (Eds.), *Human development: An interactional perspective.* New York: Academic Press.

Tinsley, B. R., & Parke, R. D. (1984b). Grandparents as support and socialization agents. In M. Lewis (Ed.), *Beyond the dyad.* New York: Plenum.

Vietze, P. M. MacTurk, R. H., McCarthy, M. E., Klein, R. P., & Yarrow, L. J. (1980, April). *Impact of mode of delivery on father– and mother–infant interaction at 6 & 12 months.* Paper presented at the International Conference on Infant Studies, New Haven, CT.

Walker, K., & Woods, M. (1976). Time use: A measure of household production of family goods and services. Washington: American Home Economics Association.

Weissman, M. M., & Paykel, E. S. (1972). Moving and depression in women. *Society, 9,* 24–28.

Wilensky, H. L. (1961). The uneven distribution of leisure: The impact of economic growth on "freetime". *Social Problems, 9,* 107–145.

Willmott, P. (1971). Family, work, and leisure conflicts among male employees: Some preliminary findings. *Human Relations, 24,* 575–584.

Yogman, M. W. (1983). Development of the father-infant relationship. In H. Fitzgerald, B. Lester, & M. W. Yogman (Eds.), *Theory and research in behavioral pediatrics* (Vol. I), New York: Plenum.

Zelazo, P. R., Kotelchuck, M., Barber, L., & David, J. (1977, March). *Fathers and sons: An experimental facilitation of attachment behaviors.* Paper presented at the Biennial Meeting of the Society for Research in Child Development, New Orleans.

CHAPTER 10

Grandparenthood in Transition

NINA R. NAHEMOW

INTRODUCTION

The framework for the discussion of grantparenthood in transition is provided by the concept of normative history-graded influences. The influences are normative to the extent that they occur to most members of a given cohort in similar ways though they may impact differently on various age cohorts at a particular time (Baltes, Reese, & Lipsitt, 1980). The normative history-graded influence of particular concern in this analysis is education in a predominantly illiterate society. Baltes *et al.* have speculated that such influences are particularly strong in adolescence and early adulthood. "Adolescence and early adulthood are the periods in which the society/individual and intergenerational dialectics are salient, and in which much of one's foundation for adulthood (family life, career, life style, etc.) is located and mediated by the nature of the current socioenvironmental climate" (Baltes *et al.*, 1980, p. 78). We are interested in the viability of grandparenthood as a meaningful role option in old age in a modernizing society. It is, therefore, important to assess how the young view this role and in what ways, if any, their confrontation with the different values and competing expectations of the modern world will affect grandparenthood today and in the future.

The life course is a progression of orderly changes from infancy through old age. Although there are rough chronological benchmarks that coincide with the transition to different stages, there is considerable variability. Indeed, in cross-cultural contexts it becomes apparent that the social meanings of age diverge even more widely.

Cross-cultural comparisons between traditional and modern societies underscore the significance of age and aging as both individual properties

Copyright © 1984 by Academic Press, Inc.
All rights of reproduction in any form reserved.
ISBN 0-12-482420-X

and as components of change. In the context of life-span transitions, individuals in traditional societies have a clearly laid out life course, whereas in modern societies they have some flexibility in creating their own life course. Consequently, the nature and timing of role transitions are a function of individual choice and social options (Neugarten & Hagestad, 1976). It is clear that society defines appropriate and inappropriate entry and exit points, but Foner and Kertzer (1978) have nevertheless noted that in both traditional and modern societies, individuals can exercise some control.

Events in the family life cycle are generally synchronized with—and, indeed sometimes, defined by—life-span transitions. Neugarten and Hagestad (1976) point out that most adult roles are achieved in modern society and also that roles entered through achievement, particularly in later life, are exited by *ascription*. With the family life cycle, for example, it is clear that marriage and parenthood are achieved or self-initiated, whereas empty nest, widowhood, and grandparenthood are ascribed. The individual has little control over the timing of those role transitions that come later in the life course. In fact, for each of these transitions the individual has even less control than for those that precede it. That is, empty nest and widowhood are predicated on earlier fertility behavior and life expectancy of the couple. Grandparenthood, on the other hand, is a role almost completely outside the individual's locus of control.

In terms of the family life cycle, grandparenthood may have several different meanings both within and between societies. Although it generally coincides with the later stages of the life span, it has been occurring earlier and lasting longer in Western societies. In traditional societies, owing to both a prolonged fertility period and joint residence norms, grandparenthood and the empty nest tend not to be mutually exclusive stages.

Grandparenthood is a role about which we do not know a great deal. Yet, because it is found in virtually all societies and has such diverse meanings from one culture to another, this stage of the family life cycle is one that deserves greater attention. However, one cannot talk about grandparenthood in any meaningful way without putting the role in the context of (1) the general position of the aged in society, (2) the role of the family or kin group in the society and, finally, (3) the position of the grandparent in the family configuration. This sequence, then, serves as the structure for the present discussion.

POSITION OF THE AGED
IN TRADITIONAL SOCIETIES

Several considerations must be kept in mind in the discussion of the aged in preindustrial societies. To begin with, definitions of age and old age are far from generally agreed upon. In a very broad sense, it can be said that *age* is a significant integrating and differentiating force in society. The *older age-sets* usually exerted some authority over the younger ones by directing their activities, either formally or informally, operating on the asymmetrical pattern characteristic of intergenerational relationships as a whole. The emphasis on respect due the aged was viewed as a "basic prerequisite for successful maintenance of social continuity" (Eisenstadt, 1959, p. 30). Thus age groups served as integrating forces whose function it was to maintain stability. This was especially true in those societies in which roles were not allocated solely on the basis of kinship, because where that was the case, descent groups were responsible for societal integration.

The concept of age can be defined in a variety of different ways, ranging from strictly biological or physiological age to a completely social definition. Simmons (1945), who wrote the seminal work on the status of the aged people in traditional societies, stated:

> The statistical data are generally inadequate to form definite conclusions concerning the time of onset for old age or the prevalence of old people in primitive societies. As to when in life old age begins, the simplest and safest rule is to consider a person "old" whenever he has become so regarded and treated by his contemporaries. (Simmons, 1960, p. 67)

One of the most pressing problems of the aged in industrialized societies is the role loss that comes with aging. Rosow (1962) maintains that the values and institutions of our society have undermined older people's position, and now the basic problem has become how to reintegrate them into society in a meaningful way.

In modernizing societies increased life expectancy coupled with shifting role structures means that the aged are now beginning to confront similar problems. Consequently, such societies afford us an arena in which to study changes in the status and roles of the aged. On the one hand, we can learn more about the process of role loss in general by studying the African situation, for under conditions of modernization parallels will no doubt exist. On the other hand, in addition to more fully understanding our own experience, we may gain new insight by studying the way in which such societies are replacing the role losses that are structurally associated with modernization.

In searching for explanations for societal variations the question of values is crucial to this discussion. *Values* can be defined as beliefs that legitimate the existence of the social structure. When demands on conduct and behavior change, can we expect values (specifically the value of respect for the aged people) to change as rapidly? That is, will societies that have traditionally had clearly demarcated roles and status for the old dramatically alter their behavior to be consistent with the demands of a money economy for achievement, education, and so forth? Because societies vary in the extent to which they revere age, we might expect considerable variation, especially because the rate of modernization is likewise variable.

There are other value orientations that we would also do well to consider. An emphasis on achievement as opposed to ascription devalues the importance of seniority, and status becomes more a function of ability than of age. Collectivism versus individualism is also a factor in assessing the status of the aged. Collectivism emphasizes the welfare of the group as a whole and the interdependence of members. On the other hand, individualism stresses independence and self-centeredness. In effect, it undermines the sense of moral duty and discourages mutual aid (Talmon, 1968).

How have the terms status, prestige, and respect been used in the literature? Simmons (1945) noted that *respect* for old age in preindustrial societies was a product of social developments; when conditions called for respect for the aged, they were accorded it; however, when these conditions changed they might lose it. Respect appears to have been accorded to people who had particular assets that were needed. There also seems to have been wide variation among societies in the number of different channels open to the aged for attaining *prestige*. Given the confusion in the literature as well as in common usage, it appears most useful for purposes of the present analysis to define *status* in a very loose sense as a synonym for prestige or honor, and it is sometimes used to denote the power, authority, rights, and obligations associated with prestige.

Part of the confusion arises out of the failure to distinguish between economic status and ritual status; the two often occur together but they need not. Although it is conceptually possible to make this distinction, it is not easy to operationalize. Much of the ambiguity grows out of a focus on *ritual status* that appears to be a transient attribute. "Theory and practice do not always agree; the old may be mocked in private and at the same time treated with outward respect. And the contrary is often to be seen—old age is honored in words and at the same time allowed to wither away in physical neglect" (deBeauvoir, 1973, p. 129).

Perhaps the finding of most interest in Simmons' (1960) work is that old age alone was not a guarantee of status or security. He concluded that the aged in some preindustrial societies have been accorded a great deal of prestige but only under culturally determined circumstances. And, this prestige did not for the most part extend to the end of a person's life; in fact, it rarely lasted into decrepitude. Looking at such factors as geography, climate, degree of residential permanence, type of economic organization, form of kinship system, and degree of religious development, he was able to describe in broad outline the most favorable cultural milieu for the old. The specification of these conditions is crucial for any analysis which seeks to account for variations among societies vis-à-vis the position of the aged.

Several conclusions can be drawn from this brief overview of the literature on the status of the aged in preindustrial societies. It seems clear that a rich old age was not automatically guaranteed to anyone. Neither is the problem of security in old age unique to industrial societies or even societies in the process of modernizing. It appears that the degree of status, respect, deference, and authority varied enormously from one society to another.

CHANGING FAMILY STRUCTURE

In virtually all African societies, the family plays a crucial role in the social organization of the group. For some societies the kinship system and the political and economic structures are intricately intertwined. In others, the social institutions are more differentiated, and the family is a buffer for the individual as he negotiates through the other spheres. But overall, the family plays a crucial role for placement and social integration in traditional societies as it does in the industrialized setting.

There is considerable variability within and among societies in family structure and organization. The general assumption has been that the traditional African family is embedded in an extended unit and that the impact of modernization has been to sever it from this tie. Many argue that the nuclear family model, similar to that found in Western societies, is the most functional structure for developed economies and is therefore the direction in which African families are evolving. This view, however, is proving to be too limited.

Africa is still predominately rural, and the tie to the land is strong. The typical pattern emerging appears to be one of erratic labor migration of males with family members left behind to cultivate the land. Women, left to their own devices, are turning to their kin rather than to their spouses for assistance. This has the effect of strengthening matrilineal ties even in societies with traditionally patrilineal structures. It would appear, then, that rigid family patterns predicated along traditional lines of authority are in flux today in societies that are modernizing (Colson, 1970).

GRANDPARENTHOOD

Intrafamilial roles constitute a significant component of the older person's social life space. There are potentially a wide variety of roles available to the aged within the family context, though obviously they vary from one society to the next and are, as Cowgill and Holmes (1972) found, modified as a function of social change. Generally speaking, we can say that the position of the aged was strongest in societies characterized by corporate kin groups in which they occupied positions of authority. Ethnographic studies also suggest that the aged fared best in the family where they could perform domestic tasks for and with the young. This link between old and young within the family context was an important one in the past and presumably has continued potential for bringing meaning into the lives of older people.

The grandparent role is the major focus of this analysis. In Western society the role of grandparent has been proposed as a potentially significant one for continued social integration. According to Kahana and Kahana, "With some 70 percent of older people in the United States having living grandchildren, grandparenthood represents an area of potential usefulness and social value for a large segment of the elderly" (Kahana and Kahana, 1971, p. 261). It is therefore of interest to investigate to what extent this is the case for modernizing society, and how viable the role of grandparent is for the older members. The argument Kahana and Kahana make is that one of the very few social roles potentially available to the majority of aged is that of grandparent. They note the shifts in emphasis in old age from achieved to ascribed status and from horizontal to vertical interactions, which go hand in hand. As a consequence, grandparenthood is viewed as an important source of ascribed status for the aged in all societies. As a concomitant of modernization, the proportion of people living to old age has increased and yet at the same time the roles open to these aged people have decreased. The question, therefore, arises as to the extent to which the grandparent role can fill the void and serve as a viable option for continued integration. To date, research on the meaning and significance of grandparenthood in the United States has suggested that it is not particularly rewarding. This is viewed as a function of (1) the separation of families (i.e., the isolated nuclear family), (2) the generation gap (age segregation), and (3) the mediating effect of intervening generations. As a consequence of such factors many young people have minimal interaction with grandparents, and the latter report dissatisfaction or lack of interest in the role.

At the other end of the modernization continuum are traditional societies characterized by corporate lineage groupings and intergenerational interdependence. Presumably in such societies the grandparent role is a more integral part of the social fabric of everyday life. The purpose of this study is to assess the meaning and significance of grandparenthood. Because we are looking at the role in transition, our concern is with the impact of modernization, especially as it is mediated through education, on the grandparent role.

BACKGROUND

Uganda is a republic in East Africa, bordered on the north by Sudan, on the easy by Kenya, on the south by Tanzania and Rwanda, and on the west by Zaire. Its total area is 91,134 square miles, which makes it about the size of the state of Oregon. According to a United Nations's estimate, the population was about 10,460,000, 99% of whom are African. It is the least urbanized of the three East African countries; according to the 1969 census, only 5% lived in urban centers, and by 1980 it was 12%. Population increase is at an annual rate of approximately 3%. Only 6% of the total population in 1968 were in wage-earning occupations outside of agriculture. This means that the majority of Ugandans grow their own food in rural areas and have not yet moved into the cash economy on anything approaching a steady basis. The vast majority of the population of working age consists, then, of peasant farmers and family members who help them. The annual cash income of the farmer is Uganda shillings: UShs) 500 (about $71), and the cash-in-kind income is estimated to be about UShs. 1200 ($170). Although the policy of Africanization has increased employment opportunities for Africans, there is still a disproportionate number of non-Africans in upper-level positions; the expulsion of large numbers of Asians in 1973 has further hastened the modernization process.

There are over 40 tribal or ethnic groups in Uganda, although English is the language of education and of government. Tribal ties have historically been strong and continue to be divisive elements in society.

The present study focuses on two Ugandan tribes. Each has different social structural characteristics that have been hypothesized to have implications for the position of the old. In addition, these two groups share a common yet distinct history. The Baganda is the largest tribe in Uganda and has been the most dominant since before the arrival of the British (1862). The Iteso, the second largest tribe, were conquered by the Baganda in 1900 and have never been particularly involved in national affairs. The Baganda fell from their dominant position when their king was overthrown in 1966 and during Obote's first regime were in disfavor. In 1971 the Amin government looked more favorably on them, but only for a short time. Despite the upheavals of the last 20 years, the history of Uganda is the history of Buganda, and the national leaders and elite came predominantly from their ranks.

In the present analysis tribal patterns and characteristics are discussed in the ethnographic present. The Baganda, a Bantu-speaking people, comprise about 25% of the population and have traditionally been a dominant tribe with a very sophisticated social organization. They are an eclectic people who for centuries have adapted their way of life to changing conditions. Thus, although they have a patrilineal kinship system in which the father–son relationship is emphasized, they are nuclear in their households, and the generations are often residentially segregated by considerable distance. This neolocal pattern reduces the power a parent exercises over his son. Equally important, it reduces the frequency of their interaction in adulthood.

Political hierarchy was the dominant factor of their social organization. Among the Baganda, unlike many other tribes, there was neither an elaborate kinship structure nor an age-grade system. According to Richards, among the Baganda, a man acquired rights over land through his political affiliations rather than through kinship ties (Richards, 1966).

The Baganda live in the fertile south central region of Uganda and enjoy both an ideal climate and a dependable food supply. This has especially important implications for the status of the old because it means that as long as they are physically able to care for themselves, they can remain independent and self-sufficient. Also, because land is fertile and plentiful, young people are not as tied to elders as they are in societies in which a son is dependent on jointly held parental property. Generally speaking, (1) neolocal residence patterns reduce the power a parent exercises over his son, and (2) extended families strengthen the status of the old people— especially when property rights are held within the family. For the Baganda, then, this source of status is absent. The Baganda are a forward-looking or future-oriented people. They have, since traditional times, placed a high emphasis on individualism and valued change and progress.

The other group we will examine are the Iteso, the second largest tribe in Uganda, though only about half the size of the Baganda. They are a Nilo–Hamitic people who live in the East Central region in a harsher environment than the Baganda; drought is a fact of life among these people. Although Nilo–Hamites are primarily herders, the Iteso are also sedentary agriculturalists. They have a strong patrilineal descent system; inheritance is through the male line and a man's heir is his eldest son, although in his own lifetime a father may subdivide his land among his sons (Lawrence, 1957). They reckon descent in the agnatic line only, so kinsmen are traced exclusively on the father's side. Marriage is ideally patrilocal, and this is further reinforced by the rigid practice of mother-in-law avoidance. However, these family patterns too are changing.

Historically there are three distinct social groupings in Iteso society. The first grouping is through kinship, the second has a territorial basis, and the third has a basis of common age-set initiation. The kinship grouping has primary importance for matters of childbirth, death, inheritance, and marriage. Kinship continues to be an important organizing principle in modern times.

The smallest kinship unit is the family consisting of the husband, his wife (or wives), unmarried children, and other dependent relatives. The extended family generally maintains a stable residence, though there is often temporary mobility in search of employment. Each extended familiy has an acknowledged elected head who is generally the senior family member in possession of his full faculties (Lawrence, 1957). Although this type of kinship organization is not as elaborate as that in other societies, it is nevertheless considerably more structured than Baganda patterns in both its traditional and modern forms. The territorial grouping was responsible for waging war, hunting and age-set initiations, but today, with limitations imposed on all of these activities, the territorial grouping has only limited significance.

Another element of sociopolitical organization present among the Iteso, yet absent among the Baganda was the age-grade system. It has long been assumed that societies with age-sets accorded their seniors higher status as they moved through higher age-grades. Although evidence to the contrary is emerging, it seems increasingly unlikely that this issue will ever be elucidated given the paucity of data from the past and the impact of change. Among the Iteso, for example, the age-grade system was formally abolished in 1900, though there are reports that it continued to exist, if in modified form. When the highly efficient and well organized Baganda conquered the Iteso, they sought to destroy the age-grade system in part because it interfered with roadmaking and other communal activities but also because age-sets had traditionally formed the basis of military organization.

The Iteso age-set system involved two initiation ceremonies. The first was a manhood initiation that took place every 2 to 5 years. It acknowledged that a group of young men had passed puberty and required adult status.

> It involved instruction of the youths in tribal duties by the old men . . . the payment of a fee in the form of an animal slaughtered to provide food for the elders at the initiation feast; a mock fight in which the retiring age-set was driven out by the incoming one. (Wright, 1942, p. 68).

The age-grades in Iteso were as follows:

Babe	for a period of roughly 2 years up to age 2
Child	for a period of roughly 4 years up to age 6
Boy	for a period of roughly 8 years up to age 14
Youth	for a period of roughly 4 years up to age 18
Young man	for a period of roughly 8 years up to age 26
Fullgrown man	for a period of roughly 16 years up to age 42
Elder	for a period of roughly 24 years up to age 65
Old man	until death

Initiation took place at puberty, so candidates were between 12 and 18 years of age.

The second initiation ceremony took place every 15 to 20 years. This involved the handing over of power and the stepping down of the elders.

> The position of dominant age-set was much coveted and it was only by the provision of much beer, and a great deal of persuasion, and the payment of a bull and a goat by each of the incoming set, that the age-set of elders could eventually be induced to retire. (Wright, 1942, p. 73)

Based on ethnographic materials, then, it appears that at least in traditional times there was a structured progression of life cycle stages marked by ritualized transactions. In addition, this account suggests upward mobility through elderhood—as distinct from old age which was a powerless position (though few lived to this stage).

To the extent that societies with age-grade systems utilize age as a principle in social organization, we would anticipate that the role configuration of the aged people would be more clearly demarcated for the Iteso than for the Baganda.

Because men generally married during the young-man-grade they were likely to become grandparents during the elder-grade. Hence, among the Iteso, grandparenthood and elderhood should be synchronized. Consequently, among the Iteso we would expect to find a better idea of the significance of age, a clearer understanding of what it means to be old and of the roles associated with age (including the grandparent role), and greater respect for old people in general and grandparents in particular.

The arrival of the British, rather than signaling a return to indigeneous Iteso practices, furthered homogenization in that Baganda agents were appointed to administer the Iteso district. Though this somewhat diminishes the distinction between the two societies, they nevertheless do have a number of differing structural characteristics. The Iteso are also an industrious people and today are considered among the most progressive farmers in Uganda.

Summary Table

Baganda	Iteso
Individualism	Collectivism
Achievement orientation	Achievement orientation
Weak patrilinealism	Strong patrilinealism
Neolocality	Patrilocality
Nuclear family	Extended family
Political hierarchy	Segmented political organization
Absence of age-grades	Age-Grade system

Thus we are comparing two societies that entered the twentieth century with divergent sociopolitical systems. The impact of some of these variations for the position of the aged population constitutes the backdrop of the present analysis. Having ascertained the relative position of the aged in these two societies, we focus on the significance and meaning of grandparenthood.

METHODOLOGY

Because interest was in assessing change, baseline measures of the position of the aged tribe members in the larger society and of their roles and status in the family were gleaned from ethnographic reports. Unfortunately, these tend to be of varying quality. They are based on a less-than-systematic conglomerate of reports, anecdotes, and tales and suffer from a lack of comparability arising out of the different anthropological paradigms of the investigators.

To address the impact of modernization, comparisons were made between these historical accounts and data more recently collected. The data presented here are part of a larger national study of the status of old people in a traditional society undergoing change. The data were collected in 1971 from a sample of approximately 7000 students in Ugandan secondary schools. A brief questionnaire was administered in a total of 15 schools in all but the northern district, owing to political upheavals in the north at the time of the study. In addition, forays outside Buganda were discouraged, contributing further to the heavier concentrations of participating schools in the central region. The intent was to secure a fairly representative sample of both the different types of schools in the country and the different tribes.

Nations in the process of modernizing allow youth access to education and jobs that are not open to older people; one result is that the young are being socialized into new ways, and this inevitably separates them from the old. As a consequence, the family may not longer be viewed as the most functional agent of socialization (Eisenstadt, 1956), and by extension the role of grandparent may also be diminished.

In a study of youth in Uganda, Wallace and Weeks rejected the premise that a new set of social values had emerged among the young. Presumably, the school is the major social institution that would disseminate these values yet their findings suggest that:

> When they return home to the village during their vacations, the role of student often becomes subservient to their other roles such as those of son, grandson, farmer, etc., as they take up their family and village lives. Many of these secondary-school leavers, if they do not obtain salaried jobs in town, do eventually

become re-integrated into the village community. (Wallace and Weeks, 1972, pp. 359–360)

This finding is significant for the present analysis because the major dimension of modernization focused on here is education.

In Uganda marked education expansion took place during the decade following independence (Bell, 1980). Consequently, except for those out of sync, the senior secondary students in our sample began their education before large numbers of people had the option of going to school, and the younger students entered when education was more available. The older students, then, are a very select group—both because senior secondary schools are highly selective and because they began their education at a time when it was not readily available. It is also of note that owing to political upheavals following this study, the percentage of 6–11-year olds attending school dropped from 61 to 53, and only 4% of 12–16-year olds were in secondary school.

There are, then, several cautions to be made at the outset: (1) This is an elite sample, given that a small proportion go on to secondary school; (2) older students are an even more select group owing to when they entered the educational system; and (3) students may either be in a stage of transition, moving in new directions, or we may have observed them in a temporary state of flux, soon to return to the traditional ways of their people.

The schools are patterned after the British education system. Thus, a child attends primary or grammar school for 7 years, at the end of which he takes the Primary Grade 7 (P7)-leaving examination. There is a high value placed on education and children are strongly encouraged to pursue all educational opportunities, although school fees are often a limiting factor. (At the time of the study, school fees for primary school were about 12% of the average family income and secondary school fees were even higher). A good grade on the P7 exam qualifies the student to attend secondary school. At the end of the fourth year of secondary school, students take the "ordinary" (0)-level examination, which must be passed in order to achieve a certificate of graduation. An especially excellent showing on this examination qualifies a student to continue into senior secondary school (S5 and S6), which is essentially a college preparatory program; at this stage the government assumes the cost of school fees. At the time of the study 69% of the population were uneducated (25% had primary education; 5% had above primary; 13% had high school certificates or higher). Twenty-seven percent of the 5–19-year olds were in school; however, the majority are not expected to go beyond primary school.

All government secondary schools are conducted in English and the questionnaires were administered to all students present in each school in their classrooms. The questionnaire took an average of 1 hour and 15 minutes to complete, though the range was from 45 minutes to 2 hours and 30 minutes, and not unexpectedly seemed to vary inversely with age and level of English proficiency.

The student subsample dealt with in the present analysis is the 1699 Baganda and 1030 Iteso secondary students, ranging in age from 12 to 21. The average age for beginning S1 was 13 and for completion of S6 was 18.

Measures of socioeconomic status (SES) in this predominantly rural society tend to be very gross. However, it is important to note that only one third of the Baganda students reported their father's primary occupation as agricultural. This compares to 70% for the Iteso. Because only 6% of the population are in wage-earning occupations, the Baganda–Iteso difference on this dimension serves as an indicator of the extent to which these two groups have moved into the modern world. Many of the Baganda students have educated parents, which distinguishes them not only from the Iteso but also from most other tribes in Uganda.

The sample consists of both males and females. As in most societies, it is the male in the family who has educational opportunities when resources are limited. So to an already select sample of male students, we have added an even more select group of females. According to the 1969 census there were half as many females enrolled in school as males, but there is a consistent decline in the number of females in the later years.

Each student was asked to recall when he or she was in the fifth grade (P5) and to discuss relationships with one grandmother and one grandfather who were living at the time. The rationale is that because we are dealing with students of different ages—a majority of whom were currently enrolled in boarding schools, as opposed to day schools—it was necessary to establish some common baseline to which they would all refer. Consequently, recall data were used to define their relationships with grandparents, or if their grandparents were not living, with another old person who was like a grandparent to them. In P5 the vast majority (over 80%) for each tribe were between 10 and 12 years old; though the range was between 9 and 18. Financial considerations, family obligations, poor school performance, and political upheavals all contribute to irregular school careers for a minority of students.

According to the 1980 census, the age distribution in Uganda is as follows: 46% between 0–14; 48% between 15–59; 6% for 60 and over. This is virtually unchanged since the 1969 census, though it must be kept in mind that population estimates are at best close approximations. Life expectancy at birth in 1970 was 48.3 years for males and 51.7 years for females, which is about 13 and 10 years longer, respectively, than it was in 1950. Unfortunately, age-specific figures are not available.

TABLE 1

Percentage of Grandparents No Longer Living (at Time of Interview)

Tribe	Father's father (FaFa)	Father's mother (FaMo)	Mother's father (MoFa)	Mother's mother (MoMo)
Baganda	68.3	52.5	53.6	35.3
Iteso	76.2	63.8	65.5	49.1

For the country as a whole, according to the 1969 census, males and females 65 and over constitute 2.5 and 1.8% of the total population. Comparable figures for the Baganda are 4.6 and 3.8%. Thus, more favorable economic and climatic conditions in Buganda appear to have an impact throughout the life cycle. Abbreviated life expectancy, the tendency of males to marry females younger than themselves, and differences in ethnic group life expectancies are reflected in Table 1. At the time of the interview, then, it is not surprising that between half to three quarters of the respondents had deceased grandparents, although when they were in P5 a majority did have living grandparents. This further highlights the need for recall data.

FINDINGS AND RESULTS

Although we are concerned here primarily with the position of the old people *vis-à-vis* the family, specifically the grandparent role, it is instructive to briefly frame this in a larger societal context. Respondents were asked: "Do old people have any special position or do different things *just because they are old?*"

Because we are dealing with elite samples, we might have anticipated that elders of both tribes would be involved in the community. The majority of the Baganda reported no special roles for old people either in the economic, social, or ritual realm. This was not altogether unexpected because the merit system that characterizes the Baganda conceivably precludes nepotism. It was surprising, however, that the Iteso responses were virtually identical. Because the Iteso had clearly demarcated age-grades, the special roles of the Iteso aged should have been more pronounced.

This absence of major societal roles is indicative of the shrinking life span of the aged and underscores the potential significance of familial roles, similar to the role configuration of the aged in industrial societies.

Before going any further, it is instructive to examine the way in which residential patterns impact on family roles for the aged. In the United States research on the quality of grandparent–grandchild relationships suggests that geographic separation is important (Gilford & Black, 1972). In the societies under study, traditional residential patterns call for neolocality among the Baganda and patrilocality among the Iteso. Indeed, 21% of the Baganda live in the same house or homestead with the paternal grandparents as compared to 61% of the Iteso. Interestingly, about 15% of each group live with maternal grandparents, a non-normative situation, especially given the strong mother-in-law taboo for both groups. This underscores again the kinds of changes African family structure is undergoing.

Grandparents were viewed by the majority (90%) of their grandchildren in a nurturant role and were characterized as kind, calm, loving, and gentle. In addition, about 60% of the students said that their grandparents were funny and/or talkative, with this being somewhat more true of grandfathers. Also, a majority of the students described their grandparents as friends. We have, then, a picture of a warm, close relationship between the respondents and the grandparents they are discussing.

Is it normative to have such close emotional ties and such a positive attitude toward grandparents in general? Or have these students chosen to discuss those grandparents to whom they feel close? Although we did not have descriptive data on all four grandparents, the students were asked to indicate how close to or how much affection they felt for each grandparent (for detailed responses see Table 2). Over 70% of the sample responded that they felt very or fairly close to each one. Both groups reported feeling closer to grandmothers than grandfathers. Overall the majority report feeling close, with this being somewhat stronger among the Iteso, particularly for paternal grandparents. There is little doubt that these students had positive feelings toward their grandparents. What is of particular significance is that Iteso are most likely to live with their paternal grandparents and at the same

TABLE 2

Perceived Closeness to Grandparents (in percentages)

	Baganda				Iteso			
	FaFa	MoFa	FaMo	MoMo	FaFa	MoFa	FaMo	MoMo
Very close	43.9	40.1	47.1	55.7	62.5	44.6	69.5	59.4
Fairly close	27.9	30.4	29.2	23.7	25.6	33.4	18.4	26.7
Not too close	24.8	25.9	20.2	19.2	9.2	19.3	10.7	12.7
Did not like	3.4	3.6	1.4	2.8	2.7	1.4	1.2	1.2
Total %	100.0	101.0	100.0	100.0	100.0	100.0	100.0	100.0
N	759	966	1001	1217	360	482	505	648

TABLE 3

Relative Affection for Grandparents
vis-à-vis Parents (in percentages)

Grandparent	Baganda		Iteso	
	N	%	N	%
Grandfather				
Closer to grandfather	334	21.4	317	33.1
Closer to father	790	50.4	312	32.4
Equally close to both	334	21.3	301	31.4
Not close to either	110	7.0	29	3.0
Total	1569	100.1	959	100.0
Grandmother				
Closer to grandmother	309	19.1	262	26.8
Closer to mother	822	50.9	325	33.3
Equally close to both	410	25.4	363	37.2
Not close to either	75	4.6	26	2.7
Total	1616	100.0	976	100.0

time report feeling closest to them. Emotionally gratifying grandparenthood then appears to be related to proximity.

Given these positive feelings about grandparents might we conclude that grandchildren felt closer to grandparents than to their own parents? Particularly among the Iteso, for whom joint residence is the norm, the opportunity for interaction is increased, and we would expect to see closer intergenerational bonds. Indeed, among the Iteso grandparent–grandchild ties seem as strong or stronger than the parent–child tie (see Table 3). This is consistent with the notion that the young and old become allies against the power of the middle generation. Among the Baganda, on the other hand, particularly when grandparents are not proximate, the parent–child bond is stronger, and grandparents seem more extraneous to their lives. Overall, though, there are close warm feelings across generations.

What implications does this have for the way grandchildren demonstrated their feelings or for their behavior in general? The relationship as outlined thus far suggests that interaction between grandparents and their grandchildren is characterized by affection. These relationships do not, for the most part, appear to be either instrumental or confidential. According to Sweetster (1956), when grandparents have power within the family their relationship with their grandchildren tends to be distant and formal. However, when they are disassociated from family authority the relationship tends to be warm and indulgent. To what extent is this applicable to the present analysis, given that close ties exist?

By and large old people were removed from the family authority structure among the Baganda. This is reinforced by the norm of neolocality and in general is inherent in the value system with its strong emphasis on individualism, so the role should be characterized by less formality. Among the Iteso, however, despite stronger values placed on extended family living, collectivism, and patrilinealism, the grandparent–grandchild tie appears even stronger than among the Baganda. This reinforces the point made previously that whatever the traditional position of the older person was in the Iteso family power structure, it is no longer a viable one. While both Baganda and Iteso grandchildren reported approximately comparable frequency of arguments (29% and 36%, respectively), the Iteso reported far more intervention by grandparents on their behalf than did the Baganda (65%), although in both cases the majority in each grandparent category did intervene. It is clear that Iteso grandparents take a more active role in the lives of their grandchildren.

What we have emerging is a picture of grandparent–grandchild relations in which grandparents appear to be relatively involved in their grandchildren's lives. These grandchildren (and their were no gender differences) view their grandparents as active participants in family relationships. This is true for both groups but particularly for the Iteso.

In P5 Iteso saw at least one grandparent much more frequently than did the Baganda (63% of the Iteso saw their grandparents weekly or more often, whereas only 40% of the Baganda had this much interaction). The older students reported the same frequency of interaction when they were in P5 as do younger ones for P5 (suggesting consistency). In terms of frequency of visits at the time of this study, each group reported seeing their grandparents about half as often as they had in P5 (19% and 37% for the Baganda and Iteso, respectively). Senior secondary students were the least likely to have frequent interaction.

To what extent have visiting patterns decreased over time? A third to half of both groups report about the same level of interaction, though the less frequent the interaction in P5, the greater the consistency at the time of the study. Given distance and school demands on time, this decrease in interaction was not unexpected and underscores again the necessity for recall data.

In neither society, then, despite their varying residential patterns and associated distribution of family authority, were the warm nurturant aspects of the grandparent relationship constrained, and in both, the majority of grandparents appeared to make positive overtures to assist their grandchildren. For both societies it seems that the removal of the grandparent from active control over the distribution of family resources (e.g., control over land is essentially absent in both societies) has served to strengthen or at any rate encourage continuance of the grandparent–grandchild tie.

TABLE 4

Signs of Respect by Grandchildren for Grandparents
(in percentages)

Signs of respect	Baganda		Iteso	
	Males	Females	Males	Females
For grandfather				
Did not respect	1	1	0	0
Obeyed/did tasks	47	30	78	57
Respectful manner	31	55	9	33
Did not laugh at	1	1	1	2
Did not call by proper name	1	1	1	2
Did not argue	4	1	4	2
Bought presents	1	2	0	0
Other	13	9	6	4
Total	99	100	101	100
N	804	557	435	123
For grandmother				
Did not respect	3	2	0	1
Obeyed/did tasks	53	39	80	70
Respectful manner	23	45	6	16
Did not laugh at	1	0	1	3
Did not call by proper name	2	1	3	1
Did not argue	3	2	3	4
Bought presents	2	1	3	2
Other	13	9	4	3
Total	100	99	100	100
N	809	571	538	158

Although grandparents are not in positions of authority, they continue to command respect. Virtually all of the respondents respected their grandparents, which is consistent with the societal norm of respect for the aged. However, respect for grandparents has taken a different form from our original conception of respect associated with high status of the elderly. The way in which respect is demonstrated diverges both within and between societies. Among the Baganda, grandsons show respect by *doing things* for their grandparents instead of by a particular *demeanor*, whereas granddaughters demonstrate their respect by kneeling or speaking in a subdued manner in their grandparents' presence (see Table 4). While Iteso girls demonstrate respect through demeanor to a greater extent than males do, the overriding pattern for both sexes is clearly to show respect by obeying their grandparents and doing what tasks are asked of them.

Because the young tend to demonstrate their respect by doing things with or for their grandparents, it is instructive to pursue at greater length the nature of these intergenerational interactions that define the behavioral components of the grandparent role.

As is to be expected in traditional societies, the basic division of labor is along the lines of gender and age. The examination of tasks sheds some light on the everyday activities in the life of older people. Roles are essentially gender-segregated with women handling domestic affairs and men being dominant in the cash-economic realm; this division of labor is further subdivided on the basis of age. Among the Baganda (for whom neolocal residence is the norm) the aged couple tend, whenever possible, to meet their own needs for day-to-day household activities. The modal pattern for tasks that require money or leaving the home is largely one of assistance by adult offspring in the more important areas followed by dependence on grandchildren for errands, such as going to the store and fetching water (Nahemow and Adams, 1974).

On the other hand, among the Iteso, for whom joint living is modal, the principles underlying the division of labor are not nearly as clear-cut. A harsher environment and a tradition of men being active in agriculture result in a much greater involvement of kin in the performance of daily household tasks. Older women in this extended family setting receive more assistance from adult offspring of both genders and Iteso men take a more active role than do Baganda men. Of note is the lesser role of Iteso grandchildren at least *vis-à-vis* their Baganda counterparts apparently owing to greater involvement by the intervening generation. In both instances, though, grandchildren do assist grandmothers with household tasks more than they do grandfathers, owing no doubt to the fact that women generally carry a heavier burden.

Although we have only minimal data on social interaction with nonkin, the material on tasks suggests that kin involvement, in varying degrees, plays an important part in the lives of the aged in both of these societies.

In turning to activities between grandparents and their grandchildren, it appears that the Iteso have more intergenerational interaction. The young people's responses do not refer to how frequently they are involved with grandparents, but rather to the things they do when they are together. Hence proximity appears to foster not only more interaction, but involvement over a broader range of activities. A sizable proportion of grandmothers and grandfathers seem to serve as companions in leisure activities such as storytelling and singing (which also have teaching functions) or in more instrumental tasks such as food collecting and herding (see Table 5). Specifically, the Baganda grandfathers are both storytellers and food collectors with their grandsons, but they are rarely more than storytellers to their granddaughters. Among the Iteso, the same general pattern emerges, although the extent of interaction is greater for both types of activities.

TABLE 5

Activities of Grandchildren with Grandparents (in percentages)

	Baganda		Iteso	
Activities	Males	Females	Males	Females
Done by/with grandfather				
Nothing	23	24	10	12
Hunt/fish	21	12	43	20
Storytelling	22	30	17	35
Bought presents	15	16	10	11
Advice/teach	4	3	2	2
Comfort	1	0	1	0
Duties/tasks	3	24	6	11
Paid fees	1	1	3	1
Just talked	4	4	1	1
Other	7	7	7	7
Total	101	100	100	100
N	795	541	407	123
Done by/with grandmother				
Nothing	27	19	12	10
Hunt/fish	20	21	33	28
Storytelling	12	19	15	27
Bought presents	15	16	11	6
Advice/teach	5	4	3	1
Comfort	3	0	3	0
Duties/tasks	10	11	17	23
Paid fees	0	0	1	0
Just talked	3	3	2	2
Other	5	6	4	3
Total	101	99	101	100
N	801	551	513	154

Grandmothers, on the other hand, are primarily food collecting companions for both grandsons and granddaughters, and although grandmothers are less often storytellers than their spouses they still tend to perform this role with granddaughters and to a lesser extent with grandsons.

Whereas there were gender differences in interaction patterns with grandparents there were no age differences. This would suggest that, at least for the time period under investigation, the grandparent role is relatively stable from a behavioral perspective.

In summary, food gathering and storytelling are the activities the two generations engage in together. Recalling that we have no measures of frequency, we can conclude only that when they get together, whether it is frequently or not, these are the things they do. Overall, though, the Iteso are involved with grandparents in a wider range of activities than are the Baganda, and this is primarily attributable to proximity.

TABLE 6

General Attitudes toward the Aged (percentage agree)

Attitude	Tribe	Year in school[a]				
		S1	S2	S3	S4	S5&6
More set in	Baganda	72	76	82	78	90
ways	Iteso	65	70	72	75	76
Wise when old	Baganda	46	53	50	50	59
	Iteso	49	51	44	42	50
Value advice less	Baganda	46	41	46	43	54
now	Iteso	38	31	42	38	43
Wrong to crit-	Baganda	56	55	56	54	39
icize grand-	Iteso	80	74	70	72	48
parents						
All right to crit-	Baganda	50	36	30	39	63
icize parents	Iteso	32	30	28	32	51
Child's responsi-	Baganda	69	82	80	85	90
bility to care	Iteso	78	78	81	83	88
for parents						

[a]S = year in secondary school.

A series of attitude questions was used to assess perceptions (1) of the aged in general and (2) of integenerational relations with kin (Table 6). Although there were no age differences with regard to behavior, it was anticipated that attitudes might prove more sensitive indicators of the status of the aged and of the changing nature of grandparenthood.

The theme running throughout much of the daily life of the young in school is one of change. They are bombarded with different values, culture content, and the related material trappings. To what extent do they view the aged as willing or able to deal with the changes they are being expected to make? To assess this, students were asked to agree or disagree with the statement: "People become more set in their ways and ideas as they become old." A majority of students agreed with this. For each year, the Baganda are somewhat more likely than the Iteso to agree. Overall, older students see the aged as more rigid, and this is particularly true among the senior secondary Baganda students.

Although they are seen as set in their ways, about half the students said that with age comes wisdom. The vast majority of students agree that old people should be consulted and asked for advice. This finding is somewhat suspicious because advice and counsel were rarely mentioned as a joint activity. When asked whether they valued the advice of old people less now than when they were young, it became apparent that although they feel obliged to solicit the opinion of the aged, they felt less constrained by them.

The Baganda were overall less likely than the Iteso to heed the advice of their elders. However, with increasing age, both groups seem to devalue the advisor role. The major shift comes at the senior secondary level. This suggests that with age and/or experience these students are changing their views. As their own base of knowledge increases, perhaps they are better able to put the old people's knowledge and advice in perspective: their conclusion appears to be that it is not too valuable.

It is difficult to make SES comparisons between the two tribes because there is not much variation, especially among the Iteso. However, some differences between white-collar students and those whose fathers are primarily agricultural should be pointed out.

For each of the areas investigated, the white-collar group exhibited less deferential attitudes *vis-à-vis* the wisdom and advice of the aged. Thus, white-collar students felt that wisdom and age do not automatically go hand-in-hand, whereas children of blue-collar workers and agriculturalists believed they did. Wisdom may well be operationally defined differently by these two SES groups. The wisdom and knowledge of old people for the life experiences of young white-collar students increasingly becomes irrelevant to their daily lives and to what they perceive to be in their future; perhaps as they age, they come to see this even more. For the blue collar and agricultural group, old people's wisdom is no doubt as inapplicable at that point in their lives as it is to the white-collar group. But many will go back to the villages, and even those who assume responsible positions at the village level will still need to draw on the advice of their elders about local and traditional matters. These things are not taught in school and to the extent that younger people need this knowledge, it will be the older people to whom they will have to turn. For the majority of students, wisdom and age are not necessarily related.

To summarize, it seems that although the vast majority of students feel that old people's advice should be asked for, there is little belief that what they have to say is worth very much or that they are wise. Put another way, in Baganda society and somewhat less so among the Iteso, one has an obligation to clear things with elders but little responsibility to take their advice seriously or act on it in any way. Perhaps old people should be consulted because of their age, but beyond that there is little commitment to following through.

In terms of intergenerational relationships there is general consensus between the Baganda and Iteso. Thus there is agreement that it is legitimate to criticize parents and grandparents, that grandparents should not spoil grandchildren, and that each individual has a responsibility to both descending and ascending generations in terms of providing for them, particularly if they are helpless.

Despite general consensus on these expectations, there is variation within the student groupings. Among students, the most interesting differences are a function of year attained in school. Once again, a large portion of senior secondary students—fifth and sixth year students—hold consistently different attitudes from their fellow students. In terms of criticizing parents and grandparents, Baganda are somewhat more likely than Iteso to agree that this is acceptable though a majority of both do agree that it is. The older the students, in each group, the more likely they are to say that it is all right to criticize their seniors. Once again the most dramatic differences are between senior secondary students and all others. There are no really consistent class differences, though the most pronounced shift in patterns comes for each SES category at the senior level. Those whose fathers are agriculturalists seem the least willing to criticize either parents or grandparents. This is consistent with the theme running throughout the data with regard to traditional ways. White-collar students seem to be more geared to modern values and the least past-oriented. Students of agricultural backgrounds express a greater sense of generational propriety and less willingness to speak out against elders. Criticizing is not especially respectful but it must be recalled that most students criticize neither their grandparents nor their parents. Rather it is primarily the senior secondary students who feel free to do so. It is therefore not anomalous that the young demonstrate respect for their grandparents and also criticize them. It is conceivable, as suggested previously, that a considerable amount of this so-called respect is really lip service paid to a societal ideal and rarely done for more than form.

These students, then, particularly as they get older, appear to be rejecting or at least questioning the link between age and respect both in the larger society and in the family context. They are not, however, forsaking the aged. When asked whether "it is a child's responsibility to care for his aged parents," the vast majority agreed that it was, and older students even more than younger ones acknowledged this obligation.

In summary, the overall pattern that emerges with regard to attitudes is as follows: The impact of education is pronounced. With each year of school there is an increase in agreement with attitudes that are consistent with individualism and that would contribute to achievement and success. Students from white-collar backgrounds have already been socialized into this mold and the process continues in school. Students from agricultural backgrounds lag somewhat behind, but with each year in school they too come to share similar views. Finally, the Iteso follow the same pattern as the Baganda but overall appear somewhat more traditional. The impact of age and education among senior secondary students appears even stronger for this group.

DISCUSSION AND CONCLUSIONS

Modernization and the advent of a money economy are associated with major changes in the status systems of society involving a shift from ascribed to achieved roles. A major intervening factor in the aged person's relationship to his juniors appears to have been the rate of technological and social change present in society. Slow change put a premium on accumulated knowledge and experience which, in turn, made possible an age-grade system which allocated the aged to less arduous positions. At the same time, these roles were still valued by the community. But the converse is that rapid social and technological change undermined their position.

Other factors which emerge, mostly from the literature review, but which jibe with the findings presented here, are that age, respectability, the accumulation of skills and knowledge are all important, but in themselves, alone or in combination, are not enough to assure high status. Wealth and social position, which are interdependent, are crucial; and without material resources, which are symbols of achievement and success as well as indicators that the old person will be an asset rather than a liability, it is highly likely that only limited respect will be given. To be rich and old generally assures high status, merely to be old rarely assures much of anything.

We can summarize the major findings by saying that old people are part of the family network, but even within this context there is little to suggest that they have any special positions or occupy any special roles. Old people do not occupy roles solely as a function of age. Few hold special positions, even in this elite sample, and those who do probably held them earlier in their life cycle. If anything, there appears to be a diminution in social life space with age, a parcelling out to kin of responsibilities and chores.

Of what, then, does the grandparent situation consist among the Baganda and Iteso? Although it is true that grandparents continue to function as a link to the past, this role is being reduced in the contemporary world. The roles of storyteller, advisor, and functionary at ceremonial occasions are rarely enacted and appear overall to be perceived as not viable for contemporary life. These are still functions the aged perform, but their utility is problematic in the eyes of youth (particularly older students) and there does not seem to be a high value placed on them because these skills are not deemed relevant for the demands of the modern world.

Grandchildren tend to be closer to grandmothers, and generally same-gender relationships predominate. There is greater interaction between grandmothers and grandchildren because the latter assist their grandmothers with chores around the house. It is also the case that grandmothers tend to be younger and more likely to be active. Also, many grandmothers' skills (in the household domain) are still very relevant to everyday life. This is especially true for granddaughters. The traditional gender division of labor cross-cuts intergenerational relationships and consequently same-sex interaction predominates. So it appears that despite a number of differences—residence patterns, family form, patrilineal emphasis, type of climate, as well as historical differences in social organization—the nature of the grandparent role is remarkably similar in the two societies. In addition, the impact of age, increased education, and social mobility appears to be predictive of even greater similarity in the future.

One effect of modernization appears to be the breakdown and revamping of traditional corporate lineage structures. It has been noted that joint residential patterns foster greater interaction and also more positive feelings toward grandparents. In a study of the aged Baganda (Nahemow, 1979), it was found that although residential separation was customary, the aged who violated this norm had higher life satisfaction and were less isolated.

Among the Baganda the nuclear unit seems to have been strengthened as a function of land reforms and the introduction of cash crops, which increased the need for economic cooperation of the family unit (Richards, 1966). In addition, a traditional pattern among the Baganda of sending children to live with a grandparent persists today. In the past it was to do service for the older person; today its purpose is so the child will remain on the land because the urban areas are deemed unfit. The end result, however, is that grandparents have a role to play.

There is also a restructuring of family organization among the Iteso. In this patrilineal, patrilocal society, relationships with maternal grandparents were warm and frequent and more proximate than anticipated. Overall, the changing family structures in both of these societies are providing options to grandparents for continued involvement.

One emphasis in this chapter has been on the life cycle as seen in three time dimensions: chronological time, social time, and historical time. In traditional societies, chronological and social time tend to be more synchronized than in modern societies in which there are overlapping systems of age-grading (Neugarten & Datan, 1973). For this reason, one must be especially cautious in drawing cross-cultural comparisons of societies at different stages of modernization. The greater proportion of older people in the United States, as well as increased life expectancy, means that although like age groups are comparable, the age structure and the social significance of age diverge considerably (Nahemow, 1979).

The meaning of chronological age, both theoretically and practically, diverges in societies at different levels of development. It should also be kept in mind, for example, that until recently, Ugandans did not keep track of years or of people's ages. In fact a substantial proportion of the sample chose to define old age in terms of characteristics other than number of years lived. Physical changes figured predominantly among the criteria for defining old age. Physical changes included baldness, grey hair, wrinkles, poor eyesight, walking-with-a-stick, bent over stance, and generally those physiological changes commonly associated with age. Among the aged Baganda (Nahemow, 1979) physical changes were found to be a more important set of definitional factors by the elders than chronological age, although this may reflect their lesser ability to deal with chronological accounting in any meaningful way. Not unexpectedly, a larger proportion of females than of males cited physical changes as important in defining old age. Southall and Gutkind (1957) make the point that a woman is often considered old between 32 and 38 both due to loss of physical attractiveness and inability to bear children.

About a quarter of the student sample defined old age as under 50; based on a *coming of age* definition that consisted of cross-over points into the status of adulthood and included both social and physical changes such as getting married, finishing school, and growing a beard. A final category used by the respondents we called *social definition,* and it includes the assumption of a broad range of roles, such as grandparent and retired person, as well as rights, obligations, and duties such as no longer paying taxes and being respected. Incorporating chronological age, physical attributes, and social roles, the students equated old age with what in Western society is generally termed middle age. Given the shortened life expectancy of these people, it is probably a fairly accurate conceptualization of old age. In a sense their definitions of age are more sensitive to interindividual differences than is the gross chronological measure we often use.

Thus, the maturational factors that accompany or define old age and grandparenthood in traditional societies are quite different from the chronological benchmarks in modern society. This is complicated by the fact that the meaning of grandparenthood is constantly in transition.

In the United States, the quickening of the stages of the family life cycle has meant that grandparenthood has become a middle-aged phenomenon. Further, increased life expectancy means that there are a growing number of four-generation families, which makes grandparenting a second rather than a first-generation phenomenon. That is, grandparents are no longer the oldest generation. Indeed, since grandparenthood is occurring earlier in the family life cycle and lasting longer, the meaning of the role itself is in flux. There are more surviving grandparents per child today, and grandchildren interact with their grandparents into adulthood, which necessitates redefinition of the role. Grandparents are juggling their time and energy between their grandchildren on the one hand and on their own aged parents on the other. In addition, many grandfathers and grandmothers are still employed and have less time to spend with grandchildren (Troll, Miller, & Atchley, 1979, p. 108).

In Uganda the picture is very different since the time lapse between generations is greater and the average life expectancy is lower. Given this lower-life expectancy (51 years), younger age at marriage (18 for females and 24 for males), higher fertility (6.1), and infant mortality (120), a larger portion of Ugandan grandparents are still in the active parent stage, with dependent offspring in the home. Also, they are much less likely than their American counterparts to live to see their grandchildren reach adulthood. Thus, the position of American grandparents is structurally quite different from that of Ugandan grandparents who tend to be older, first generation and closer to the end of their life cycle (Nahemow, 1983).

What does the future hold for the aged in these modernizing societies? That is, how are they replacing role losses that are structurally associated with social change? It has been suggested that one of the roles that has the potential to assume primacy in the lives of older people is that of grandparenthood.

Until recently there has been little systematic research on grandparenthood in the United States, and the picture which emerges is at best inconclusive, although it appears that the grandparent role is not highly significant for most older people (Troll *et al.*, 1979). The work of Neugarten and Weinstein (1964) and Wood and Robertson (1976) suggests that those people who enact the grandparent role in the future are likely to do so when they are younger, and that they will also tend to be less constrained by formal role demands. The grandparent role does not appear to incorporate the functions of primary socializing agent, advisor, or companion. Rather it appears to be evolving into a largely socioemotional role. This is the case for the United States, and it appears to be similar in the two societies under investigation here. Thus, the emergent pattern of grandparent–grandchild relationships is based on intermittent contact, informality, and playfulness. Rather than concern/anxiety over transmission of values and socialization, grandparents freed of this responsibility focus more on having fun with their grandchildren. Atchley (1980) reports that grandmothers and granddaughters have a better chance than their male counterparts of developing such a relationship because the housewife role for women is far more stable than the occupational roles for men. That is, grandmothers' skills and knowledge are still often relevant to their granddaughters, whereas grandfathers' are often obsolete both for industry and for their grandsons. This is changing in the United States with the advent of societal shifts in the role of women, but in modernizing nations such major gender-role reallocations are a long way off. The greater relevance of grandparenting among grand-mothers (who are younger than their husbands both chronologically and socially) is a pattern that is likely to persist.

Modifications in family patterns at earlier stages of the life cycle have implications for enactment of the grandparent role. Rising divorce and remarriage rates in conjunction with later age at marriage and delayed fertility may be predictive of a bimodal distribution for the onset of grand-parenthood. Individuals may become grandparents later in the life cycle than they do today if their offspring postpone parenthood, or they may be discouraged from playing the role in the event of divorce. On the one hand, middle-aged grandparents may be unable or unwilling to enact the grand-parent role. On the other hand, these same people are subsequently likely to be confronted anew with this option as a consequence of reconstituted families at a point in the life cycle in which fewer responsibilities make the role more attractive.

In conclusion, the variation in grandparenthood can be conceptually represented along a continuum of modernization using the ascription–achievement dichotomy discussed previously. In traditional societies the more corporate the kin network, the higher the status of the elderly in the society and within the family. In the extreme case, at one end point of the continuum, elders exercise complete control over the family-life cycle of their kin. Thus, for example, they control the timing of marital choice and the fertility behavior of their offspring. Theoretically, this makes grand-parenthood an achieved role (particularly in societies that practice infan-ticide). At the other end of the continuum are older people who lack control altogether, such as those whose adult offspring remain voluntarily childless.

For most of the distance along this continuum, however, grand-parenthood is an ascribed role from which the role incumbent is increasing-ly removed from control. In fact for the most part, the transition into the grandparent role depends on the actions of others. It may be that to the extent that the individual relinquishes control over assuming a role, the role itself may become less significant in his or her life. Conceivably under conditions of modernization, grandparenthood may prove a viable option for the aged population in the absence of other roles. On the other hand, in modern societies in which grandparenthood is increasingly occurring at a point in the life cycle when individuals are more fully integrated in other age-status systems, this role may prove less important in the future.

REFERENCES

Atchley, R. (1980). *Social forces in later life.* Belmont, CA: Wadsworth.
Baltes, P., Reese, H., & Lipsitt, L. (1980). Life-span developmental psychology. *Annual Review of Psychology, 31,* 65–110.

Bell, M. (1980). Patterns of youth mobility in Uganda. *Journal of Asian and African Studies*, XV, 3–4, 203–216.

Colson, E. (1970). Family changes in contemporary Africa. In John Middleton (Ed.), *Black Africa*. Toronto: MacMillan.

Cowgill, D., & Holmes, L. D. (1972). *Aging and modernization*. New York: Appleton-Century-Croft.

deBeauvoir, S. (1973). *The coming of age*. New York: Warner.

Eisenstadt, S. N. (1956). *From generation to generation*. Glencoe, IL: Free Press.

Foner, A., & Kertzer, D. (1978). Transitions over the life course: Lessons from age-set societies. *American Journal of Sociology, 83* (5), 1081–1104.

Gilford, R., & Black, D. (1972). *The grandchild–grandparent dyad: Ritual or relationship?* Paper presented at the meetings of the Gerontological Society, San Juan, Puerto Rico.

Kahana, E., & Kahana, B. (1971). Theoretical and research perspectives on grandparenthood. *Aging and Human Development, 2*, 261–268.

Lawrence, J. C. D. (1957). *The Iteso*. London: Oxford University Press.

Nahemow, N., & Adams, B. (1974). Old age among the Baganda: Continuity and change. In J. Gubrium (Ed.), *Late life: Communities and environmental policy*. Springfield, IL: Thomas.

Nahemow, N. (1979). Residence, kinship and social isolation among the aged Baganda. *Journal of Marriage and the Family, 41* (1), 171–183.

Nahemow, N. (1983). Grandparenthood among the Baganda: Role option in old age. In J. Sokolovsky (Ed.), *Growing old in different societies: Cross-cultural perspectives*. Belmont, CA: Wadsworth.

Neugarten, B., & Datan, N. (1973). Sociological perspectives on the life cycle. In P. Baltes & K. W. Schaie (Eds.), *Life-span Developmental Psychology: Personality and Socialization*. New York: Academic Press.

Neugarten, B., & Hagestad, G. (1976). Age and the life course. In R. Binstock & E. Shanas (Eds.), *Handbook of aging and the social sciences*. New York: Van Nostrand.

Neugarten, B. L., & Weinstein, K. K. (1964). The changing American grandparent. *Journal of Marriage and the Family, 26*, 199–204.

Richards, A. I. (1966). *The changing social structure of a Ganda village*. Nairobi: East African Publishing House.

Rosow, I. (1962). Old age: One moral dilemma of an affluent society. *Gerontologist, 2* (December), 182–191.

Simmons, L. (1945). *The role of the aged in primitive society*. New Haven: Yale University Press.

Simmons, L. (1960). Aging in preindustrial societies. In C. Tibbetts (Ed.), *Handbook on Social Gerontology*. Chicago: University of Chicago Press.

Southall, A., & Gutkind, P. C. W. (1957). *Townsmen in the making*. Kampala: East African Institute of Social Research.

Sweetser, D. A. (1956). The social structure of grandparenthood. *American Anthropologist, 58*, 656–666.

Talmon, Y. (1968). Social aspects of aging. *Encyclopedia of social sciences*. New York: MacMillan.

Troll, L., Miller, S., & Atchley, R. (1979). *Families in later life*. Belmont, CA: Wadsworth.

Wallace, T., & Weeks, S. G. (1972). Youth in Uganda: Some theoretical perspectives. *International Social Science Journal, 24*, 354–365.

Wood, V., & Robertson, J. F. (1976). The significance of grandparenthood. In J. Gubrium (Ed.), *Time, Roles and Self in Old Age*. New York: Human Science Press.

Wright, A. C. A. (1942). Notes on the Iteso social organization. *Uganda Journal, 9*, 57–80.

Author Index

Numbers in italics show the page on which the complete reference is cited.

A

Abramson, L. V., 171, *201*
Adam, J., 3, *14*
Adams, B., 267, *277*
Ainsworth, M. D. S., 90, *102*
Allen, F. L., 8, 9, *14*
Allport, G. W., 9, *14*, 18, *42*, 61, *69*
Ambrose, J. A., 92, *102*
Anderson, B., 208, 209, 223, 224, *246*
Annis, L. F., 37, *42*
Annis, R. C., 85, *103*
Antonis, B., 206, *247*
Antonovsky, A., 150, *159*
Arenberg, D., 3, *14*
Aschenbrenner, B. G., 219, *243*
Asimov, I., 48, 49, *69*
Atchley, R. C., 58, *69*, 275, 276, *277*
Augustyniak, S., 168, *199*

B

Baldwin, W., 215, *242*
Ball, S., 34, 35, 36, *43*
Baltes, P. B., 2, 3, 6, 8, *14*, 18, 26, 39, 40, 42, *43*, *44*, 47, *69*, 73, 79, 83, 84, *103*, 249, 276
Bandura, A., 173, *199*
Barber, L., 238, *248*
Barker, R. G., 21, *103*
Bartlett, F. C., 114, *127*
Bashman, R. B., 218, 219, *247*
Becker, M., 96, *103*
Bee, R. L., 87, 88, *103*
Bell, M., 260, *277*
Bell, R. Q., 42, *43*
Bem, D. J., 168, *199*

Bengtson, V. L., 136, *140*
Berger, B., 132, *140*
Berger, P., 132, *140*
Berger, P. L., 99, 100, *103*
Bergmann, G., 29, *43*
Berry, J. W., 75, 76, 79, 85, *103*, *107*
Biller, H., 237, *242*
Birren, J. E., 63, *71*
Bischof, N., 90, *103*
Black, D., 263, *277*
Blanchard-Field, F., 125, *127*
Block, J. H., 162, 169, *199*
Blood, R., 221, *243*
Bloom, A., 110, 113, *127*
Bloom-Feshbach, J., 205, 213, 219, 223, *243*
Boas, F., 75, *103*
Boeckmann, M. E., 23, 24, *45*
Boesch, E. E., 96, 97, 99, 101, *103*
Bogatz, G. A., 34, 35, 36, *43*
Bohen, H., 226, *243*
Bolin, R., 34, *43*
Bonk, W. J., 25, 31, *44*
Boole, G., 119, *128*
Bormann, F. H., 18, *43*
Bottoms, S. F., 208, *243*
Botwinick, J., 3, *14*, 111, *128*
Boukydis, C., 210, *245*
Brackbill, Y., 212, *243*
Brassard, J. A., 204, 205, *243*
Braudel, F., 51, 68, *69*
Brenner, M. H., 171, *199*
Brown, G. W., 167, *200*
Brim, Jr., O. G., 18, *43*, 239, *243*
Bringuier, J. C., 115, *128*
Bronfenbrenner, U., 84, *103*, 204, 220, 226, 239, *243*

279

Subject Index